OXFORD ENGLISH MONOGRAPHS

General Editors

The Graphics of Verse

*Experimental Typography in
Twentieth-Century Poetry*

DANIEL MATORE

OXFORD
UNIVERSITY PRESS

Great Clarendon Street, Oxford, OX2 6DP
United Kingdom

Oxford University Press is a department of the University of Oxford.
It furthers the University's objective of excellence in research, scholarship,
and education by publishing worldwide. Oxford is a registered trade mark of
Oxford University Press in the UK and in certain other countries

© Daniel Matore 2023

The moral rights of the author have been asserted

Published in the United States of America by Oxford University Press
198 Madison Avenue, New York, NY 10016, United States of America

British Library Cataloguing in Publication Data
Data available

Library of Congress Control Number: 2023935800

ISBN 9780192857217

DOI: 10.1093/oso/9780192857217.001.0001

Printed and bound by
CPI Group (UK) Ltd, Croydon, CR0 4YY

Links to third-party websites are provided by Oxford in good faith and
for information only. Oxford disclaims any responsibility for the materials
contained in any third-party website referenced in this work.

For my mother and my grandmother

Acknowledgments

The principal debt this book owes is to the tireless support of my doctoral supervisor Prof Rebecca Beasley. The Leverhulme Trust, Harvard University and the Houghton Library, the Arts and Humanities Research Council, Royal Holloway, University of London, and the University of York have all provided funding and support without which the book couldn't have been written. I'd like to thank each one of my colleagues and mentors at my current department, the Department of English and Related Literature at the University of York, for their ongoing, invaluable friendship, collaboration, and advice. I would like to acknowledge the formative influences of Dr Louise Joy, Dr David Clifford, and Mr Steve Watts, my undergraduate tutors at Homerton College, Cambridge, on my critical thinking and their profound kindness. Prof Matthew Bevis should be thanked for his very early encouragement of my academic work and the enduring impression his approach to literature has had on my scholarship. Dr Fiona Green has been a source of sage advice, trenchant criticism, and practical assistance. Dr Ian Patterson made crucial counterarguments to my initial hypotheses about typography and poetics. Prof Michael Hurley offered formidable help to an earlier incarnation of my work on typography. I would like to thank Prof Derek Attridge, Dr Hannah Sullivan, Prof Michael Whitworth, and Dr Stephen Hebron for their invaluable responses to my work in its formative stages. I am especially grateful for the recommendations, insights, and mentorship of Dr Sullivan and Prof Attridge. I'd like to thank the librarians of the Houghton Library, Harvard University, who awarded me a Joan Nordell Fellowship to undertake the archival work contained in this book, and provided expert bibliographical advice during my time there, as did the librarians of the Beinecke Library at Yale University. Melissa Watterworth Batt of the University of Connecticut was immensely kind during my stay in Storrs and offered crucial help with navigating the papers of Charles Olson. Dr Natalie Ferris and Dr Alison Rosenblitt have offered much insight during our discussions of modernist studies. I'd like to thank my former colleagues at the Department of English at Royal Holloway for their support, encouragement, and assistance. My editors at Oxford University Press, especially Aimee Wright and Ellie Collins, have been a stalwart source of expertise and assistance. Dr Giles Bergel and Dr Judith Priestman have made bracing suggestions from the perspective of history of the book and bibliographical studies. I'd also like to thank Prof Matthew Reynolds and Prof Fiona Stafford for their advice, support, and encouragement. And I'd like to sincerely thank my two anonymous peer-reviewers for their expert feedback and suggestions. My sincere apologies to anyone I've unjustly omitted from the list—the fault is mine alone.

'the sky was' in *Complete Poems: 1904–1962* by E. E. Cummings, edited by George J. Firmage is reproduced by permission. Copyright © 1973, 1983, 1991 by the Trustees for the E. E. Cummings Trust. Copyright © 1973, 1983 by George James Firmage, 'the/ sky/ was'. Copyright 1925, 1953, © 1991 by the Trustees for the E. E. Cummings Trust. Copyright © 1976 by George James Firmage. Used by permission of Liveright Publishing Corporation.

Excerpts from unpublished materials by E. E. Cummings from the Cummings Collection at Houghton Library, Harvard University are reproduced by permission. Copyright by the Trustees for the E. E. Cummings Trust. Used by permission of Liveright Publishing Corporation.

Works by Charles Olson published during his lifetime are copyright the Estate of Charles Olson; previously unpublished works are copyright the University of Connecticut. Used with permission.

'In A Station of the Metro' by Ezra Pound, from *Personae*, copyright ©1926 by Ezra Pound is reprinted by permission of New Directions Publishing Corp.

Extracts from the Ezra Pound Papers, Beinecke Rare Book and Manuscript Library, Yale University, by Ezra Pound are reproduced by permission. New Directions Pub. acting as agent, copyright ©2022 by Mary de Rachewiltz and the Estate of Omar S. Pound. Reprinted by permission of New Directions Publishing Corp.

Extracts from the letters of Jeremy Prynne are reproduced by permission of Jeremy Prynne.

A version of a section of the first chapter first appeared as an article in *Modernism/modernity*. Copyright© 2019 The Johns Hopkins University Press. This article first appeared in *MODERNISM/MODERNITY*, Volume 26, Issue 2, April, 2019, pages 351–373.

An earlier version of the first part of the second chapter was previously published in *Textual Practice*. Copyright© 2017 Informa UK Limited, trading as Taylor & Francis Group. *Textual Practice* Volume 31, Issue 7, 2017, pages 1509–1531.

Contents

List of Illustrations

Note on Translations

All translations are my own unless otherwise specified.

Note on Manuscripts

Drafts are not necessarily blueprints for printed editions, nor do printed editions always manifest the intended design of the poet. Editorial incursions and the creative additions of book designers are not the subject of this book. What it contends is that many twentieth-century poets not only thought of typography as part of versification, they also elaborated means of producing it. This book reads a communicative intent in typescripts and drafts because so many of their graphical aspects are blueprints for their publication. Layouts in notebooks become layouts in print. It is crucial to look at texts both prior to and after publication not only to furnish the empirical proof that such typography is the work of the poet, but also to see how their designs evolved. Elaborating means of production does not mean that they took over publishing houses or set up their own presses as the Woolfs did. What it entailed was the employment of an annotatory apparatus of numbers, lines, and diagrams appended to drafts, manuscripts, and typescripts; the exploitation of new technologies like the typewriter and the xerox machine; exhortatory correspondence with typesetters and publishers; and the correction and emendation of proofs.

Introduction

1. 'Le vers n'est très beau que dans un caractère impersonnel: c'est-à-dire typographique': Mallarmé's *impressions*

Writing to the poet and editor Catulle Mendès about the inclusion of thirteen of his lyrics in the journal *Le Parnasse Contemporain*, Stéphane Mallarmé makes two requests: first, that Mendès voice any criticisms he may have of recent revisions to the poems; second, that the typography of his verse be arranged in a particular fashion:

> Seconde prière, qui se rapporte — je n'ose pas dire à l'impression, mais à l'imprimerie. Je voudrais un *caractère assez serré*, qui s'adaptât à la condensation du vers, mais *de l'air entre les vers, de l'espace*, afin qu'ils se détachent bien les uns des autres, ce qui est nécessaire encore avec leur condensation. J'ai numéroté les poèmes, est-ce utile? En tout cas, je voudrais, aussi, un grand blanc après chacun, un repos, car ils n'ont pas été composés pour se suivre ainsi, et, bien que, grâce à l'ordre qu'ils occupent, les premiers servent d'initiateurs aux derniers, je désirerais bien qu'on ne les lût pas d'une traite et comme cherchant une suite d'états de l'âme résultant les uns des autres, ce qui n'est pas, et gâterait le plaisir particulier de chacun.[1]

Prescriptive though he is, Mallarmé in one sense does not know what he is asking for; he hesitates over the category of his demand before it is even uttered, qualifying the already periphrastic relative clause. Hardly reputed

---

[1] 'Second request, which is connected to – I daren't say to the impression, but to the printing. I would like a fairly dense typeface, which befits the density of the verse, but some air and space between the lines, so that they each stand apart clearly, which is necessary given their density. I've numbered the poems, is that useful? In any case, I would like, in addition, a large white space after each one, a break, as they weren't written to follow one after the other, and, although, thanks to the order they're in, the first ones function as precursors to the final ones, I would very much wish that they weren't read in one go, as though the reader were seeking a sequence of sensations resulting one from another, which wouldn't be fitting, and would spoil the peculiar pleasure of each poem.'

The Graphics of Verse. Daniel Matore, Oxford University Press. © Daniel Matore (2023).
DOI: 10.1093/oso/9780192857217.003.0001

for timidity in literary experiment, it is rare to hear what Mallarmé dare not say, yet he withdraws the first term which he is minded to speak, erasing '*impression*' in favour of '*imprimerie*'. What this book will examine is how poets came to elide the distinction between those two terms; how poetics and printing became interwoven. For what resides in Mallarmé's discrimination between *impression* and *imprimerie* is the conviction that poetry and typography are separate, that the substance of poetry is detachable from the accidents of its arrangement in print. In this lexical nuance lies the belief that the size of typeface and the distance between lines of print, as well as their spacing and arrangement, do not constitute the inner essence of poetry. *Impression* can mean printing, just as *imprimerie* does, but it also connotes feeling, apprehension, sensation, which the latter term—able to signify a printing works, press, or office—does not. *Impressions*, for Mallarmé, are the lifeblood of verse. Of his incomplete verse drama 'Hérodiade', he writes: 'J'ai, du reste, là, trouvé une façon intime et singulière de peindre et de noter les impressions très fugitives. Ajoute, pour plus de terreur, que toutes ces *impressions* se suivent comme dans une symphonie'.[2] The value of these *impressions* is their evanescence, though even here the hard matter of typography is palpable, as the art of fixing and notating these feelings, impressing these *impressions*, is broached. Likewise in Mallarmé's celebrated letter of 1866, where he speaks of hollowing out poetry to its cerebral minima, the abyss he encounters is only filled out by 'toutes les divines impressions pareilles qui se sont amassées en nous depuis les premiers âges'; only the glorious falsehoods of 'impressions poétiques' paper over the underlying nothingness Mallarmé apprehends.[3] In relegating his typographical stipulations to the nuts and bolts of the *imprimerie*, Mallarmé is safeguarding the immaterial substance, the inner sanctum of *impressions*, poetry is supposed to constitute. Typography is kept at the threshold of verse.[4]

It is serendipitous that in French, in the polysemy of *impression*, the membrane between typography and poetry should be so porous, since it is in Mallarmé's *oeuvre*, in the long poem *Un coup de dés*, that the two

[2] 'Furthermore, I've found in this instance an intimate and particular way of painting and notating especially transient impressions. Add to this, to compound the sense of dread, that all these impressions follow on from one another like in a symphony'.

[3] 'All such celestial impressions which have accumulated in us since the first ages'; 'poetic impressions'.

[4] Stéphane Mallarmé, 'Letter to Catulle Mendès, 24 April 1866', 'Letter to Henri Cazalis, 15 January 1865', and 'Letter to Henri Cazalis, 28 April 1866', in Stéphane Mallarmé, *Correspondance complète 1862–1871 suivi de Lettres sur la poésie 1872–1898 avec des lettres inédites*, ed. Bertrand Marchal (Paris: Gallimard, 1995) 292–96 (p. 293); 219–22 (p. 220); 296–301 (p. 298).

dramatically collapse together.[5] In *Un coup de dés* it becomes impossible to distinguish the typography of the poem from its style. This book will be concerned with typographical experiment in English-language poetry, but the exemplar of Mallarmé's work needs to be taken into account first because it is the archetype of its kind; it prefigures and typologizes what later poets will attempt, even when they are ignorant of the French poet's example. It predates the *parole in libertà* of the Italian Futurists, the *calligrammes* of Guillaume Apollinaire, and the heterodox mise-en-page of Anglo-American modernists. Mallarmé's influence on poets writing in English, as with their European counterparts, fluctuates; and, indeed, this book will go on to argue that poets are often at pains to discount the influence of their predecessors and contemporaries' typography on their own work and to think of typography as a *tabula rasa*, a virginal canvas on which to paint a wholly personal language. However, Mallarmé's work and his writings on it adumbrate the suppositions and tensions which will animate the typographical investigations of succeeding generations of modernists. Typography merits being undertaken as an autonomous subject because, despite the idiosyncrasies of its practitioners, it elicits and stimulates recurrent concerns across literatures and generations: free verse, notation, advertising, optics, and other such preoccupations resurface time and again when poets think about what mise-en-page might do.

What does it mean for typography to be experimental? Modernist typography is a somewhat misleading term, since the stanzaic layout of a poet such as Wallace Stevens diverges from the thoroughgoing dislocations of E. E. Cummings, even though both are regularly labelled modernists. This book will be concerned chiefly with poets who, prior to the publication of their work, prior to their collaboration with typesetters and printers, deliberately chose to design and plot the layout and arrangement of their poetry against the grain of inherited typographical conventions, and whose manipulations of mise-en-page were sustained and elaborated over the span of their career. Experimental typography is a provisionally useful phrase, but it ought not to be employed to fence off a certain area of verse. Our inherited critical vocabulary in this field—terms like *concrete poetry* and *visual poetry*—is ghettoizing. Poets like Ezra Pound, William Carlos Williams, or David Jones, who do not shape their poems like the Eiffel Tower or interlocking circles in the manner of Guillaume Apollinaire or Ian Hamilton Finlay, cannot properly be said to be concrete poets, but much of their verse is

[5] 'A Throw of the Dice'

typographically experimental. What this book will claim is that typographical experiment is bound up with the preoccupations of modernist poetics:
the preservation of the poet's voice as metre is abandoned; the regulation of
free verse; the instability of the category of poetry as it becomes receptive
to myriad, often foreign, documents; and the safeguarding or dissolution of
intentionality in polyglossic and polyphonic textures of verse.

   Poems like *Un coup de dés* seem at first glance so exorbitant as to be
cut off from the corpus of typographically normative verse. Surveying the
orthodox typography of the works that precede that poem, *Un coup de dés*
seems to emerge like Minerva sprung fully formed from the head of Jove;
a poetic experiment with no organic gestation. Yet, in a germination that
foreshadows that of other visually pioneering poets, this work can be read
as having its seeds much earlier in the poet's career. For when Mallarmé
makes this distinction between *impression* and *imprimerie*, he is writing
in 1866, thirty years before the publication of *Un coup de dés*. Likewise,
his typographical suggestions, though he wishes to consign them to the
afterthought of the printer's shop, are not merely functional. In desiring 'un
caractère assez serré, qui s'adaptât à la condensation du vers, mais *de l'air
entre les vers, de l'espace*, afin qu'ils se détachent bien les uns des autres, ce
qui est nécessaire encore avec leur condensation', he is sketching a theory
of typographical affect and mimesis.[6] Once again in his lexis typography
and poetics cohabit, 'caractère' denoting both typeface and the personality
of the verse. Typography ought not just harmonize with the style of
poetry—serried lines of type for dense textures—it should orchestrate the
reader's apprehension; govern the tempo of impressions; punctuate a series
of states of mind, 'une suite d'états de l'âme'. This inspection of the contours
of type is brought to bear on conventionally disposed verse; that is to say,
Mallarmé does not believe typography only becomes expressive when
dramatically reworked. Apprehensive though this letter to Mendès is, *Un
coup de dés* can be thus seen as a radicalization of these premonitions of
what mise-en-page might effect. Years later, in 1891, as he is negotiating the
publication of his collected verse with Edmond Deman, Mallarmé avers
that the durability and the beauty of his whole corpus depends on its proper
typographical realization. A manuscript edition, he opines, would give his
poems a subjective, personal aura quite at odds with the self-abnegation
he has attempted to practise. He goes on: 'Le vers n'est très beau que dans

---

[6] 'a fairly dense typeface, which befits the density of the verse, but some air and space between
the lines, so that they each stand apart clearly, which is necessary given their density'.

un caractère impersonnel, c'est-a-dire typographique: sauf bien entendu à faire graver si l'on veut donner à l'édition quelque chose d'immuable et de monumental. C'était, je crois, votre impression quand vous parlâtes de gravure autrefois, et, me semble-t-il, la vraie.'[7] Mallarmé had long yearned to endow himself with a 'caractère impersonnel'. After a trial of self-examination to purify his poetry, he declared to Henri Cazalis: 'je suis maintenant impersonnel, et non plus Stéphane que tu as connu'.[8] From this vantage point, typography is no faddish, latter-day interest; it is wedded to the telos of Mallarmé's aesthetics. The poet assumes the impersonal character he longs to be through the impersonal character of print.[9]

The work of Mallarmé, in this regard, is prophetic. Pound, Williams, Olson, Jones: from tentative beginnings, these poets became more and more audacious in their typography. Works such as *The Pisan Cantos, Paterson, Maximus IV, V, VI*, and *The Anathemata* are not freak occurrences in these authorships; they are the culmination of years of exploration. Yet the instability of utilizing the printed page to remould poetry is never quite exorcized. Typography, both in critical reflection and poetic practice, veers between poles of magisterial control and aleatory risk. Writing to Cazalis in 1864, Mallarmé uncannily prefigures the imagistic cosmos of *Un coup de dés*:

Henri, qu'il y a loin de ces théories de composition littéraires à la façon dont notre glorieux Emmanuel [Des Essarts] prend une poignée d'étoiles dans la Voie lactée pour les semer sur le papier, et les laisser se former au hasard en constellations imprévues! Et comme son âme enthousiasme [sic], ivre d'inspiration, reculerait d'horreur devant ma façon de travailler! Il est le poète lyrique, dans tout son admirable épanchement. Toutefois, plus j'irai, plus je serai fidèle à ces sévères idées que m'a léguées mon grand maître Edgar Poe. Le poème inouï du 'Corbeau' a été ainsi fait. Et l'âme du lecteur jouit *absolument* comme le poète a voulu qu'elle jouit. Elle ne ressent pas une impression autre que celles sur lesquelles il avait compté.[10]

---

[7] 'Verse is only truly beautiful when it has an impersonal character, that is to say, typo-graphical: unless, of course, you were to have the edition engraved, if you wanted to endow it with something unchangeable and monumental. That was what you had in mind [lit. your impression] when you spoke of engraving the other time, and it seems to me to be correct.'
[8] 'I have now assumed an impersonal self, and I am no longer the Stéphane which you once knew.'
[9] Stéphane Mallarmé, 'Letter to Catulle Mendès, 24 April 1866', 'Letter to Edmond Deman, 7 April 1891', and 'Letter to Henri Cazalis, 14 May 1867', in *Correspondance complète*, 292–96 (p. 294); 609–11 (p. 610); 341–46 (p. 343).
[10] 'Henri, how far away we are from those theories of literary composition which belong to our glorious Emmanuel [Des Essarts], where he snatches a fistful of stars from the Milky Way

Not only is it remarkable how the lexis—'hasard', 'constellation'—foreshadows its iconic reappearance in *Un coup de dés*, again suggesting the work has a much longer gestation than its idiosyncrasy would imply, but it is also illuminating how this dichotomy between the poetics of Des Essarts and that of Edgar Poe is reawakened in Mallarmé's typographical experimentation and that of his successors. *Un coup de dés* is a poem that is hyperconscious of its style, but one which writes its anxieties about that style into the text.[11] In an explicatory preamble that accompanied the poem in its original publication in *Cosmopolis* as well as its publication in 1914, Mallarmé entrusted two very different species of exactitude to the layout. The disposition of typography is now that of prismatic subdivisions of the Idea 'dans quelque mise-en-scene spirituelle exacte'.[12] No longer the mere matter of *imprimerie*, the printed page is now the stuff of pure cerebration; the very schema of *impressions*. Yet, at the same time, typography is to inhabit a second nature. It is, for the careful recitant, 'une partition', a perfect score for the intonation and speed of the reading voice. This hybrid nature—at once a transcription of pure thought and a transcription of the human voice—will vex debates about typographical experiment for decades to come.

Confident though he is in the technical precision of his work, Mallarmé is dubious about its legacy. From it may spring 'rien ou presque un art'.[13] At the helm of *Un coup de dés* is a forgotten man with no inheritance to bequeath; a skeletal captain on a shipwrecked vessel who holds a 'legacy in disappearance'—*legs en la disparition*. This tussle between poetic mastery and poetic chance, whether the art of verse is to scatter ideas on a page like a fistful of stars in the manner of Des Essarts or to notate inerrantly a suite of impressions in the manner of Poe, is what concerns the typography of this poem. Belying his title 'LE MAÎTRE', Mallarmé's persona is a reckless

in order to scatter them on the paper and to let them form by chance into unforeseen constellations! And how his passionate soul, drunk with inspiration, would recoil with horror when confronted with my way of working! He is the true lyric poet, in all his admirable effusions. But the further along I go, the more faithful I am to the austere notions which my great master Edgar [Allan] Poe has bequeathed to me. The astonishing poem "The Raven" was written in such a way. And the reader's spirit exults in the exact manner in which the poet wished that it would. Their spirit receives no impression other than those which the poet anticipated that it would'; Stéphane Mallarmé, 'Letter to Henri Cazalis, 7 [?] January 1864', in *Correspondance complète*, 160–63 (p. 161).
   [11] 'chance ... constellation'.
   [12] 'in some precise spiritual mise-en-scene'; Stéphane Mallarmé, 'Observation relative au poème', *Cosmopolis*, 17 ([May] 1897) 417–18 (p. 417); Stéphane Mallarmé, *Un coup de dés jamais n'abolira le hasard* (Paris: Gallimard, 1914), n.p.
   [13] 'nothing or almost an art in itself'

gambler, a figure lost to chance, and the poem concludes with a statement that stays any current of exact premeditation: 'Toute Pensée émet un Coup de Dés'.[14] Contra the Mallarmé of the 'observation relative au poème', we might say that the triumph of the poem's typography rests on its dissolution of inherited certainties. When 'LE MAÎTRE' appears in the poem, it isn't clear what we are next to read. The eye wavers between reading down the page to the postmodifiers 'surgi / inférant', a direction closer to normative reading habits but still enjoining us to knit together floating words, or over to the recto, on to the phrases 'hors d'ancien calculs / où la manoeuvre avec l'âge oubliée'.[15] On this decision, accordingly, hangs the mastery of The Master; whether we read him first as a resurgent calculator or a senescent and floundering dotard. The re-routings of the reading eye which the typography induces disorient prepositional fixities. What might have been a climactic affirmation for a poem dependent on a metaphysical dice throw, the phrase 'C'ÉTAIT LE NOMBRE', is undercut by a broad space between copula and complement across the fold of the page and the mirroring in italicization and capitalization of 'C'ÉTAIT' by 'CE SERAIT', the latter phrase located further down the page and towards the left-hand margin, so that the indicative of the former is shadowed by the conditional of the latter and the typography bifurcates stability.[16] Flawless mastery and careless risk collide in *Un coup de dés*, and the poem prefigures the dialectics of typographical experiment in the coming century, of poets torn between hubristic self-assurance and crippling self-doubt. The achievement of Mallarmé's poem is not intonational certainty or an exact mapping of the intellect, but a calculated art of doubt, the heir to a body of work that eroded the bonds of syntax and punctuation.[17]

2. 'Io inizio una rivoluzione tipografica': Typographical Revolutions and English Poetry

Uncertain legacies haunt the history of typographical experiment. Mallarmé's poem is, in a sense, intestate. Though, as Pound later observed, the poem was published in the 'Anglo-International' journal *Cosmopolis* in 1897—a forum that exhibited Mallarmé's poem as a contribution to

---

[14] 'Each thought emits a throw of the dice.'
[15] 'arisen / inferring ... bereft of his ancient calculations / the right manoeuvre forgotten with age'
[16] *'IT WAS THE NUMBER'* / *'IT WAS'* / *'IT WOULD BE'*
[17] Stéphane Mallarmé, *Un coup de dés*, n.p.

world literature, not a peculiarly French endeavour—this version of the poem is compromised.[18] The antiphony of text spliced between verso and recto, cardinal to the mechanics of the typography, is deadened by being squashed onto the single leaves of the journal. So too are typefaces native to advertising, the arabesques of ornamented lettering, grafted onto the poem, against the poet's design, in such a way that commercial print and display typography infiltrate the poet's codex.[19] Mallarmé's mise-en-page, though experimental, is emphatically allied to book typography and the graphical idiolect of the lyric poet. This tussle between display typography and book typography, between the poet's printed voice and the clamour of mass advertising, will come to dominate the imagination of much modernist verse. When, in 1914, Mallarmé's poem is committed to the more lapidary format of book publication and appears disposed according to his original scheme, his legacy has been brought into question. Other voices have proclaimed their own typographical revolutions, some wishing to claim that *Un coup de dés*, far from being ahead of its time, is a work stuck in the nineteenth century.

Was there a typographical revolution in poetry written in English? A principal contention of this book is that typography becomes part of the style, the expressive repertoire, of poetry in English in the twentieth century. To design the layout of verse becomes second nature, a right that was neither taken for granted nor commonly exploited in previous centuries. Poets were able to experiment with the page before the twentieth century, but they rarely did so, and such experiment either produced the pictorial verse of poets like George Herbert, whose seraphic wings and altars have little in common with the abstract geometry of the modernist page, or it happened within the confines of typographical tradition, as in the exploitation of the line break in John Milton's blank verse. Critical discussion of *technopaegnia*, or pattern poems, existed sporadically before the twentieth century, and critics like Seth Swanner have observed how Renaissance writers such as Michel de Montaigne and Gabriel Harvey often condemned them as vain subtleties or 'madde gugawes'. Investigating the complex textual history of Herbert's 1633 *The Temple*, Swanner also compellingly explores how conflicting theologies of the image might have swayed the poet and his posthumous compositors and editors in their determinations of margins

---

[18] Ezra Pound, 'The Island of Paris: A Letter', *The Dial* (September 1920), 406–11 (p. 407).
[19] Stéphane Mallarmé, 'Un coup de dés jamais n'abolira le hasard', *Cosmopolis*, 6 (1897), 417–27 (pp. 423–25).

and indentations.[20] One of the fullest treatments of a poetry for the eye prior to 1900 in English verse is Richard Bradford's *The Look of It: A Theory of Visual Form in English Poetry*, which argues for an acute sensitivity to the shape of poetry arising in Milton's blank verse and discernible in Wordsworth, where the line ending, though fixed, is in subtle sycopation with syntax and sound.[21] Book design has attracted various poets over the centuries. Much scholarly work has been done on how William Blake brought his training as a printmaker, painter, and engraver to bear on his illuminated books.[22] Walt Whitman, apprenticed like Blake in the stuff of book production, was intimately involved in the choice of a Scotch Roman typeface for the 1860 edition of *Leaves of Grass*, seemingly guided by the fonts of nineteenth-century periodicals and advertising.[23] Experimental typography in twentieth-century poetry, though, diverges from these antecedents in three principal ways. First, it favours abstract over pictorial typography and is often as contemptuous as Montaigne of the 'madde gugawes' of depicting shapes in verse. Second, unlike the work of Blake, for example, it turns to book design only secondarily, to safeguard or elaborate poetry that is already graphically innovative at the manuscript stage. Third, in contrast to the visual acuity of Milton or Wordsworth's blank verse, it expands the graphical vocabulary of verse well beyond typographically fixed line endings into a near-limitless repertoire of spacing, layout, and symbology. Because of this fertile prehistory, it would be short-sighted to claim that visual poetry only emerges in English verse in 1900, but in its thoroughgoing prosodic abstraction, radical graphical complexity, and transcendence of particular editions and book design alone, the experimental typography of the twentieth century was emphatically *sui generis*.

There is no singular catalyst for why typography was radicalized in the early twentieth century. The typewriter facilitated graphical adventure, but since some of this work is sketched in pencil or pen, it cannot be said to have caused it. To claim otherwise would be a *post hoc ergo propter hoc*. However, the discerning of landmarks in this English-language poetry is not

---

[20] Seth Swanner, 'The Beauty of Ho(me)liness', *Studies in Philology*, 3 (2018), 544–79 (pp. 551, 553).

[21] Richard Bradford, *The Look of It: A Theory of Visual Form in English Poetry* (Cork: Cork University Press, 1993).

[22] Eden Bass, 'Songs of Innocence and Experience: The Thrust of Design', in *Blake's Visionary Forms Dramatic*, ed. David V. Erdman and John E. Grant (Princeton, NJ: Princeton University Press, 2017), 196–213.

[23] Barbara Henry, 'The Design and Typography of Leaves of Grass (1860)' *Huntington Library Quarterly*, 4 (2010), 601–12 (p. 604).

as straightforward as in French, Italian, or Russian literature. Unlike their European counterparts, British and American poets in the 1910s did not announce a revolution in typography. This is not to say they were out of step or behind the times. Early versions of Cummings's lyrics, written in 1916, and Pound's *Homage to Sextus Propertius* of 1917 are unmistakeably audacious in their typography, but the former remain unpublished and the latter attracted more attention for its translational liberties than its layout. Works such as Blaise Cendrars and Sonia Delaunay's *La Prose du Transsibérien et la petite Jehanne de France* or F. T. Marinetti's *Bataille: Poids + Odeur*, both published in 1912, have few equivalents in English, except for Hope Mirrlees's 1920 *Paris: A Poem*. Mirrlees's phantasmagoric tour of signage and desire, though published by the Hogarth Press, was relatively overlooked in the Anglosphere, a fact compounded by her abandonment of graphical experiment after the poem's publication. Despite its myopic neglect by her contemporaries, Mirrlees's clairvoyant poem, though, heralds and anticipates some of the most rarefied linguistic distillations of poetic typography of later decades.

The closest to a manifesto for a rejuvenated page space in English is Wyndham Lewis's *BLAST*. The bold unserifed capitals, cavernous white spaces, and vertiginous asymmetries of *BLAST* call for an aesthetic and political revolution *in* revolutionary typography, though the journal does not make any prescriptions for mise-en-page. It does rather than says. Assertively individualist, it is in fact in its rejections of parentage and kinship with concurrent schools of the avant-garde that *BLAST* is most typical and most European. No mention is made of Mallarmé, and Marinetti's Futurism is castigated: 'AUTOMOBILISM (Marinetteism) bores us. We don't want to go about making a hullo-bulloo about motor cars, anymore than about knives and forks, elephants or gas-pipes.'[24] Refuting the fraternity their graphics seem to declare is a trope common to the *manifesti* of the European avant-garde.

Denouncing Futurism and claiming that 'The futurist is a sensational and sentimental mixture of the aesthete of 1890 and the realist of 1870', the journal is announcing the colouring of its own typography: it is not draped in Marinetti's banners but in the house style of its Anglo-Saxon anarcholibertarian politics.[25] Wittingly or not, *BLAST* is recapitulating the rhetoric

[24] Wyndham Lewis, 'Long Live the Vortex', in *BLAST: Review of the Great English Vortex*, 1 (1914), n.p.
[25] Wyndham Lewis, 'Long Live the Vortex', in *BLAST: Review of the Great English Vortex*, 1 (1914), n.p.

of a Futurist manifesto of the previous year. In 'Distruzione della sintassi –
Imaginazione senza fili – Parole in libertà', Marinetti seeks to govern the
reception of his own typography and ward off the presence of his rivals.[26]
Typographical experiment, it should be remembered, had played no part in
the first Futurist manifesto of 1909, nor did it figure even amongst the stylistic prescriptions of the 'Manifesto tecnico' of 1912, but Marinetti wishes to
claim the policy as his own. In a section headed '*Rivoluzione tipografica*', he
writes:

> Io inizio una rivoluzione tipografica diretta contro la bestiale e nauseante
> concezione del libro di versi passatista e dannunziana, la carta a mano sei-
> centesca, fregiata di galee, minerve e apolli, di iniziali rosse a ghirigori,
> ortaggi, mitologici, nastri da messale, epigrafi e numeri romani. Il libro
> deve essere l'espressione futurista del nostro pensiero futurista.[27]

Typographical experiment impels writers to an amnesiac and territorial
individualism, and Marinetti's pronouns are telling here. Belligerent though
he is, Marinetti tends to style himself as the *porte-parole* of a movement,
not as a lone renegade. Impersonal constructions like 'bisogna' or 'si deve'
preceded the tenets of previous *manifesti*, as well as appeals for a collective
endeavour—'Noi inventeremo insieme'.[28] In his declaration of a typographical revolution, however, excepting that single gesture to 'nostro pensiero
futurista', Marinetti articulates himself in the first person singular, referring to 'la mia rivoluzione', as though he were a one-man revolutionary.[29]
BLAST describes itself, even as it announces the birth of movement, as an
'art of Individuals', and the language of typographical experiment with its
propensity to disavow comity and filiation thus befits its atomistic individualism: this is a language that wants not to be shared.[30] To lay sole claim

[26] 'Destruction of syntax – Imagination without wires – Words in freedom'
[27] 'I am declaring a typographical revolution against, above all, the ghastly, sickening, and
passé notion of the book of poems in the manner of D'Annunziano, with its hand-made,
seventeenth-century style paper, decorated with galleys, Minervas, Apollos, red initials and
flourishes, vegetables, mythological missal ribbons, and Roman epigraphs and numerals.
The book should be the Futurist expression of our Futurist thought'; F. T. Marinetti, 'Distruzione della sintassi—Immaginazione senza fili—Parole in libertà', in *I manifesti del futurismo*
(Firenze: Edizioni di Lacerba, 1914), 133–46 (p. 143).
[28] 'There is need of'; 'it is necessary to'; 'we will discover together'; F. T. Marinetti, 'Manifesto
tecnico della letteratura futurista', in *I manifesti del futurismo* (Firenze: Edizioni di Lacerba,
1914), 88–96 (pp. 88, 94).
[29] 'Our Futurist thought ... my revolution'
[30] Wyndham Lewis, 'Long Live the Vortex', in *BLAST: Review of the Great English Vortex*, 1
(1914), n.p.

to *the* typographical revolution, as though such a singular event could take place, Marinetti has to exorcize the ghost of Mallarmé. Having set out his typographical programme, he goes on:

> Combatto l'estetica decorativa e preziosa di Mallarmé e le sue richerche della parola rara, dell'aggettivo unico insostituibile, elegante, suggestivo, squisito. Non voglio suggerire un'idea o una sensazione con delle grazie o delle leziosaggini passatiste: voglio anzi afferrarele brutalmente e scagliarele in pieno petto al lettore.[31]

This juxtaposition is a shrewd attempt to revise literary history. In a 1914 article entitled 'Nos Amis Les Futuristes', Apollinaire figures Marinetti as the emissary of French poetics: 'La nouvelle technique des mots en liberté sortie de Rimbaud, de Mallarmé, des symbolistes en général et du style télégraphique en particulier, a, grâce à Marinetti, une grande vogue en Italie.'[32] Gallicizing Futurist *parole in libertà* as 'mots en liberté', Marinetti is imagined as broadcasting the discoveries of Mallarmé and the Symbolists. Marinetti, though, severs this lineage. Usurped from his role as the progenitor of experimental typography, Mallarmé is cast as the last scion of a superannuated bibliographical tradition. Paired with D'Annunzio, his recherché lexis symptomatizes the same Decadent aesthetics that furnishes the *fin-de-siècle* 'book of verse'. Far from being ahead of its time, Marinetti implies that *Un coup de dés* is a typical publication of the 1890s, closer to *The Yellow Book* or the Kelmscott Chaucer. 'La mia rivoluzione è diretta contro la così detta armonia tipografica della pagina, che è contraria al flusso e riflusso, ai sobbalzi e agli scoppi dello stile che scorre nella pagina stessa', Marinetti states.[33] Yet the asymmetries and fluctuations of *Un coup de dés*, its ruptures with the 'armonia tipografica nella pagina stessa', are reinterpreted as decorative excrescences which are the natural heir to

---

[31] 'I am fighting against the ornamental and recherché aesthetic of Mallarmé and his search for the rare word, the one, unique, irreplaceable adjective, elegant, pregnant and exquisite. I do not want to suggest an idea or a sensation with old-fashioned airs and affectations: I want to snatch them savagely and hurl them right at the heart of the reader.' F. T. Marinetti, 'Distruzione della sintassi—Immaginazione senza fili—Parole in libertà', in *I manifesti del futurismo* (Firenze: Edizioni di Lacerba, 1914), 143.

[32] 'Our Friends the Futurists'; 'The new technique of words in freedom which comes from Rimbaud, Mallarmé, the Symbolists in general and the telegraphic style in particular, enjoys, thanks to Marinetti, a great vogue in Italy'; Guillaume Apollinaire, 'Nos Amis Les Futuristes', *Les Soirées de Paris* (1914), 78–79 (p. 78).

[33] 'My revolution is directed against the so-called typographical harmony of the page, which is contrary to the ebb and flow, to the jumps and jerks of the style that traverses the page itself'.

the Minervas and Apollos and embellished initials of the frontispieces of the Renaissance codex. Futurist typography, *BLAST* implied, was 1890s aestheticism; Marinetti says the same of the work of Mallarmé and even roots *Un coup de dés* in the seventeenth century.[34]

It is the conspicuousness of typography, its apparent conscription of the poet to this or that school, that prompts these proprietorial reflexes. Orphists, Futurists, and Vorticists are drawn to typographical experiment as a means to break with past literary traditions, yet they fear that such graphics might ally them with the wrong contemporary faction. Particular to modernism in English, in addition, is an unease about the autonomy of poetry and an anxiety that typographical experiment opens up verse to foreign cultures of print: to signage, commerce, and advertising. Ezra Pound betrays this distinctly Anglophone disquiet, even as he leads the vanguard of typographical pioneers. When Marinetti proclaims, 'Combatto inoltre l'ideale statico di Mallarmé', claiming that his typography enables him to harness the velocity 'degli astri, delle nuvole, degli aeroplani, dei treni, delle onde, degli esplosivi, dei globuli della schiuma marina, delle molecole, e degli atomi', he is refiguring the tempi and semantics of Mallarmé's lines.[35] Dynamic though they appear, the fractured phrases of *Un coup de dés* are reread as static emblems of the poet's idealism. When Pound decries the 'fancy type, broken lines, hosiery-ad fonts, valentine wreaths or other post-Mallarmé devices' of contemporary poetry in 1925, he too is remapping the semantics of typography. The 'broken lines' of Pound's corpus, which he had been employing for over a decade, are emphatically not to be read as 'post-Mallarmé devices', and his verse is not to be read as a close cousin of 'hosiery-ad fonts'.[36] The full panoply of graphic culture—ticketing, advertising, signage, telegrams—is synthesized, held in collage, in the European poetry of the 1910s, in works like Apollinaire's 'Lettre-Océan'. Marinetti's poems often read like *manifesti*, featuring undigested slogans like 'superiorità della mia poesia su tutte le altre'.[37] British and American poetry, though it will imbibe all manner of documentation in Pound's *Cantos* or Williams's *Paterson*, jealously guards

---

[34] F. T. Marinetti, 'Distruzione della sintassi—Immaginazione senza fili—Parole in libertà', in *I manifesti del futurismo* (Firenze: Edizioni di Lacerba), 133–46 (p. 143).

[35] 'Moreover I am fighting against the static idealism of Mallarmé'; 'of stars, of clouds, of aeroplanes, of trains, of waves, of explosives, of gobbets of marine spume, of molecules, and of atoms' F. T. Marinetti, 'Distruzione della sintassi—Immaginazione senza fili—Parole in libertà', in *I manifesti del futurismo* (Firenze: Edizioni di Lacerba), 133–46 (p. 143).

[36] Ezra Pound, 'Mr. Dunning's Poetry', *Poetry*, 6 (1925), 339–45 (p. 341).

[37] 'the superiority of my poetry above all others'; F. T. Marinetti, *Zang Tumb Tuuum* (Venezia: Edizioni Futuriste di Poesia, 1914), 36.

the autonomy of verse at first. Pound's appraisal of *BLAST*, to which he was co-signatory and to which he contributed several poems, is evidence of this. If *BLAST* trumpeted an English typographical revolution, then Pound, for one, wants no part in it. In his homage to the sculptor Gaudier-Brzeska, he writes: '*Blast* has behind it some of the best brains in England, a set of artists who know quite well what they want. It is therefore significant. The large type and the flaring cover are merely bright plumage. They are the gay petals which lure.'[38] And in a letter of 1917, he circumscribes his place in the journal: 'My corner of the paper is *BLAST*, but *BLAST* covered with ice, with a literary and reserved camouflage'. Pound judges the typography of *BLAST* to be no more than a branding exercise, and his wording betrays a fear that the journal's house style is hegemonic. *BLAST* is a grouping of 'a set of artists who know quite well what they want', he remonstrates, as though the 'large type and flaring cover' would override authorial intentionality and corral individual artists into a homogeneous printed chorus.[39] This is a timely protest. Modernist poets, even in the midst of their experiments with print, will worry that typography stifles or even drowns out the lyric voice of the poet.

Lyric is the cradle of typographical experiment in English. The iconic works of European visual poetics—*Un coup de dés*, *La Prose du Transsibérien et la petite Jehanne de France*, *Zang Tumb Tuuum*—are too lengthy and generically ambivalent to be classed as lyric, and even the *calligrammes* of Apollinaire, brief though they are, are too divorced from sonnet, song, or ballad to be judiciously cast as such. It is in poems that are unmistakeably lyrics, though, that most modernists writing in English begin to experiment with typography, as is the case with Ezra Pound, E. E. Cummings, Marianne Moore, William Carlos Williams, Charles Olson, Barry MacSweeney, and J. H. Prynne. (Hope Mirrlees and David Jones, who devote their graphical energies to longer poems, are notable exceptions). On the one hand, this allows for local, heuristic experimentation before confronting the larger canvas of epic. Though much of this book will be concerned with epics such as *The Cantos*, *Paterson*, and *The Maximus Poems*—canvases where poets can work their boldest designs—lyrical exercises are where most of these writers begin to rethink the page. It is less of a gamble to chip away at the lines of a sonnet than to undertake Mallarmé's

---

[38] Ezra Pound, *Gaudier-Brzeska: A Memoir* (London: Laidlaw & Laidlaw, [1939]), 127.
[39] Ezra Pound, 'Letter to Edgar Jepson, 29 May 1917', in *The Letters of Ezra Pound 1907–1941*, ed. D. D. Paige (New York: Harcourt, Brace, 1950), 112.

large-scale throw of the dice. On the other hand, lyric, as the sanctum of the singing voice and the individual subject, is the genre that seems the most inimical to typography. Pound's defence of his 'corner of [...] BLAST' against the incursions of 'large type' miniaturizes this broader conflict. To say his lyrics in BLAST are vested in 'literary and reserved camouflage' is freighted with ambivalence. It is to maintain a severance between poetry and typography, as Mallarmé did in dividing *impressions* from *imprimerie*, to say that the latter is merely clothing for the former, but it is also to uphold a typographical decorum, to claim that the poems exhibited still adhere to the propriety of a lyric typography. Yet Pound's term 'camouflage' subverts any such clear demarcations of literary and non-literary typography by suggesting that the poems are hiding their true colours. 'Salutation The Third', one of the lyrics from the first edition of BLAST, betrays these divided loyalties:

> Let us deride the smugness of "The Times" :
> GUFFAW !
> So much the gagged reviewers,
> It will pay them when the worms are wriggling in their vitals ;
> These were they who objected to newness,
> HERE are their TOMB-STONES.
> They supported the gag and the ring :
> A little black BOX contains them.
> SO shall you be also,
> You slut-bellied obstructionist,
> You sworn foe to free speech and good letters,
> You fungus, you continuous gangrene.

Far from being deaf to BLAST's vociferous large type, this poem is tuned to the stentorian and proto-fascist tones of the journal at large. Words are hammered out with capitals in the manner of a manifesto, shaped like the angular emphases of BLAST's sloganeering. Nor can typography be divorced from the lyric voice here or sheltered from collusion in racist politics as the poem goes on to emblazon and capitalize viciously anti-Semitic slogans. These capitals aren't outlining a recitation implicit in the text. Repeated words are in majuscules in one instance and not in the next, dictating rhetorical stress like cues for a far-right orator. In lines like 'HERE are their TOMB-STONES', the capitalization seems to warp the contours of voicing; to stress the clearly demoted second syllable of 'TOMB-STONES' and give it equal weight to the first is to strain the rhythms of speech.[40] Lyric here is not 'covered in ice', insulated from the visual dynamism of *BLAST* and from proximity with newsprint and manifestos. Typography is fracturing the idea of 'literary and reserved' lyric; stressing and stretching the singing voice. Print amplifies the jarring dynamics of anti-Semitic demagoguery. Insinuated in the texture of this short poem, and implicit in Pound's apologia for *BLAST*, is the febrile potential of typography, its capacity to distort, envenom, and destroy the lyricism of verse.

Positioned against the popular press from its opening line, vaunting its pugilistic typography against the complacent newsprint of *The Times*, yet at the same time supposedly a reserved, lyric refuge from *BLAST*, 'Salutation The Third' adumbrates the schisms and fractures of modernist poetry, fault lines that are largely due to typographical experiment.[41] Is poetry written for the ear or the eye? Ought the printed page to be employed solely as a script for the voice? Is verse which is broken across the page, splintered and spaced, really verse anymore? These aporias inhabit the typographical ruptures of this lyric; preliminaries to the typographical dramas of the inclusion of diplomatic correspondence in the Malatesta Cantos or the amorphous hybridity of prose and verse in David Jones's *In Parenthesis*. Typographical experiment, despite seeming at odds with the speaking voice, was not always seen as anti-lyric by English poets. One of the most resilient, though highly contestable, theories of mise-en-page is that it provides a means to better record and preserve the poet's voice and, the analogy of the phonograph prevailing, that it augments the possibilities of prosody through a newfound notational exactitude. Free from adherence to inherited metres, typography is repeatedly proffered as the means to articulate the unbounded rhythmical vistas modernists envisaged.

Aptly, then, one of Pound's earliest experiments with layout is a bel canto solo, his 1911 poem 'Aria':

[40] Ezra Pound, 'Salutation The Third', in *BLAST: Review of the Great English Vortex*, 1 (1914), 45.
[41] Ezra Pound, 'Salutation The Third', in *BLAST: Review of the Great English Vortex*, 1 (1914), 45.

My love is a deep flame
　　　　that hides beneath the waters

—My love is gay and kind,
My love is hard to find
　　　　as a flame beneath the waters.

The fingers of the wind
　　　　　　　　meet hers
With a frail
　　　　swift greeting.
My love is gay
　　　　and kind
　　　　　　　and hard
　　　　　　　　　　of meeting,
As the flame beneath the waters
　　　　hard of meeting.

Characteristic of Pound's earliest verse is this effort to inflect poetry Deca-dent in its tropes and lexis through typographical mutation. As in the Swinburnean 'Night Litany', the phraseology of this poem is passé, but its angularity on the page is new as it syncopates syntax, severing noun-phrase from verb and adjective from adjective. Propelling the innovation of modernist poetics, as per Pound's critical account, is a quasi-technological commitment to exactitude, commonly styled as a commitment to ever more minute nuances of rhythm. The singer of this aria is singing an old song, but its modernity is the variegation of the voice through typographical manip-ulation. The layout of a poem like 'Aria' is not supposed to sabotage lyric or the musicality of verse but rejuvenate it. Yet even here, in this demon-stratively cantabile offering, critics might cavil and protest. What are these broken lines supposed to sound like? Printed poems do not notate the voice as the score to an aria does. Such verse may be forged by a will for precision, but, being cut off from the interpretative and graphical inheritance of sheet music—that a line of verse is not quantifiable like the stave and bar—what lingers is a pregnant polysemy. A more celebrated lyric, Pound's 'The Return', is testament to this and to how reading such pages divided modernists. The poem is shaped by the same kind of broken lines Pound had essayed in 'Aria' and elsewhere:

> Slow on the leash,
>
> pallid the leash-men !⁴²

The eye of W. B. Yeats, a poet unaffected by the typographical experiments of his peers, passes over the unorthodox shape of Pound's lines.⁴³ He hears, instead, sounds from Antiquity: the quantitative rhythms of a Greek chorus. For E. E. Cummings, this brief poem is for the future. It is a revolution in lyric, presaging '[t]he inaudible poem—the visual poem—the poem not for ears but eye', the founding vision of his lifelong typographical poetics.⁴⁴

3. 'Vers libre be damned': Typographical Experiment and Free Verse

Typography was invoked as the saviour of modern versification throughout the twentieth century. Versions of this credo are voiced by Pound in the 1910s and the 1930s, by Williams and Olson in the 1950s, and by Levertov in the 1970s.⁴⁵ Resolute though many modernists are that accentual-syllabic and stress metres have obsolesced, that new rhythmic paradigms should be assumed, they often recoil from the term *vers libre*, or its belated Anglicization free verse, to describe their poetry. In 1917, Pound reiterates Eliot's famous dictum that 'No *vers* is *libre* for the man who wants to do a good job', and, judging the technique an exception, casts a sceptical eye over much of his own lyric achievements: 'As a matter of detail, there is vers libre with accent heavily marked as a drum-beat (as par example my "Dance Figure"), and on the other hand I think I have gone as far as can profitably be gone in

---

⁴² Ezra Pound, *Canzoni* (London: Elkin Mathews, 1911), 37; Ezra Pound, *Ripostes* (London: S. Swift and Co, Ltd., 1912), 54.
⁴³ Though Yeats's verse remains typographically conservative insofar as he doesn't employ broken lines like Pound does, he does experiment with relineating prose in his introduction to *The Oxford Book of Modern Verse* [see *The Oxford Book of Modern Verse: 1892–1935* (New York: Oxford University Press, 1936), p. xxx. Yeats's contribution to the typographical reforms of the Irish Arts and Crafts Movement and the design of his own books via the Cuala Press has been explored by Nicola Gordon Bowe in her chapter on the printed book in Ireland at the turn of the century (see Nicola Gordon Bowe, 'The Iconic Book in Ireland, 1891–1930', in *The Oxford History of the Irish Book, 1891–2000* (Oxford: Oxford University Press, 2011), 390–412.
⁴⁴ Christopher Sawyer-Lauçanno, *E.E. Cummings: A Biography* (London: Methuen, 2005), 73.
⁴⁵ Ezra Pound, 'Letter to Harriet Monroe, 30 March 1913', in *The Letters of Ezra Pound*, 17–18 (p. 17); Ezra Pound, 'Letter to Hubert Creekmore, February 1939' in *The Letters of Ezra Pound*, 321–23 (p. 322); William Carlos Williams, *The William Carlos Williams Reader*, ed. M. L. Rosenthal ([London]: Macgibbon and Kee, 1966), 406–9; Charles Olson, *Collected Prose*, ed. Donald Allen and Benjamin Friedlander (Berkeley: University of California Press, 1997), 245; Denise Levertov, *New & Selected Essays* (New York: New Directions, 1992), 94.

the other direction (and perhaps too far). I mean I do not think one can use to any advantage rhythms much more tenuous and imperceptible than some I have used. I think progress lies rather in an attempt to approximate classical quantitative metres (NOT to copy them) than in a carelessness regarding such things.'[46] What Pound fears is that his prosody, premised on exca-vated verse forms and rarefied rhythmic nuances, unanchored in common English metres, is scarcely audible. This spectre of prosodic unintelligibility, of rhythmic idiolects peculiar to each poet, monadic musics drifting in iso-lation, vexed modernist poets. Unsettled by this presence, Eliot summons up traditional metre as a watchful phantom, and even Mallarmé, writing to the putative inventor of *vers libre* Gustave Kahn, asserts the resilience of French syllabics as the 'rythme officiel de la langue' and 'monument pub-lic', as a municipal warden enforcing a prosodic communality.[47] Pound, though, refuses to ballast free verse with pentameters or alexandrines. Yet his invocation of quantitative metre hardly seems to ward off the shadow of imperceptible rhythms, since classical prosody is not readily apprehensible by the Anglophone ear. Dactyls and anapaests do pattern Pound's verse, but quantitative metre cannot be said to reinstitute a shared prosody or solve the problem of communicability he himself articulates. Typography, though, seemed to chart even his wildest excursions into the prosodic wilderness of free verse: in 1912 he speaks of his experimental mise-en-page as a 'rhythmic system' and in 1938 he claims his layout articulates the full suprasegmental complexity of *The Cantos*.

Williams reaffirms this modernist distrust of *vers libre*. In 'The History of a Coterie' he writes: 'The modern versifier must not however be deceived by what I say: science may be one thing but knowledge is another. You must know. *Vers libre* be damned. It was a passing, necessary phase. To write it now is not to know. It would do good to go back to some of Ezra Pound's original don'ts for the Imagists. Work, study, try, experience, and reject. Almost everything else is worthless.'[48] Critical though he is of Eliot's conservatism, Williams's denunciation of free verse is familiar from the latter's 'Reflections on Vers Libre'. Free verse is a nullity. For Eliot, it is ontologically inexistent since, though predicated on the absences of pattern, rhyme, and metre, all poetry, he sophistically opines, can be analysed into

[46] Ezra Pound, *Pavannes and Divisions* (New York: Alfred A. Knopf, 1918), 108.
[47] T. S. Eliot, 'Reflections on Vers Libre', *New Statesman* (3 March 1917), 518–19; 'the official rhythm of the language [...] public monument'; Stéphane Mallarmé, 'Letter to Gustave Kahn, [7] June 1887', in *Correspondance complète*, 594–96 (p. 595).
[48] William Carlos Williams, *The Embodiment of Knowledge*, ed. Ron Loewinsohn (New York: New Directions, 1974), 33.

feet and as such free verse is a metaphysical phantasm. Eliot's argument smacks of sophistry because, even though any line could be translated into stressed and unstressed syllables, this scansion would not necessarily correlate with any form of prosody; a hundred-syllable line with wholly arbitrary accents cannot be judged by the same criteria as a ballad. Labelling units of loose, prosy text as 'iambs' doesn't elide metrical and non-metrical verse. For Williams, *vers libre* is epistemologically inexistent; it is to write poetry without practical knowledge of versification. Free verse as such is antipathetic to Williams's oft-stated empiricism; his 'No ideas but in things' mantra; his anti-idealist epistemology founded on accumulated particularities and experiences. Empiricism functions through heuristic experiment, and that is what Williams prescribes to the modern versifier: 'Work, study, try, experience, and reject [...]'. Yet the lofty fiat that *vers libre* had officially ended by the late 1920s, at odds with Williams's anti-teleological model for literary progress, is contestable. *Vers libre* had not passed away. All this assertion does is to exorcize the phantom of a licentious free verse, an imagined poetry without rules; for Williams cannot extricate himself from free verse understood as non-metrical verse, a prosodic condition with which he is inescapably bound up. What Williams does do from the late 1920s onwards, however, is to rework his verse through experiment, in particular experiments with typography. This is not to say Williams starts afresh. Critics such as Henry Sayre have convincingly argued that earlier work like *Spring and All* (1923) manifests a visual poetics where lineation, rather than demarcating a particular rhythm, instead patterns the optics of phrasing and imagery.[49] By 1929, though, Williams betrays an unease with the ocular lineation of *Spring and All*. If lineation is for the eye more than the ear, why not further exploit the dimensions of the printed page? Consequently, if modern lineation is chiefly for the eye, then hasn't poetry become fully typographical, a disposition of text on a page unguided by the ear? This is to play devil's advocate somewhat, and I do not intend to claim Williams abandons musicality wholesale in favour of a 'poetry for the eye'. Rather, it is to understand that these questions surface in the texture of his verse; and that they seemed like reasonable objections to his critics. 'Simplex Sigilium Veri: A Catalogue', published in the same year, is apprised of such discomforts with modern verse:

[49] Henry M. Sayre, *The Visual Text of Williams Carlos Williams* (Urbana; Chicago: University of Illinois Press, 1983), 6.

> pen holder rest on the brown
> mottled crust of the stained blotter
> by an oystershell smudged
> with cigarette ash, a primrose plant
>
> in a gold ringed saucer, flowerless,
> surfaces of all sorts
> bearing printed characters, bottles,
> words printed on the backs of
>
> two telephone directories
> The Advertising Biographical
> Calendar of Medicine, Wednesday 18
> Thursday 19, Friday 20, papers[50]

This is an inventory of the poet's bureau, an audit of their atelier. Like Yeats's survey of the symbolic stock of his homestead in 'My House', it is also an act of poetic housekeeping. Williams tidies these disparate objects into neat four-line stanzas. But the asyndeton of this assemblage, the loose parataxis of these things, accentuates the artifice of the lineation. These objects spill out of their stanzaic containers such that the lineation seems no more than shallow domestic orderliness. That so much of this paraphernalia consists of assorted paper and text—'surfaces of all sorts / bearing printed characters'—makes the verse, and verse more generally, seem incommensurate with the unruliness of print culture at large. The inclusion of 'two telephone directories' here is timely. Randall Jarrell, referring to Part III of *Paterson*, denounces Williams's chopped-up prose and visual mimicry of blank verse, fearing 'that the guidebook of today is the epic of tomorrow; and a more awing possibility, the telephone book put into accentual verse, weighs upon one's spirit.'[51] That the modernist poet was just a typesetter who lineated any old scraps of print, telephone books, or calendars, is an anxiety that Williams felt acutely.

---

[50] William Carlos Williams, *An Early Martyr and Other Poems* (New York: Alcestis Press, 1935), 55.

[51] Randall Jarrell, '... "Paterson" has been getting rather steadily worse', *Partisan Review*, 6 (1951), in Charles Doyle (ed.), *William Carlos Williams: The Critical Heritage* (London: Routledge & Kegan Paul, 1980), 238–41 (p. 239).

The free-verse lineation of Williams's poems of the late 1920s is fringed by alien, destabilizing print cultures. Verse lines are pressed up against ads and slogans such that the conventions of poetic typography seem in jeopardy. *Spring and All*, with its interweaving of verse and prose, and occasional iconic arrangements on the page, foreshadows these explorations. It is not until around 1930, however, that Williams decisively essays typography that sets him apart from the free verse of poets like H.D., Amy Lowell, or D. H. Lawrence, whose mise-en-page remains orthodox even if some of them abandon normative metre. Poems of this period, such as 'Della Primavera Trasportata al Morale', figure an interpenetration of the printed page of verse and the graphics of the metropolis. The perennial lyric idyll of springtime is repeatedly perforated by the city's hectoring typography: 'BUY THIS PROPERTY'; 'Stop : Go'; 'THIS IS MY PLATFORM'. Pastoral tropes eventually reform into signage—'Winter : Spring'—and propositional statements of personal belief, lyric subjectivity, collapse:

I believe

Spumoni	I.00
French Vanilla	.70[52]

Experimental typography, figured often as foreign visual interpolations, unsettles free verse that retains conventional mise-en-page—conventional in that the visual grammar of the page is limited to the line break and verse paragraph. As with H.D. and Lowell, much of William's early work falls under this latter bracket of non-metrical verse that is visually regular. British poets such as Basil Bunting and D. H. Lawrence slough off accentual-syllabic metre but eschew graphical innovation, as do some of the New York poets, for example John Ashbery (unlike Frank O'Hara or Barbara Guest) or even some of the Black Mountain poets such as Robert Creeley. There is a sizeable corpus of poetry from the 1910s to the present day that does not turn to typographical experiment in the absence of metre. There is no firm date, though, when poets opted for or turned away from graphical orthodoxy. Though many of Williams's lyrics after the late 1920s are visually orthodox, the arc of his oeuvre bends decisively to ever more audacious experiments in typography, culminating in the hybridity of his late epic *Paterson*. What it meant, though, to graduate from free verse to typographical experiment varies from

[52] William Carlos Williams, 'Della Primavera Trasportata al Morale', in *Imagist Anthology 1930* (London: Chatto & Windus, 1930), 129–36.

literature to literature and from poet to poet. The typography of 'Della Primavera Trasportata al Morale' recalls the textual promiscuity of Marinetti and Apollinaire in its inclusion of receipts and industrial signage. Both poets had declared the obsolescence and even death of free verse much earlier than Williams, and both are more explicit than English-language modernists in declaring its supersession by experimental typography. Marinetti's 1913 manifesto extolling the advent of his *paroliberismo*, 'Distruzione della sintassi', announces the '*Morte del verso libero*':

Morte del verso libero

Il verso libero dopo avere avuto mille ragioni d'esistere è ormai destinato a essere sostituito dalle parole in libertà.

L'evoluzione della poesia e della sensibilità umana ci ha rivelati i due irrimediabili difetti del verso libero.

1. Il verso libero spinge fatalmente il poeta a facili effetti di sonorità, giochi di specchi previsti, cadenze monotone, assurdi rintocchi di campana e inevitabili risposte di echi esterni o interni.

2. Il verso libero canalizza artificialmente la corrente della emozione lirica fra le muraglie della sintassi e le chiuse grammaticali. La libera ispirazione intuitiva che si rivolge direttamente all'intuzione del lettore ideale si trova così imprigionata e distribuita come un'acqua potabile per l'alimentazione di tutte le intelligenze restie e meticolose.[53]

Both poets writing in English and European poets saw typographical poetics as an advance on and evolution from free verse, but whereas poets like Marinetti and Apollinaire storied *mots en liberté* as a further logical liberation of verse, succeeding the emancipations from rhyme, metre, and syntax, poets including Pound, Williams, Zukofsky, and Olson thought of

---

[53] 'Words-in-freedom'; 'Destruction of Syntax'; '*The Death of Free Verse*: After having had a thousand reasons to exist, free verse is now fated to be supplanted by words-in-freedom. The evolution of poetry and human sensibility has revealed to us the two irremediable deficiencies of free verse: 1. Free verse inevitably inclines the poet to facile sound effects, predictable mirroring devices, monotonous cadences, silly tintinnabulations, and inevitable iterations of internal and external echoes; 2. Free verse artificially channels the flow of lyric emotion between the walls of syntax and the sluices of grammar. That free intuitive inspiration which addresses itself to the intuition of the ideal reader thus finds itself imprisoned and dosed out like a drinkable water to nourish all those minds which are stubborn and fastidious'; F. T. Marinetti, 'L'Immaginazione senza fili e le parole in libertà', *Lacerba*, 12 (1913), 121–24; F. T. Marinetti, 'Distruzione della sintassi – Immaginazione senza fili – Parole in libertà', in *I manifesti del futurismo*, 137.

typography as a rationalization and a regulation of free verse; an imposition of limits on poetic liberty. Free verse, for Marinetti, is a debilitating hindrance, less free almost than traditional metre, since its proponents resort to compensatory strictures, pseudo-metres, in the forms of cadential repetitions and parallel phrasing. Only a break with inherited typographic conventions offers true freedom in verse. Typographical manipulation, though, for most British and American poets of the last century was a means of governing and mapping the uncharted soundscape of free verse; it was supposed to preserve, albeit in an expanded and complicated mode, the quantifiable music of prosody.

How British and American poets diverged from European poets on the relationship between free verse and typography can be illustrated by comparing the essays and poetry of Apollinaire with those of Williams. What distinguishes Apollinaire's vision of typographical order from that most commonly espoused by modernists writing in English (and entertained in Mallarmé's 'Préface') is its synthetic amplitude. Apollinaire's response to the liberties of free verse is not to impose restrictions on verse but to open it up even further.

Il eût été étrange qu'à une époque où l'art populaire par excellence, le cinéma, est un livre d'images, les poètes n'eussent pas essayé de composer des images pour les esprits méditatifs et plus raffinés qui ne se contentent point des imaginations grossières des fabricants de films. Ceux-ci se raffineront, et l'on peut prévoir le jour où le phonographe et le cinéma étant devenus les seules formes d'impression en usage, les poètes auront une liberté inconnue jusqu'à présent. Qu'on ne s'étonne point si, avec les seuls moyens dont ils disposent encore, ils s'efforcent de se préparer à cet art nouveau (plus vaste que l'art simple des paroles) où, chefs d'un orchestre d'une étendue inouïe, ils auront à leur disposition : le monde entier, ses rumeurs et ses apparences, la pensée et le langage humain, le chant, la danse, tous les arts et tous les artifices, plus de mirages encore que ceux que pouvait faire surgir Morgane sur le mont Gibel pour composer le livre vu et étendu de l'avenir.[54]

---

[54] 'It would have been strange if, in an age where the foremost popular art form, cinema, is a book of images, poets had not tried to construct images for the more refined contemplative minds who are not in any way satisfied by the crude imaginations of filmmakers. These people will become more sophisticated, and you can foresee the day when, the gramophone and the cinema having become the sole forms of expression in usage, poets will have a liberty hitherto unknown. We should not be at all surprised that if, even with the particular forms currently

How Apollinaire hopes to compass these heterogeneous materials in verse is that he already conceives of the world as though it were bibliographical. This brave new world unfolds like the pages of a book or a musical score. Cinema does not supersede literature through its technological advancement since it is still figured as a codex, indeed little more than a glorified flipbook. Gramophones and cinemas are placed under the category of *impression*, of printing. Typographical experiment, then, for Apollinaire, is prophetic. History is seen in and through the expanding dimensions of a book.

This 'livre vu et étendu de l'avenir', though, is also imagined as a score and the poet as a conductor at the podium before an ever-expanding orchestra. However, there are two different scores in the history of typographical experiment, and their dissimilarity manifests two different species of verse. The score of Apollinaire is unhindered by technical prescriptions. The conductor soon becomes Morgane la Fée; their baton a magic wand. Metaphor prevails over specificities. The score which British and American modernists most often hold up is earnestly literal. Sheet music is gestured to as a readily available blueprint for the schematics of typography. Spaces on the page are reckoned interchangeable with the crotchet rests of a stave or bits of text with minims. Empirical pragmatism and a cavalier disregard for detail commingle in this theory of typography as notation. An unprecedented precision is sought through a framework that is inherently imprecise.

These differing scores, one magical and one musical, typify a pervasive dissimilarity between typographical experiment in English and European typographical experiment which can be discerned by comparing a poem by Apollinaire (see Figure 1) and a poem by Williams (below), both on the subject of rain:

---

within their means, they strive to prepare themselves for this new art (vaster than the simple art of words) where, conductors of an orchestra of unimaginable amplitude, they shall have at their disposal: the whole world, its noises and phenomena, thought and human language, song, dance, all the arts and all their devices, more apparitions than those which Morgane la Fée could conjure up on Mount Gibel to compose the tome of sights and sounds of the future'; Guillaume Apollinaire, 'L'Esprit nouveau et les poètes', *Mercure de France* (1918), 385–96 (p. 386).

As the rain moistens
everything
so does
          your love

bathe every
          open
object of the world—

In houses
the priceless dry
          rooms
of illicit love
where we live
hear the wash of the
                    rain—

There
          paintings
and fine
          metalware
[w]oven stuffs—[55]

Where the nature of the two poems' typography differs is that the former's plasticity is answered by the latter's abstraction. While the motions of precipitation are implicit in the layout of Williams's lyric, he does not imitate the pattern of raindrops as Apollinaire does. Apollinaire bends the lines of type, works a haphazard contingency into the mise-en-page, plies angular print into the curviness of the autograph hand. This elasticity typifies the art of the *calligrammes*. They iconize their subjects with ludic naiveté, incorporate ink squibs and a patchwork of typefaces, and later abandon print altogether for the fluidity of penmanship. Williams almost never allows his typography to bend and flex like the tumbling lines of 'Il pleut'. His lines jut and intersect with geometrical calculation. He exploits the rigidity of print rather than twisting it into something almost graphological. Angles prevail over curves.

It is this typography, angular and abstract, that most poets writing in English adopt. This is not to say that there is a school of British and American typography, as might be said of the Italian Futurists. British and American poets of the twentieth century elaborate typographical idiolects, and

---

[55] William Carlos Williams, 'Rain', in *Imagist Anthology*, 145–48 (pp. 145–47).

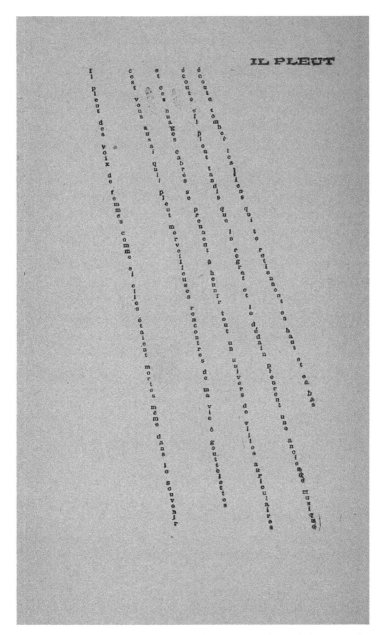

Figure 1. Guillaume Apollinaire, *Calligrammes: poèmes de la paix et de la guerre (1913–1916)* (Paris: Mercure de France, 1918), p. 62.[a]

[a] It is raining women's voices as though even the memory of them were dead / it is raining you also, my life's wondrous encounters, O droplets / and these reared-up clouds begin to whinny a whole universe of auricular towns / listen whether it is raining while regret and disdain weep an ancient music / listen to the wires fall which clutch you high and low

the layout of many passages of verse cannot be mistaken for the work of any other writer. Amongst the myriad idiosyncrasies, nevertheless, a style consisting of stepped, broken lines and elongated spacing, both within and between lines, is discernible; not a house style, nor an accepted lingua franca as such, since such terms would imply more conscious agreement or codi-fication than ever existed, but a familiar *cantus firmus* around which more melismatic descants unfold. Modulations of typeface, contrasts in font size, and sloping, curving or diagonal lines, common in European typography, are much more rarely employed.

Counting and measurement, a conviction that verse must not be free, exercises typography in English across the twentieth century. The analogy of the musical score, which is so resilient in critical discourse about visual poetry, tells us two things: first, that the dictum that poetry is for the voice is never quite abandoned, even as typography renders such verse effectively unpronounceable; second, that quantification as an autotelic ideal, derived from the chronometry of sheet music, is sought through typographical exactitude. This quantifying through typography is exem-plified in Williams's late verse epic *Paterson*. Often the voice of *Paterson* sounds like someone beating time.

> Two—
>   disparate among the pouring
> waters of their hair in which nothing is
> molten—
>
> two, bound by an instinct to be the same:
> ribbons, cut from a piece,
> cerise pink, binding their hair: one—

Score and text commingle ambivalently throughout:

> Stale as a whale's breath: breath!
> Breath![56]

Those 'breaths' hover between being cues and being words, as though Williams were alphabetically writing out rests for the recitant. Strolls in the park in the poem are described as though the speaker were perusing a vocal score:

---

[56] William Carlos Williams, *Paterson: Book One* (New York: New Directions, 1946), n.p.

(He hears! Voices . indeterminate! Sees them
moving, in groups, by twos and fours—filtering
off by way of the many bypaths.)

Indeterminacy is the presiding condition of this text. What is to be said, heard, or seen is kept in suspense. Counting often supplants singing; keeping time does not mean any sounds are actually uttered. Williams exhorts even the tone-deaf reader to hear tempi in his landscapes:

> Stand at the rampart (use a metronome
> if your ear is deficient, one made in Hungary
> if you prefer)
> and look away north by east where the church

Feet throughout the poem's many ambulations are reminiscences of the prosody of the past, but it is hard to determine whether they have been resettled in Williams's pages or are merely lost:

> It is all for
> pleasure   .   their feet   .   aimlessly
>   wandering[57]

These dots are scattered throughout *Paterson*, and they concretize the elusiveness of modernist typography. Their usage in this manner is unique to the poem, as though the work is conversant in its own private language. These are symbols at once familiar and alien; they look like full stops, but their placement transfigures them. It is as though Williams believes he can infuse his verse with systemic order by inserting these typographical quanta, as though totting up points on the page would render this liberated verse measureable.[58]

Williams often speaks as though the printed line and spoken line of verse are quite separate, and critics of Book III of *Paterson*, indeed, acquiesced to this dissociation between line and rhythm when reviewing the poem. Hayden Carruth wrote in 1950:

---

[57] William Carlos Williams, *Paterson: Book Two* (New York: New Directions, 1948), n.p.

[58] As the first edition to which I refer and which I quote is unpaginated I have added the following citation to a later complete edition for ease of reference. Williams's typography is faithfully reproduced in the later edition: William Carlos Williams, *Paterson* (Manchester: Carcanet, 1992), 18, 19, 45, 55, 54.

Twenty-five years ago Eliot felt that he should explain some of the symbols and meanings of 'The Waste Land' in accompanying notes; for Dr. Williams this is not necessary. We are better readers now [...] But I think we should call on Dr. Williams for another kind of note – a definite note on prosody. He himself sees the trouble, and at one point he says to the reader, rather sharply: 'Use a metronome if your ear is deficient, one made in Hungary if you prefer.' I think he misses the mark, for any reader with an ear for poetry will easily discern Dr. Williams's astonishingly pure feeling for the rhythms of the American language. It is not meter that bothers me, but the line. These lines are not run over, in the Elizabethan sense; nor are they rove over, in the Hopkinsian sense; they are hung over, like a Dali watch. They break in the most extraordinary places, with no textual, metrical, or syntactical tension to help us over. If this is done for typographical effect, as it sometimes appears, it is inexcusable, for it interferes with our reading. If it is done to indicate a certain way to read the poem, then we should be told what it is.[59]

Try as he might, Carruth cannot unsee Williams's typography, though this account betrays a reading practice which earnestly tries to do so. To reach the conclusion that Williams's speech rhythms subsist wholly apart from the fractures, dots, and gaps of *Paterson*, Carruth must have read the poem as though it were text entirely unmediated by typography, as though it might as well have been laid out as prose. Typography here is just white noise for the eye; it 'interferes with our reading' rather than forming it. It is as if there is an untainted oral tradition of modern American verse, a fabric of homespun rhythms, which exists apart from the physical presence of this poetry, as though, however much poets interfered with the written word, rhythm and metre lived on inviolate.

Line and metre were once in step; they were commensurate. The span of the printed line was the span of the verse line. Carruth deliberately obscures this norm by referring to the atypical cases of hypermetrical lines in Elizabethan poetry and the *sui generis* prosody of sprung rhythm. Hypermetrical lines compensate for the spillages of rhythm; they allow some give in the temporality of the poem, without metre coming apart.

[59] Hayden Carruth, 'Hung Over Like a Dali Watch', *Nation*, 8 April 1950, in Charles Doyle (ed.), *William Carlos Williams: The Critical Heritage* (London: Routledge & Kegan Paul, 1980), 218–21 (p. 220).

Pursued by the whirlpool-mouths, the dog
descends toward Acheron   .   Le Néant
    .   the sewer
          a dead dog
                turning[60]

Lines like these, though, leak. Contradicting his own dictum that the pure rhythms of speech tick along apart from the page, Carruth likens these 'hung over' lines to a 'Dali watch'. Devoid of the propulsion of accentual-syllabic metre, spaces and broken lines deflate whatever dynamism the poem retains. Far from imposing time and quantity upon free verse, typographical experiment is read as a dissolution of the chronometry of verse.

This critique of the typography of Williams's *Paterson* is so timely because it voices deep-seated anxieties in modernist poetics, doubts and misgivings that few poets could ignore, even if they remain unspoken. Carruth continues:

The question of 'Paterson's' [sic] value as poetry should at last put the critics face to face with the problems they have been dodging for twenty years: What kinds of lines and sentences does one put next to each other to create a long poem? Is it an arguable prosodic concept that the metrical beat, to the exclusion of the line, is the basic unit of poetry? What, precisely, has experimental technique added to our knowledge of ways to say our thoughts?[61]

The period Carruth demarcates, from roughly 1930 to 1950, is when the typographical experiments of the 1910s and 1920s are being consolidated: Hart Crane's metrical but visually amorphous long poem *The Bridge* is published in 1930; Williams is substituting the spare layout of his early lyrics for the hybridity that will typify *Paterson*; Cummings will decisively adopt a 'poetry for the eye' in his 1935 volume *No Thanks*; and Pound is increasingly drawn to radical theories of printing in the 1930s and 1940s.

The commonplace to which so many poets and critics of this period give credence—that typographical innovation will shore up free verse and endow verse with a solidity it lost in losing metre—might well be wholly inverted. For a consequence of this ferment of graphical experiment in

[60] William Carlos Williams, *Paterson: Book Three* (New York: New Directions, 1949), n.p. [cf William Carlos Williams, *Paterson* (Manchester: Carcanet, 1992), 132].
[61] Hayden Carruth, 'Hung over, like a Dali Watch', in Charles Doyle (ed.), *William Carlos Williams: The Critical Heritage* (London: Routledge & Kegan Paul, 1980), 221.

poetry written in English is that the 'basic unit of poetry' becomes hard to define. To ask what 'kind of lines and sentences does one put next to each other to create a long poem' is to ask what the stuff of poetry is and how is it to be put together. It is the plea of a craftsman who is sure of neither their materials nor how they might be assembled. Surveying free verse, which he terms 'the most characteristic poetic form of the twentieth century', Derek Attridge lucidly demonstrates this problem by comparing a limerick with a poem from Williams's *Pictures from Breughel* and makes the distinction between 'lines' and 'segments'.[62] The admission of prose into poetry, of which Pound's Malatesta Cantos are the *locus classicus*, only leads to a clear binarity, an unambiguous alternation of *lines* and *sentences*, in certain poems or collections of verse, such as Williams's *Spring and All*. Vast tracts of modernist poetry are a hinterland where the frontiers between verse and prose are thoroughly blurred. That this hinterland comes about is not only because poets want to include other types of text aside from rhythmical verse in their *oeuvre*. Its formation is as much due to the fact that we cannot *see* what is a verse line and what is not. We cannot see where the line ends and the sentence begins. To this binary taxonomy need to be added broken lines; stepped lines; diagonal lines; vertical lines; and words, phrases, and even letters that hang in graphical isolation. The question which Carruth's contemporary critics have dodged might be formulated more radically and tersely. Twenty years of 'experimental technique' lead to the question: What is a line?

Depending on their response to this question, poets and critics read the same lines in wholly divergent ways. The poetry of Marianne Moore is an index of this divergence. Moore, it might be objected, is an outlier in her prosody, as she composes in syllabics but is more conventional in her typography, with its meticulous symmetries but lack of more thoroughgoing experimentation. Yet Moore's syllabics implicate her in the very same ambivalences endemic to the period. Prosody and typography, in fact, are indissolubly wedded in her poetics. Interviewing Moore many years before she will prepare an edition of the poet's verse, Grace Schulman does not find her own attentiveness to typography is endorsed in the way she anticipates:

Late in her life, in 1967, Marianne Moore told me that the sound of the verse was more important to her than its visual pattern. She remarked that

[62] Derek Attridge, *Moving Words: Forms of English Poetry* (Oxford: Oxford University Press, 2013), 204–7.

'it ought to be continuous,' and that she has always wanted her verse to sound 'unstrained and natural, as though I were talking to you.' At the time she told me of her distaste for the commonplace that she wrote in syllabic verse, in which the line lengths of a repeated stanza pattern are determined by the numbers of syllables, rather than stresses. 'Syllabics? Oh, I repudiate that.' All the same, she added, 'I like to see symmetry on the page, I will confess.' At the time, her statement confirmed my way of reading her poems for sound *and* visual pattern. In preparing this edition, though, I have found myself applauding the balletic turns of the visual patterns, especially those created in the poet's earlier years.[63]

There is a syncretism and conciliatoriness in Schulman's account of this interview that ought to be probed further, for it is evident that her and Moore's ways of reading are flatly antipathetic. Like many readers of Moore's poetry, Schulman thinks that the type line and the verse line are in harmony; that prosody and typography are commensurate. Line breaks are a cue for the voice to pause, however briefly, and, as importantly, to mark the metrical identity of the line. If a recurrent number of syllables are grouped in one line of print, however irregular the accents in that line, however much the syntax would have us read across the break, the typography ordains that the poem is written in syllabics, a metre foreign to English phonology but still nominally a species of versification. Syllabics only exist because of typography; to the English ear they are virtually inaudible. Moore reads her own typography, though, in a quite different manner. Just as Carruth hears Williams's rhythms ebb and flow unimpeded by the printed page, Moore refuses to let her line breaks interrupt her reading voice. Sound has nothing to do with the printed page, in her estimation, and accordingly, Moore's model for verbal transmission is face-to-face conversation, without the mediation of the written word. You ought to hear my verse, she tells Schulman, as you hear me now in this interview.

Lines do not do what most readers think they do; this is the nub of Moore's reproof. Typography does not, in this instance, regulate free verse; it cannot transmute irregular speech rhythms into syllabics. Mise-en-page does not create metre. This is the very antithesis of the notational theory so commonly proffered in the last century. Stepped lines and abrupt breaks are

---

[63] Marianne Moore, *The Poems of Marianne Moore*, ed. Grace Schulman (London: Faber and Faber, 2003), xxvii.

not cues for recitation. Typographical symmetry and conversational fluency exist simultaneously, each a self-sufficient aesthetic independent of the other. This is no general rubric. As this book will suggest, typography can at times inflect the recitation of verse. Moore's dicta do, though, gesture to a less frequently acknowledged liberty in modernist verse. There is not just free verse in twentieth-century poetry; there is at the same time *free lineation*. Far more than regulating non-metrical verse, experimental typography generates more hermeneutic possibilities and more graphical ambiguities. If *vers libre* frees rhythm from metre, then experimental typography frees the printed line from framing metre. The span of the line doesn't need to measure out a pentameter or even a breath unit. Lines unbound from demarcating metre are free to become vectors of all manner of errant, eccentric, and transitory thoughts or, indeed, iterative structures quite unlike rhythm. This is what this book will investigate. Poetry for the ear and poetry for the eye can cohabit the same text.

1

Pound's Transmissions

1. Pound's Typographical Legacy

It is doubtful whether Pound would have welcomed a critical study of
his typography. Pound, whose poetics Derrida famously described as
'irréductiblement graphique', was doggedly phonocentric in his recognition
of literary value.[1] While his pantheon is peopled by figures like the blind
bard Homer, the itinerant troubadours, and the phonetician Dante of *De
Vulgari Eloquentia*, those pioneers of visual poetry who were his immediate forebears and contemporaries are routinely disparaged or overlooked.
The Italian Futurists are cast as charlatans and blasted as the enemies of
Vorticism; Apollinaire is deemed unworthy of the book-length study Zukofsky devotes to him; and Mallarmé's *Un coup de dés* is never read carefully
enough for Pound to correctly cite its title, recurrently misnaming it 'Un
Jeu de Dés' in his Parisian dispatches.[2] Even those American poets, Cummings and Zukofsky, whom Pound patronizes and supports, are labelled as
'technical kids', *enfants terribles* of a succeeding generation too 'abstract' for
Pound to comprehend.[3] Pound, were we to credit these accounts, would be a
poet insulated from the typographical revolutions surrounding him: 'fancy
typography' is best left to the French, the Italians, or overly cerebral young
Turks.

Pound's attempts to exempt himself from the contemporary strains of
visual experimentation merit scepticism. In separating himself from the
typographical enthusiasms of the 1920s, he could not have chosen a more
unconvincing adjective than 'technical'. On the evidence of the body of

---

[1] 'irreducibly graphic'; Jacques Derrida, *De la grammatologie* (Paris: Éditions de Minuit,
1967), 140.
[2] Ezra Pound, 'Letter to Louis Zukofsky, 8 January 1933', in *Pound/Zukofsky: Selected Letters
of Ezra Pound and Louis Zukofsky*, ed. Barry Ahearn (London: Faber and Faber, 1987), 141;
Ezra Pound, 'The Island of Paris: A Letter', *The Dial*, 69 (1920), 406–11 (p. 407).
[3] Ezra Pound, 'Letter to Louis Zukofsky, 22 December 1931', in *Pound/Zukofsky*, 122–24
(p. 122).

The Graphics of Verse. Daniel Matore, Oxford University Press. © Daniel Matore (2023).
DOI: 10.1093/oso/9780192857217.003.0002

essays and articles achieved by 1920, when he first makes this generational distinction, Pound had advertised himself as a historian and critic of the technicalities of verse far more explicitly than any other poet of his stature. Moreover, those very 'technical kids' Pound affects to misunderstand see him as their parent: Cummings claims that it was Pound's 1912 lyric 'The Return' that catalysed his typographical imagination just as Charles Olson will canonize Pound alongside Cummings and Williams in 1950 as a pioneer whose spatial notation illuminates new prosodic vistas.[4] Pound may omit his own name from a history of typographical experiment, but succeeding modernists saw him as its *fons et origo*.

Why, then, would Pound, a poet hardly reticent about the progressiveness of his verse, seek to play down one of its most modern aspects? Pound did not enjoy being misheard. The elusiveness of genre in *Homage to Sextus Propertius* occasioned *ex cathedra* pronouncements on the poem's purpose, and even in the case of *The Cantos* Pound reiterates that he is not being intentionally obscure and will 'start exegesis' on the poem once done.[5] Visual experiments leave Pound vulnerable to such misapprehensions: that he has some kinship with Futurist typography even as he denounces Marinetti or that he is employing Mallarmean notation even as he formulates an aesthetics hostile to French Symbolism. Pound's opus appears more absorbent of continental currents, less rigidly shaped by a selective literary heritage, when such visual similarities are discerned. Typography unsettles Pound, though he is recurrently drawn to it. It is a technique that is too modern to fit his aesthetic lexicon. It cannot be subordinated to those trans-historical categories of poetic creation, *phanopoeia*, *melopoeia*, and *logopoeia*, which enable him to weigh Propertius with Gautier and Homer with Yeats. Despite Jerome McGann's exhortation to see the visuality of Pound's pages as a subset of *phanopoeia*, there is no evidence that he ever employed the term to denote anything other than the 'casting of images upon the visual imagination.'[6] The tenor of his scattered remarks on the topic is, uncharacteristically, tentative and unsure. What this chapter will strive to do is think through

[4] Christopher Sawyer-Lauçanno, *E.E. Cummings: A Biography* (London: Methuen, 2005), 73; Charles Olson, *Human Universe and Other Essays*, ed. Donald Allen (San Francisco: The Auerhahn Society, 1965), 53.
[5] Ezra Pound, 'Letter to Hubert Creekmore, February 1939' in *The Letters of Ezra Pound 1907–1941*, ed. D. D. Paige (New York: Harcourt, Brace, 1950), 321–23 (p. 322).
[6] Jerome J. McGann, *The Textual Condition* (Princeton, NJ: Princeton University Press, 1991), 106.

the apprehensiveness that tinges so many of Pound's discussions of typography, to contextualize this anxiety about poetry's burgeoning graphicness, and to understand why, in spite of this uncertainty, Pound persevered with typographical experiment from some of his very earliest lyrics in the 1910s to the late cantos of the 1960s.

2. Tired Eyes and Typographical Fatigue

Over a decade before the documentary reproductions and epistolary mimicry of the Malatesta Cantos, Pound muffles the poet's voice with script and paper. Though possessed of a Swinburnean sonic wealth and often framed as Browningesque dramatic monologues, Pound's early poems deny us direct access to lyric song. These debut volumes are further nourished by his incipient researches into the troubadours and their eminently bardic poetry, and Pound stages this interest by making these figures speaking personae. Yet the first troubadour to step into the limelight in *A Lume Spento*, the fictional Miraut de Garzelas, is a mumbling geriatric who is soon stifled by senility:

> Once when I was among the young men . . . .
> And they said I was quite strong, among the young men.
> Once there was a woman . . . .
> . . . . but I forget . . . . she was . . . .
> . . . . I hope she will not come again.
>
> . . . . I do not remember . . . .[7]

Browning makes recourse to ellipses to punctuate the elastic vocals of his speakers, and aposiopesis has a classical pedigree, but the lacunae tend to come at the end of the line so that it can be heard as a verse line that trails off. However, the fourth line here has disintegrated to fragments too bitty to even be grouped as *vers libre*, and the two strophes contain nine ellipses in seven lines. In the subsequent poem, Cino grumbles about his incapacity to retain the objects of his poetry during his peregrinations on the open road—'Eyes, dreams, lips, and the night goes. / Being upon the road once more, /

---

[7] Ezra Pound, *A Lume Spento* (Venice: A. Antonini, 1908), 4.

They are not'—and after finally bursting into stanzaic, tetrametric song he trails off:

> Seeking e'er the new-laid rast-way
> To the gardens of the sun . . . .
>
> . . . .
> . . . .[8]

Browning's monologues utilize italics, ellipses, and dashes to score an internal drama of recollected refrains, hesitations, and ventriloquism, but Pound uses the printed page not to invigorate his characters' vocal range but to expose their fragility. This rash of ellipses critiques the oral culture of the troubadours in two ways: first, it shows that their repertoire of songs is prey to old age and physical destitution; second, it underlines the voice's dependence on, but discomfort with, a material script. These dots are not readily articulable cues: how can two successive ellipses be voiced? What does a two-line pause sound like? Do we count the syllables that we imagine hearing? Pound excessively punctuates these poems to the point that such marks do not ease the transcription of sound but question how far such transcription is possible. What these early lyrics, sketches, and homages communicate is how long-standing Pound's preoccupation with the graphics of verse was. They demonstrate, in part, how he distorts some of the stanzaic and punctuational characteristics of Victorian poets like Browning and Swinburne into unfamiliar typographical shapes, and, in part, how he experimented with radical forms of mise-en-page without a clear antecedent. What I wish to argue by dissecting these early lyrics is that Pound's concern with how typography could transmit sound and thought, a preoccupation that on a larger canvas animates the drama of his epic verse, is already feverishly awake in his short poetry. Recording, inscription, and notation, the energies that animate the typography of the *Cantos*, already exercise the style of the lyrics, epigrams, and hokkus.

A dissatisfaction with stable typography and regular print marks exercises the early volumes; they long for a better script. It is often eyes that are tired rather than voices. It is a degeneration of ocular proficiency, not just a rupture in oral transmission, that symptomatizes the air of decline. 'Masks' speaks of 'Old poets skill-less in the wind-heart runes' and figures

---

[8] Ezra Pound, *A Lume Spento*, 5–6.

the world—archaizing its orthography as 'earth's queynt devyse'—as a cabbalistic script. The speaker of 'Vana', another jaded bard, laments that 'the wandering of many roads hath made my eyes / As dark red circles filled with dust', and after a brief iridescence that spirals from 'little red elf words' to '[l]ittle green elf words', the poem's imagined script wilts to 'words [. . .] as leaves, old brown leaves in the spring time'. Eyes voice their complaint directly in 'The Cry of the Eyes':

> Free us, for we perish
> In this ever-flowing monotony
> Of ugly print marks, black
> Upon white parchment.[9]

Beneath the superannuated conceit of this poem, that the eyes would rather behold their beloved mistress than scholarly tomes, lies more timely aesthetic unease. In 1907, T. E. Hulme articulated a similar sense of the constriction of reading:

> Enlightenment when first see [sic] that literature is not a vision, but a voice, or a line of letters in a black border.
> Vision the sight of the quaint shadows in things, of the lone trees on the hill, and the hills in life; not the deed, but the shadow cast by the deed.
> The art of literature consists exactly in this *passage from the Eye to the Voice*. From the wealth of nature to that *thin* shadow of words, that gramophone. The Readers are the people who *see* things and want them expressed. The author is the Voice, or the conjuror who does tricks with that curious rope of letters, which is quite different from real passion and sight.
> The Prose writer drags meaning along with the rope.
> The Poet makes it stand on end and hit you.

Hulme's notes overall formulate an optical aesthetics concerned with the transfer of fully fleshed, sculptural images, as Vincent Sherry has outlined, but his presentiments of *phanopoeia* are stimulated by the monochrome poverty of the printed page.[10] Hulme is hyperconscious of the typographical presence of texts, of 'words seen as a physical thing like a piece of string', that

---

[9] Ezra Pound, *A Lume Spento*, 40, 30, 25.
[10] Vincent Sherry, *Wyndham Lewis, Ezra Pound and Radical Modernism* (New York: Oxford University Press, 1993), 40.

literature's attempts to convey a plethora of colour and affect are thwarted by its entrapment in invariant lines of print like bands of binary code.[11]

Sound, in Hulme's account, is not the organon of poetry's material richness, but is already abstracted to transcribed sound, to 'that *thin* shadow of words, that gramophone'. Music is already whittled down to the lines of notated melody or the squiggles scored by a gramophone's stylus. How Hulme's writer, later imaged as a 'snake charmer', makes 'the living worm' of print stand on end is beyond the remit of the fragmented drafts of 'Notes on Language and Style', but Pound's early lyrics have the space to work through and find solutions to their own vexation with graphical constriction and transcribing sound.[12] 'Vana', despite the speaker's tired eyes, aerates the page with mid-line spatial pauses, and it is in 'Night Litany', first published in 1908's *A Quinzaine for this Yule* and reprinted in 1909's *Exultations*, that this dissatisfaction with normative typography becomes most pronounced. Swinburne's 'A Litany', a major source for the poem, is propelled by the rhyming alternation of three-beat triple rhythms with an indented two-beat line, syntactical completion often being tautly held in check over the line break.[13] Pound echoes Swinburne's metre, but quells its systole-diastole pulse by omitting the rhyme, adding more offbeats and finally extricating itself from the binaries of its forerunner by modulating to a tripartite line grouping:

> Upon the shadow of the waters
> In this thy Venice.
>   And before the holiness
> Of the shadow of thy handmaid
> Have I hidden mine eyes,
>   O God of waters.

As with his destabilizing extension of Browning's ellipses, Pound dilates the slight indentations of Swinburne's poem. 'Night Litany' alerts us to its lineation from start, praising its aestheticized 'Dieu' for 'the lines thou hast laid unto me', and this stepped indentation attempts to confect a new rhythmic shape where, without rhyme or clear metrical urging, three lines can be

---

[11] T. E. Hulme, *The Collected Writings of T. E. Hulme*, ed. Karen Csengeri (Clarendon Press: Oxford, 1994), 31.
[12] T. E. Hulme, *Collected Writings*, 31–2.
[13] Algernon Charles Swinburne, *Poems and Ballads* (London: John Camden Hotten, 1866), 102–7.

apprehended as a cohesive unit. The tone of the poem is one of confected rarefaction as Anglican versicles are gallicized and transplanted onto a hymn of praise to Venice, the city being aestheticized to the point of saturation, glimpsed as the shadow of a watery reflection. This yearning for rarefaction climaxes in the final strophe:

> *(Fainter)*
>   Purifiez nos coeurs
> O God of the silence,
>   Purifiez nos coeurs
> O God of waters.[14]

That tonal nuance sought by the remoulded lineation is further qualified by an indication of dynamic markings, as a composer would note *piano* on a score. Rather than dramatizing typographical dissatisfaction as in earlier lyrics, Pound here turns to the modus of the musical score to do tricks with 'that curious rope of letters'.

Pound's scoring of the page in 'Night Litany' heralds a long-standing interest in notation in the broadest sense of the word, in how sound and emotion can be inscribed not only in musical manuscripts but in the printing of poetry. This imbrication between musical notation and typographical experiment is again made explicit in 'Aria', a lyric from 1911 that presents its quasi-operatic solo in the *fioritura* of broken lines and spacing.[15] It is through research into the history of notation that Pound rationalized typographical innovation. By 1912, as he was flouting typographical convention in his poetry, Pound would have learned that musical notation was not an immutable form but was historically conditioned, as he became acquainted with the neumes of medieval musical notation through the pianist and composer Walter Morse Rummel. The greatest influence on Pound's knowledge of notation, however, was the musical antiquarian, instrument maker, and early music revivalist Arnold Dolmetsch. Dolmetsch, as he emerges in Robert Merritt's book-length study, is rightly remembered as an advocate for a musicology that tried to excavate the minutiae of historical performance practice and a figure who furnished modernist poets with antique instruments, constructing a clavichord for Pound and fashioning a psaltery

---

[14] Ezra Pound, *A Lume Spento*, 30; Ezra Pound, *Collected Early Poems*, ed. Michael John King (London: Faber, 1977), 60–61; cf Ezra Pound, *Exultations* (London: Elkin Mathews, 1909), 10–11.

[15] Ezra Pound, *Canzoni* (London: Elkin Mathews, 1911), 162.

at the request of W. B. Yeats for Florence Farr to accompany recitations of his poetry.[16] Dolmetsch's project, though, did not consist only in adducing performance directions from eighteenth-century treatises; he also embarked on a critique of notation. In the introduction to his 1915 *The Interpretation of the Music of the XVII & XVIII Centuries*, after a brief genealogy of modern sheet music, Dolmetsch writes:

> For nine hundred years notation has progressed, and still it is far from perfect [...] A hundred years ago people wrote their music still less accurately than we do now, so that if we want to play in the original style a composition of Beethoven, for example, we find the text incomplete and imitative interpretation perplexing, for the leading players of our time do not agree in their readings.[17]

Dolmetsch has a positivist view of musical notation, where the written text has inerrantly evolved and will in time emerge as a perfect score in which no aspect of compositional intention is left unrecorded. Impatient with the common stock of symbology, Dolmetsch re-notates a selection of keyboard pieces in the appendix to his monograph, crowding the page with idiosyncratic glyphs for lost nuances of ornamentation.

Pound, however, does not claim Dolmetsch as the musicological equivalent of his own typographical re-notation. Conversely, despite Dolmetsch's own complication of the stave, Pound first hears a call to notational streamlining. In his 1917 article in *The Egoist*, he writes:

> Dolmetsch strikes at the root of the trouble by showing how music has been written, more and more, for the stupid; how the notation or rather the notators have gradually ceased to trust to, or to expect, intelligence on the part of the interpreters; with the result that the whole major structure of music, of a piece of music, is obscured; the incidental elements, the detail show on the score equally with the cardinal contentions of the composer.

Though he complains contemporary music is excessively prescriptive, that 'the eye is confused by the multitude of ornamental notes and trappings, lost in the maze', once Pound himself tries to convey the performances he's

---

[16] Robert Merritt, *Early Music and the Aesthetics of Ezra Pound: Hush of Older Song* (Lewiston: Edwin Mellen Press, 1993), 113, 13.

[17] Arnold Dolmetsch, *The Interpretation of the Music of the XVII & XVIII Centuries* (London: Novello, 1915), v.

tasked with reviewing as music critic for *The New Age*, under the *nom de plume* William Atheling, he falls far short of his own maxims.[18] Reviewing a recital of Hebridean songs, Pound hears and sees a rhythmic shape which he at first posits as unwriteable, and then attempts to set down:

> It is just possible that this curious "Figure eight" rhythm cannot be conveyed to the contemporary musician by contemporary musical notation.
>
> Éárly puts the sún   greeting on Strōā, [macron over 'S in 'Stroa']
> Éárly chant the birds   the béauty of Donnan.

For all his discontent with 'blobs and splotches' the preceding year, Pound's only recourse when articulating Gaelic song is to crowd the page with diacritics and to turn to the same notational micromanagement he affected to disdain.[19]

Pound's thesis that Dolmetsch is an exponent of 'major form', a scholar who wishes to declutter printed music, not only misrepresents Dolmetsch but also tries to tidy up his own aesthetics. Far from positing a hierarchy of cardinal themes and inessential ornaments, Dolmetsch elevates every attribute of the musical work, from tempo to phrasing; every *acciaccatura* and *staccato* is indispensable. Dolmetsch's wish to recuperate Baroque performances leads him not to licensing improvisation and spontaneous invention, but rather to reworking the written score so that every inflection of sound can be graphed and preserved. As Pound relegates some sounds to ornamentation, his wish to be unencumbered by detail is an impulse that he will manifest throughout his poetic life, most memorably when convinced of the urgency of disseminating political and economical ideals in the late 1920s and early 1930s. Dolmetsch's fastidious musicology, however, is consonant with Pound's own theory of absolute rhythm, suppressed in the 1917 article but gestating since at least 1910, that all facets of music, from dynamics to pitch, are interlinked and essential. In his diacritical tinkering or his attempts to graph a Rubenstein concert with equation signs and virgules, Pound's infidelity to 'major form' and the resilient meticulousness of absolute rhythm is made evident. Atheling's typographical eccentricities, his frustration that a singer's dynamic mismanagement 'cannot be rendered by any capital letters at our disposal', his ambitious attempts at idiosyncratic

---

[18] Ezra Pound, 'Arnold Dolmetsch', *The Egoist*, 7 (1917), 104–5 (p. 104).
[19] William Atheling, 'Music', *The New Age*, 28 March 1918, 434; additional accents over 'puts', 'chant', and 'birds'.

notation, are a microcosm of Pound's typographical experiments in his own poetry.[20] This fastidiousness as a music critic manifests Pound's attempts through typographical experiment to make verse into a rhythmical and affective record. Typography registers the fluctuations in Pound's aesthetics, from extremes of formal scrupulousness where the smallest nuance is prized to extremes of political urgency where detail is eyed with suspicion. Typography is often derided as ornament, but what Pound deems as ornament is far from stable: what may at one point be a speck of surface detail is elsewhere a luminous detail miniaturizing artistic refinement.

3. Recording Instruments: Typography, Phonography, and Perfect Notation

What typography could register, and what poetry was thought capable of notating, was susceptible to technologically charged optimism and technologically stimulated misgivings in the 1910s. Writing in 1918, Pound sounds a cautionary note as to what both poetry and music have the power to record:

> Music is not speech. Arts attract us because they are different from reality; yet differ in some way that is proportionate to reality. Emotions shown in actual speech poured out under emotion will not go into verse. The printed page does not transmit them, nor will musical notation record them phonographically; but, for all that, a certain bending of words or of syllables over several notes may give an emotional equivalent.[21]

Pound's alliance of print literature, musical scores, and sound technology typifies a language where books and manuscripts are conceived of as a form of recording apparatus. Pages, like antennae, transmit. Yet at the same time, the very machinery whose lexicon has infiltrated how Pound talks about art is a pejorative adverb. This simultaneous ingestion of and aversion to technological language is symptomatic of Pound's technological poetics, where poetry's proximity to machinery is enticing for a poet pursuing a programme of radical reform but where a mechanical poetics is still eyed with revulsion.

---

[20] William Atheling, 'Music', *The New Age*, 7 March 1918, 377–78 (p. 377); William Atheling, 'Music', *The New Age*, 9 December 1920, 68.
[21] William Atheling, 'Music', *The New Age*, 7 March 1918, 378.

Pound's sense of a technical hitch in affective transfer, articulated in the mismatch between the production process of pouring emotion into the mould of verse as if in a foundry and the aerial precisions of modern acoustics, is unusually pessimistic and hinges on a distinction between real and aesthetic emotion that is uncommon in his prose. Five years earlier, Pound's faith in what the printed page could transmit was much more sanguine. He repeatedly volunteers accounts of the composition of his lyrics as the effort to record momentary densities of feeling; and in 1913, the year of the poem's publication, he narrates the genesis of 'In a Station of the Metro':

> I tried to write the poem weeks afterwards in Italy, but found it useless. Then only the other night, wondering how I should tell the adventure, it struck me that in Japan, where a work of art is not estimated by its acreage and where sixteen syllables are counted enough for a poem if you arrange and punctuate them properly, one might make a very little poem which would be translated as follows[22]

The punctuation of this very little poem is unremarkable if we take it that Pound is referring to commas and full-stops, but its punctuation of the page in its original printing in *Poetry* is striking:

> The apparition   of these faces   in the crowd :
> Petals   on a wet, black   bough .[23]

In Pound's account a radical diminution in poetic scale is justified if that space is allotted with sufficient acuity. The typography of this hokku more than just underscores the rhythm units of these lines: it opens up apertures. The space between 'black' and 'bough' is not the most natural juncture, while the preceding consecutive stresses of 'wet' and 'black' after three unstressed syllables invite a pause. Even more conspicuous is the spacing between words and punctuation marks at the end of both lines. In effect, Pound's typography creates spaces in the voicing of this poem that but for this layout would not otherwise exist.

Pound's wording in the 1913 article is notable for its confidence in how sound can be manipulated. Syllables are spoken of as if they have no cohesive force of their own, no inherent adhesion at the level of the word or phrase,

[22] Ezra Pound, 'How I Began', *T.P.'s Weekly*, 6 June 1913, 707.
[23] Ezra Pound, 'In a Station of the Metro', *Poetry*, 1 (1913) [Volume II], 12.

but rather are monadic particles to be arranged and disposed at will. Pound speaks of them as if they were graphical counters rather than phonetic units.

Just prior to the discussion of 'In a Station of the Metro', Pound makes an even more audacious assertion of what level of control the poet can exercise:

> I knew at fifteen pretty much what I wanted to do. I believed that the 'Impulse' is with the gods; that technique is a man's own responsibility. A man either is or is not a great poet, that is not within his control, it is the lightning from heaven, the 'fire of the gods', or whatever you choose to call it. His recording instrument is in his own charge. It is his own fault if he does not become a good artist – even a flawless artist.[24]

Poets have perennially spoken of their instruments, whether barbitos, lute, or lyre, but those are the vessels of unmediated poetic performance, of the oral culture of pastoralized bards. But a *recording* instrument is an instrument of notation rather than performance—or, rather, both at once. For recording instruments belong to the age of the phonograph, where the production and storage of sound are no longer separate functions; as Friedrich Kittler articulates: 'Unlike Gutenberg's printing press or Ehrlich's automatic pianos in the brain metaphors of Taine and Spencer, [the phonograph] alone can combine the two actions indispensable to any universal machine, discrete or not: writing and reading, storing and scanning, recording and replaying.'[25] Its typographical notation inscribing patterns of sound that are otherwise inaudible, 'In a Station of the Metro' is one such recording instrument, a poem apprised of the idea that the writing and production of sound are no longer discrete processes.

'[T]he first articulate return of the selfsame voice' that recording instruments channeled, claims Douglas Kahn, and the 'machined fusion of orality and literacy' propelled modernist writers to totalizing visions of their technical powers—a prosodic hegemony 'during the heyday of imperial expansion.'[26] The manifold possibilities of typographical manipulation led Pound to think like an architect of systems. Corresponding with Harriet Monroe in 1913, Pound both insists that his experimental spacing be adhered to

---

[24] Ezra Pound, 'How I Began', *T.P.'s Weekly*, 6 June 1913, 707.
[25] Friedrich A. Kittler, *Gramophone, Film, Typewriter*, trans. Geoffrey Winthrop-Young and Michael Wutz (Stanford, CA: Stanford University Press, 1999), 30.
[26] Douglas Kahn, 'Histories of Sound Once Removed' in *Wireless Imagination: Sound, Radio and the Avant-Garde*, ed. Douglas Kahn and Gregory Whitehead (Cambridge, MA: The MIT Press, 1992), 5.

and indicates that 'In a Station of the Metro' is not an isolated essay in typography, but part of a global scheme:

> Dear Miss Monroe: I'm deluded enough to think there is a rhythmic system in the d—stuff, and I believe I was careful to type it as I wanted it written, i.e., as to line ends and breaking *and capitals*. Certainly I want the line you give, written just as it is.
>
> > *Dawn enters with little feet*
> > *like a gilded Pavlova.*
>
> In the 'Metro' hokku, I was careful, I think, to indicate spaces between the rhythmic units, and I want them observed.[27]

Though the spacing of 'In a Station of the Metro' is omitted in later editions, the 1913 experiment in *Poetry* foreshadows the graphical innovation which became part of Pound's poetic language; the hokku is highly unusual in having its layout ironed out in later editions. Normalizing typography in later editions is not typical of Pound's lyrics, long poems, or, indeed, *The Cantos*; graphical experiment tends to endure. More representative of Pound's newfound graphical vocabulary than the spacing of the hokku, at least in terms of the typography of his lyrics, is the line breaking of 'The Garret', the poem referred to in his letter to Monroe. Line breaking is ubiquitous in the poet's lyrics; it is a resource Pound turns to again and again. The delusion referred to might be read as the undercurrent of the ambition here exhibited. Systematizing prosody, reworking how the printed page communicates without any recourse to literary tradition, invites the self-reproach of hubris. Pound, though, is not alone in advancing such hubristic claims for how typographical experiment might renovate the communicative medium of poetry. In the year following Pound's letter to Monroe, Filippo Marinetti publicly announces his own typographical system in an article free of Pound's admixture of self-doubt:

> [. . .] mediante uno o più aggettivi isolati tra parentesi o messi a fianco delle parole in libertà dietro una riga perpendicolare (in chaive), si può dare successivamente l'atmosfera generale del racconto e il tono (di colore, suono, odore e rumore) che lo governa. **QUESTO AGGETTIVO-ATMOSFERA O AGGETTIVO-TONO NON PUÒ ESSERE RIMPIAZZATO DA UN**

---

[27] Ezra Pound, 'Letter to Harriet Monroe, 30 March 1913', in *The Letters of Ezra Pound*, 17.

SOSTANTIVO. Si tratta anche qui di convinzioni intuitive difficilmente dimonstrabili. Credo però che isolando per esempio il sostantivo *ferocia* (o mettendolo in chiave) in una descrizione di strage, si otterrà uno stato d'animo di ferocia isolato e chiuso staticamente in un profilo netto.[28]

Marinetti, referencing the broader symbology of the musical score with its lines and clefs, as Pound did in 'Night Litany', is more audacious than Pound in his belief in the linguistic bonds that can be unloosed in reordering the space of the page. Marinetti's proposals are an extreme version of Pound's sense of the control that can be exerted in co-opting the arrangement and punctuation of syllables, regardless of natural phonological pressures. Syntactical links and grammatical class, the sinews of language, can be dissolved and reengineered simply by sectioning off and segmenting the body of text. The title of Marinetti's article, 'Geometric and Mechanical Splendour', is telling, for in his linguistic imagination spatial ordering and technological progress are twinned. The gay abandon with which Marinetti sweeps away cultural inheritance in favour of a mechanistic year zero is consonant with his belief that the spatial language of typography can cut up and resuture the tissue of poetic language. More cautious though he is, Pound's rhetoric of 'the flawless artist', rhythmic systems wired through typography and the free arrangement of syllables, conspires in the notion that typography might be the instrument of a quasi-technological mastery of poetic language, the means of systematizing rhythm or reengineering syntax and grammar.

The systematicity of typography Pound alludes to in 1913 is the heir of a rhythmic idea he has been nurturing since at least 1910: the concept of absolute rhythm, vocalized in the introduction to *The Sonnets and Ballate of Guido Cavalcanti*:

> When we know more of overtones we shall see that the tempo of every masterpiece is absolute, and is exactly set by some further law of rhythmic accord. Whence it should be possible to show that any given rhythm implies about it a complete musical form, fugue, sonata, I cannot say what

---

[28] 'By means of one or more adjectives isolated between parentheses or set next to words-in-freedom behind a perpendicular line (in clefs) one can give the different atmospheres of the story and the tones that govern it. **THIS ADJECTIVE-ATMOSPHERE OR ADJECTIVE-TONE CANNOT BE REPLACED BY A NOUN.** They are intuitive convictions difficult to explain. I nevertheless believe that by isolating, for example, the noun *ferocity* (or putting it in a clef) when describing a slaughter, one will create a mental state of ferocity, firmly enclosed within a clean profile'; F. T. Marinetti, 'Lo splendore geometrico e meccanico nelle parole in libertà', *Lacerba*, 6 (1914), 81–83 (p. 82).

form, but a form, perfect, complete. *Ergo*, the rhythm set in a line of poetry connotes its symphony, which, had we little more skill, we could score for orchestra.[29]

This passage typifies Pound's insistence in the early 1910s that rhythm in art can be perfected and that artistic mastery is achieved through engineering a flawless concinnity of sonic attributes. But importantly, in Pound's conception, this harmonious soundscape is not realized by heuristically tinkering with dynamics and tempi, adding a *forte* here and a *rallentando* there, but through rhythm alone. The verse line is deceptively linear; latent within it is a polyphonic score; each line is a symphony in miniature. This notion that the poetic line is pregnant with other dimensions takes root in Pound's imagination. Bringing this musicological seed to fruition in the 'credo' from his 'Treatise on Harmony', Pound reflects: 'In 1910 I was working with monolinear verbal rhythm but one had already an adumbration that the bits of rhythm used in verse were capable of being used in musical structure, even with other dimensions.'[30] Analytical geometry, with its monolinear equations denoting spatial constructions, is a favoured metaphor for the work of poetry, which Pound articulates in his review of the scientist turned literary critic Hudson Maxim in 1910 and which he reiterates in 'The Wisdom of Poetry' and *Gaudier Brzeska*.[31] Similarly, as he discovers Arnaut Daniel at this time, the cadential nuance that catches his ear is Daniel's quasi-polyphonic rhymes set in monolinear verse, achieved through stanzaic repetition; and his 1911 translation of 'Canzon: Of Incense' uses experimental line breaking to figure this polyphony. The deconstruction and stratifications Pound exerts on the verse line owe part of their genesis to this eccentric musicological conviction that the singular poetic line defined by conventional typography is an optical illusion, that encoded within it is the spatial breadth of a symphonic score.

This preoccupation with scoring and perfect recording is not just a musicological and prosodic hobby horse. Psychophysics, through its musical

---

[29] Guido Cavalcanti, *Sonnets and Ballate of Guido Cavalcanti*, trans. Ezra Pound (London: Stephen Swift, 1912), 11.

[30] Ezra Pound, *Antheil and the Treatise on Harmony* (Paris: Three Mountains Press, 1924), 7.

[31] Ezra Pound, 'A review of *The Science of Poetry and the Philosophy of Language* by Hudson Maxim', *Book News Monthly*, 4 (1910), in *Ezra Pound's Poetry and Prose: Contributions to Periodicals*, ed. Lea Baechler, A. Walton Litz, and James Longenbach, 11 vols (New York: Garland Publishing, Inc., 1991), I: 40–41 (p.41); Ezra Pound, *Gaudier-Brzeska: A Memoir* (London: Laidlaw & Laidlaw, [1939]), 105–6.

analogues for the human body, gives an emotional justification to Pound's aesthetics of recording. For absolute rhythm is as much a psychological and affective theory as it is a stylistic one, as Pound makes clear in his 'Prolegomena', a prosodic credo of 1912:

> *Rhythm.*—I believe in an 'absolute rhythm', a rhythm, that is, in poetry which corresponds exactly to the emotion or shade of emotion to be expressed. A man's rhythm must be interpretative, it will be, therefore, in the end, his own, uncounterfeiting, uncounterfeitable.[32]

A unique rhythmic signature is allied to a unique emotional signature. This key association in Pound's prosody between rhythmical and emotional quiddities is nourished by the assumptions of psychophysics in the late nineteenth and early twentieth century. Ian F. Bell has unearthed the unacknowledged debt of Pound's critical thought to Hudson Maxim's *The Science of Poetry and the Philosophy of Language*, and Maxim's tome, constructing a theory of poetry from 'natural' phenomena, exposits this tenet of sonic affect from the outset: 'All sounds are nerve stimuli and are, consequently, emotional stimuli. All vocal sounds, then, used as signs of ideas in all languages, are nerve stimuli, and emotional stimuli, independently of the thought exprest.'[33] Maxim's utilitarian claims that sound is a mood inducer and his sharp demarcation between the musicality of verse and the intellection of poetry will have less bearing on Pound's thinking, and Pound singles out Maxim's crudeness of taste in his 1910 review.[34] Maxim, however, quotes a key source for his idea of sonic affect, William James's *Principles of Psychology*, at the beginning of his own work, and if we attend to James's articulation of this concept, the proximity of psychophysical thought and Pound's absolute rhythm becomes apparent:

> To begin with, no reader of the last two chapters will be inclined to doubt the fact that *objects do excite bodily changes* by a preorganized mechanism, or the farther fact that *the changes are so indefinitely numerous and subtle that the entire organism may be called a sounding-board*, which every

---

[32] Ezra Pound, 'Prolegomena', *Poetry Review*, 2 (1912), 72–76 (p. 73).

[33] Ian F. A. Bell, *The Critic as Scientist: The Modernist Poetics of Ezra Pound* (London: Methuen, 1981), 27; Hudson Maxim, *The Science of Poetry and the Philosophy of Language* (New York: London: Funk and Wagnalls, 1910), 3.

[34] Ezra Pound, 'A review of *The Science of Poetry and the Philosophy of Language* by Hudson Maxim', in *Contributions to Periodicals*, I: 41.

change of consciousness, however slight, may make reverberate. The various permutations and combinations of which these organic activities are susceptible make it abstractly possible that no shade of emotion, however slight, should be without a bodily reverberation as unique, when taken in its totality, as is the mental mood itself.[35]

James's metaphor of the sounding board, one to which he returns repeatedly in this chapter, betrays a key interdependence in psychophysics and art. Not only is Pound's absolute rhythm ballasted by the psychophysical framework James erects here, but psychophysics grounds its science in a musicalization of the human body. Indeed, Alexandra Hui's recent monograph, *The Psychophysical Ear*, has demonstrated that this reciprocity between psychophysics and music developed throughout the latter half of the nineteenth century and into the twentieth.[36] Psychology, trying to establish itself as an empirical science, needs some measurable quantum to record the vagaries of emotions, and the quantum it adopts is rhythm. Rhythm, understood as an infinitely variable spectrum of frequencies, records and concretizes an infinitely variable spectrum of emotions, so that such affective nuances, rather than being the airy speculations of the psychologist or the poet, can be measured or registered.

Emotional vibrations, though, can be most evidently concretized, solidified into empirical data, in the form of a written record. John Durham Peters, in his history of the idea of communication, *Speaking into the Air*, has claimed that the gamut of the body's idiosyncrasies was broadened by the recording capacities of new media: 'Just as the photograph and the phonograph allowed for new personal phantasms in the late nineteenth century, they also revealed hitherto unexplored worlds, incidentals of motion and action that were never visible before—the gaits of horses and humans, the varieties of human earlobes, or the split-second expressions on the face. Media spelled not only disembodiment, but a new focus on bodily singularities.'[37] The phonograph, the recording instrument which already furnished theories of consciousness in the later nineteenth century, has an iconic weight here in that it realizes the first example of a non-artificial notation

---

[35] William James, *The Principles of Psychology*, 3 vols (Cambridge, MA: Harvard University Press, 1981), II: 1066.

[36] Alexandra Hui, *The Psychophysical Ear: Musical Experiments, Experimental Sounds, 1840–1910* (Cambridge, MA: MIT Press, 2013).

[37] John Durham Peters, *Speaking into the Air: A History of the Idea of Communication* (Chicago: University of Chicago Press), 190.

of sound; with its oscillating stylus, it spools out reams of non-symbolic writing. James's sounding board, a wooden plane overwrought with strings, visually evokes the wirework of a printed stave, but the psychophysicists who preceded him often explicitly thought of the body as a score to be notated. As Hui notes, 'Like the kymograph, which recorded blood pressure through a stylus on a graph on a rotating band of paper, [Ernest] Mach believed that the ear drew (*zeichnen*) the sound waves in the fluid of the inner ear labyrinth.'[38] Friedrich Kittler reports the account of Jean-Marie Guyau, the nineteenth-century philosopher and poet, who proposed that the phonograph models a psychophysical theory of memory and affect via a kind of inscription: 'Upon speaking into a phonograph, the vibrations of one's voice are transferred to a point that engraves lines onto a metal plate that correspond to the uttered sounds—uneven furrows, more or less deep, depending on the nature of the sounds. It is quite probable that in analogous ways, invisible lines are incessantly carved into the brain cells, which provide a channel for nerve streams.'[39] In the quest to bring the human psyche and its emotions into the realm of empirical measurement, then, psychophysics begins to conceive of the body itself as a kind of phonograph, a recording instrument that inscribes its notation in the flesh. Rainer Maria Rilke, in his 1919 essay 'Primal Sound', contemplates a hybridic fusing of the human body and the phonograph. Just as Pound fantasizes about a poetic mastery through perfecting the recording and typography of verse, Rilke prophesies that 'the perfect poem' can only be engineered through experimental notation. New scores for verse, Rilke posits, lie in the creases of the skull, and he imagines that if the stylus of a phonograph were to trace the coronal suture, atavistic sounds, unheard for aeons, would issue forth.[40]

4. Phonoscopy: l'Abbé Rousselot, the Post-Mallarmeans, and Experimental Typography

With his relocation from London to Paris, Pound finds a literary milieu where typographical experiment, in the wake of Guillaume Apollinaire's *calligrammes* and the rediscovery of Stéphane Mallarmé's *Un coup de dés*, is far more conspicuous and well established than in Anglo-American letters. The

---

[38] Alexandra Hui, *The Psychophysical Ear*, 95.
[39] Friedrich Kittler, *Gramophone, Film, Typewriter*, 30.
[40] Rainer Maria Rilke, 'Primal Sound', in Friedrich A. Kittler, *Gramophone, Film, Typewriter*, 38–42 (p. 41).

ferment around visual poetry in 1920s Paris elicits from Pound his first, and indeed most sustained, public statements about mise-en-page, and by 1925 he will speak, with reactionary unease, as though experiments in printing are endemic in contemporary literature. Mallarmé's radical work *Un coup de dés*, despite Pound's inattentive reading of it, has a talismanic force, which he sees exerted on his French contemporaries and whose historical importance cannot be ignored. In one of his 'Island of Paris' dispatches for *The Dial*, which appears in October 1920 but is signed September of that year, Pound relates the poem's rediscovery, deploying its publication date to discredit the Futurists' claims of typographical innovation:

> The young and very ferocious are going to "understand" Guillaume Apollinaire as their elders "understood" Mallarmé. They have raked up Mallarmé's Jeu de Dés, which was published in an Anglo-International periodical called Cosmopolis before the Futurists had cut their eye-teeth.[41]

Pound's careful ascription of *Cosmopolis* as an 'Anglo-International periodical' might be taken as an indication that Mallarmé had broadcast his achievement to a global audience, and that he had, as it were, clearly patented his discovery. In the following month, Pound translates a short sketch of Mallarmé by the French avant-garde writer Fernand Divoire, which again emphasizes Mallarmé's singular foresight:

> Imagine the author of Un coup de dé [sic] living in our time. We should expect him really to produce poetic *symphonies* rich in sonorities and with distinct architectonic form; symphonies which would have routed the Mallarméens of 1880. Mallarmé came to the threshold of this art. He saw over the threshold. But all his age, all his surroundings, every thing that he had formed, combined together to prevent him from incubating the egg he held in his hand. The Coup de dé was forty years beyond the time in which it was written. It comes to us young with all the future it contained, weighted with the defects of the time in which it was put together. If there is among us any one who can shed his friends and disciples three times running. Gain: 40 x 3 = years 120.[42]

With his extravagant synchronization of formal innovation and literary chronology and his fantasy of a poetic maverick time-travelling in isolation

---

[41] Ezra Pound, 'The Island of Paris: A Letter', *The Dial* (September 1920), 406–11 (p. 407).

[42] Fernand Divoire, 'Case: Mallarmé', trans Ezra Pound, *The Dial* (November 1920), 514.

from his lesser peers, Divoire, apparently reckoning that the poem is written in 1880, calculates that *Un coup de dés* is only truly at home in 1920. It is a guiding light for twentieth-century poetry that had the misfortune of being conceived forty years too early. In his final 'Island of Paris' article of the year, in December 1920, Pound again refers to Mallarmé, acknowledging the poem's gravitational pull and the immense promise its typography was seen to herald: 'There are no prohibitions, there are only questions of degree. Mallarmé's Jeu de dés is permissible, one does not perhaps consider it as a New Light or the basis for the only possible poetry of to-morrow.'[43] Pound, unsurprisingly, is not willing to wager the course of all future poetry on one work. His own poetry never quite reaches Mallarmean heights of graphical complexity, but *Un coup de dés* remains an extreme and tutelary presence in Pound's poetical firmament whose force magnetizes the less dramatic efforts of the post-Symbolists with whom Pound socializes, poets whose mise-en-page is demonstrably similar to his own.

Divoire's claim that were Mallarmé living in the 1920s he would be composing poetic symphonies gestures to one of his principal legacies for French poetry of the 1910s and the 1920s. Apollinaire's 1914 essay 'Simultanéisme-Librettisme' depicts his contemporaries as striving to break free of the solo line of lyric poetry and construct polyphonic textures native to music, their principal means of achieving this being typographical. Apollinaire remarks that Henri-Martin Barzun, one of the founders of *simultanéisme*—a movement dedicated to creating stereoscopic, polyphonic textures in painting, theatre, and literature—will remain unable to break free of monolinear succession in his poetry so long as he employs 'des lignes typographiques habituelles'. Barzun is contrasted with the poet Blaise Cendrars and the artist Sonia Delaunay:

Blaise Cerdrars et Mme Delaunay Terck ont fait une première tentative de simultanéité écrite où des contrastes de couleurs habituaient l'œil à lire d'un seul regard l'ensemble d'un poème, comme un chef d'orchestre lit d'un seul coup les notes superposées dans la partition, comme on voit d'un seul coup les éléments plastiques et imprimés d'une affiche.[44]

[43] Ezra Pound, 'The Island of Paris: A Letter', *The Dial* (December 1920) [article signed November], 635–39 (p. 638).
[44] 'Blaise Cendrars and Mrs Delaunay Terck pioneered a first attempt at written simultaneity where contrasts in colour conditioned the eye to read in a single glance the whole of a poem, just as a conductor reads at a single glance the tiered notes of a score, or as you would read at a single

Mallarmé's 'Préface' to *Un coup de dés* had propounded the idea that the printed page should be read as a score, but that supposed the reader was a recitant modulating their delivery according to spatial oscillations of words and phrases. Apollinaire, quite differently, takes the musical score as a model of stereoscopic reading, where, like superimposed staves and instrumental lines of sheet music, a page striated with chromatic contrasts can facilitate a simultaneous experience of counterpointed lines of verse.

This endeavour amongst the French avant-garde to amplify poetry to symphonic proportions persists in the writers that Pound frequents and reports on in the early 1920s. Pounds himself avers that the verse line encodes a miniaturized symphony in its rhythmic intricacies 'which, had we little more skill, we could score for orchestra', and, as we have already seen, speaks of Arnaut Daniel as achieving a species of polyphony in poetry through stanzaic rhymes, a dimension Pound graphs with experimental line breaks.[45] Pound's interest in poetry becoming polyphonic is confined to Daniel, and in his musicology he obstinately opposes the idea that music has a vertical dimension, arguing that even harmony should be thought of in terms of horizontal lines. Moreover, though he may have come across coloured staves in his research into Guido d'Arezzo, the tenth-century pioneer of notation to whom he frequently alludes, it is unlikely he would have been interested in the chromatic stereoscopy of the *simultanéistes*. Rather, the type of poetic symphonies to which Pound is privy in 1920 are still realized by solo recitation and do not venture into the synaesthetic counterpoint or poster art to which Apollinaire and his circle is drawn.

In his 'Island of Paris' article of December 1920, Pound summons up Arnaut Daniel and his polyphonic rhymes as a contrast to André Wurmser, whom he hears reciting his poem 'Denise' earlier that year:

> Thus in a *grenier* on l'Isle St Louis, in a gathering of young men for the most part allied to Lettres Parisiennes and to René Doyen's revue Connaissance I heard André Wurmser read his Denise, with perfectly modest doubts as to whether it had any literary value whatsoever, but with an execution which demonstrated that he had thought perhaps more about verbal orchestration or at least felt more than any one else in Europe. I found there was nothing historic in this, he had apparently not heard of Arnaut Daniel,

glance the plastic and printed constituents of a poster'; Guillaume Apollinaire, 'Simultanéisme-Librettisme', *Les Soirées de Paris* (1914), 322–25 (p. 323).

[45] Guido Cavalcanti, *Sonnets and Ballate of Guido Cavalcanti*, 11.

or the Provencal rhyme sequences [. . .] his Denise compares to Arnaut Daniel's work as a Beethoven symphony to a Bach fugue; the modes are not mutually exclusive.

Wurmser's poem in this account is not symphonic in the sense of being an orchestration of multiple voices or attempting a kind of simultaneity, but it does pose a typographical quandary:

> Wurmser had considerable doubt as to whether any graphic representation of his *opus* was possible, it departs from the modern modes, it approaches the *chantefable*, he lifted and lowered his voice, he sang, and the whole thing with its four distinct sections or movements made an entirety, of extreme interest to any one who had sufficient musical and verbal knowledge to follow it.[46]

By virtue of its intonational suppleness, its oscillation between speech and song, and the idiosyncrasies of its voicing, Wurmser's poem is deemed unprintable. Crucially, like Dolmetsch's conception of the musical work, the poem's performance is not considered a free variable where tone and pitch are accidentals at liberty to vary from delivery to delivery; this recitation, in all its suprasegmental complexity, *is* the poem itself. Pound reiterates that his idea of *melopoeia* is not simply the rhyme and metre of a poem: it is the total acoustics of a poem, including whether it is to be spoken, chanted, or sung. As Pound is venturing into the uncharted vocal terrain of *The Cantos*, a polyglossic epic where the boundaries between song and speech, epistle and lyric, one voice and another are more unstable than ever, it is clear that Wurmser's problem applies to his own, much more ambitious, *chantefable*. And when tasked with accounting for the typography of *The Cantos* in 1939, Pound not only refers to 'facilitating the reader's intonation', but he hopes that in due course he will be able to mark 'breaks into song'.[47]

Though Wurmser may think his poem is singularly oral and inassimilable by the medium of print, Pound is more optimistic about the typographical advances of the post-Symbolists. Indeed, in this article, Pound betrays an exceptional attentiveness to the mise-en-page of his contemporaries and a sophisticated level of theorization about what it manifests. After

[46] Ezra Pound, 'The Island of Paris: A Letter', *The Dial* (December 1920), 635–36.
[47] Ezra Pound, 'Letter to Hubert Creekmore, February 1939', in *The Letters of Ezra Pound*, 322.

the comparison of Wurmser and Daniel, Pound introduces an even more unexpected point of reference:

> The art of fitting words to tunes is not to be confused with the art of making words which will be "musical" without tunes. All of which statements will greatly bore Mr Cummings, but it can't be helped; English and other criticism is constantly vague and entangled for the lack of a few such uninteresting dissociations.[48]

This allusion to Cummings, three years before the publication of his debut collection *Tulips and Chimneys*, is strikingly prescient. Pound is likely to have encountered Cummings in the five poems published in *The Dial* in January 1920 and the seven poems published in the same review in May 1920. From this handful of lyrics, Pound has already figured Cummings as the most conspicuous proponent of typographical experimentation in English and thought of him in relation to the mise-en-page of the post-Symbolists. Further, Pound has already elaborated an incisive critique of Cummings's poetics, although its exact terms are ambiguous. One reading would be that Cummings's typography is trying to generate musicality by itself, rather than to record the desired recitation of the verse or notate a possible musical accompaniment. This distinction is of capital importance because a species of typography that does more than simply record or notate a pre-existent musicality is incongruous with Pound's fundamentally phonocentric conception of poetry.

Considering how Wurmser's *chantefable* might be recorded in a manner faithful to the fluctuations and contours of its soundscape, Pound explicitly synthesizes his preoccupations with typographical experiment, musical notation, and voicing, concerns implicitly interlinked with some of his earliest lyrics but never before consciously amalgamated in his critical prose:

> Every one has been annoyed by the difficulty of indicating the *exact* tone and rhythm with which one's verse is to be read. One questions the locus of degrees, *sic:* at what point is it more expeditious to learn musical notation and to set one's words to, or print them with the current musical notation, rather than printing them hind-side-to and topsy-turvy on the page. And musical notation? Has been of all man's inventions

---

[48] Ezra Pound, 'The Island of Paris: A Letter', *The Dial* (December 1920), 636.

the slowest to develop, and people have tried various devices from our
very unsatisfactory own, to the circular bars of the Arabs, divided, like
unjust mince-pies, from centre to circumference. Yet Souza has in Terp-
sichore presented a method of printing which might record a good deal
of Wurmser's orchestration, and there are possibly changes of voice, man-
ners of speaking, and intonation which are not expeditiously transcribable
by the present convention of "music": minims, quavers, tonic sol fa, and
the like. All of which is a very nice play-ground for "technical kids," but
it cannot be dismissed in its entirety as unworthy of the serious author's
attention.

The example of Robert de Souza's 'method of printing' which Pound gives
is as follows:

>"—Songes...
>   or sur bronze,
>   gong ! —

The rhythmical and tonal precisions of modern poetry, in Pound's estimation, are not communicable through conventional typography; the poet
is obliged to either incorporate musical notation in their verse or innovate methods of unorthodox printing. Pound's opaque phrase here, 'the
locus of degrees', which follows on from his assertion about Mallarmé's
Un coup de dés that 'There are no prohibitions, only questions of degree',
expresses a paroxysm of spatial and experimental uncertainty: these are
both degrees of experimentalism, on a scale where Mallarmé's poem is an
extreme outlier, and degrees of prosodic and typographical measurement.[49]
By what notational or diagrammatic gauge can the poet transmit their voicing? Pound's vision of the mise-en-page to which he and his contemporaries
make recourse is one of vertiginous disorientation, of a text 'hind-side to and
topsy-turvy'. Even musical notation, though, does not offer a stable or neutral stock of characters. Branches such as Arabic notation have fostered their
own alien geometries with crossed circles 'like unjust mince-pies', and Western notation, which Pound already believes has corrupted modern music, is
impervious to the subtleties of voicing. Underlying this passage is the implication that an insatiable refinement of prosody undertaken by both French

[49] Ezra Pound, 'The Island of Paris: A Letter', *The Dial* (December 1920), 637–38.

and English poets has led to a realization of the insufficiency of conventional printing and the inadequacy of current notation. The printed page is no longer a trustworthy map. The topography of writing needs to be reoriented, even if that entails the dizziness of entering a foreign typographical space.

That the printed page was an ossified convention, incapable of authentically communicating sound, is not only a realization reached by modernist and post-Symbolist poets. Having exhorted his readership not to dismiss the technicalities of typography, Pound immediately segues into a seemingly remote and unconnected discipline, as if the transition were perfectly self-evident:

> I admit that many people did "dismiss" l'Abbé Rousselot; it is, for example, impossible to imagine God's own Englishman with one tube pushed up his nose, reciting verse down another, and God's own Parisian, and God's own supporter of the traditional alexandrine made a good deal of fun of the phonoscope; until M l'Abbé made such handy little discoveries for the locating of boche cannon, and for the locating of submarines, and until his star pupil was so amiable as to locate hostile air craft.[50]

Often hailed as the father of experimental phonetics, Jean-Pierre Rousselot was a French linguist who invented the phonoscope, a mechanism comprising tubes affixed to the speaker's nostrils and mouth, a revolving cylinder, and a stylus inscribing the vibrations onto a paper graph. Pound's interest in Rousselot has been carefully documented by Michael Golston in relation to race and rhythm. Rousselot has, I wish to argue, a particular connection with Pound's typographical poetics. The Frenchman first appears in Pound's critical writings as a direct comparison with experimental typography, as the coda to an article on the graphical innovations of Mallarmé, Cummings, and de Souza.[51] Rousselot's experimental phonetics intends to transform linguistics, hitherto a historical study like philology, into a science by bypassing the authority of alphabetic writing, by no longer trusting that print authentically registers sound. A 1901 article by Rousselot that announces the advent of experimental phonetics tracks the existence of previously unimagined

[50] Ezra Pound, 'The Island of Paris: A Letter', *The Dial* (December 1920), 638.
[51] Michael Golston, *Rhythm and Race in Modernist Poetry and Science* (New York: Columbia University Press, 2008), 63–72.

consonant sounds in certain French dialects like *le parler Marseillais* and, having graphed them with the aid of the phonoscope, concludes:

> Il existe des *z, j* forts, medio-sourds, nasalisés, et des nasales à début sourd. Les qualités propres à ces consonnes, échappant à l'oreille et n'étant révélées que par l'expérimentation, n'ont pu être notées dans l'écriture[...][52]

Rousselot's experimental notation not only supersedes conventional writing, it reveals, validates, and gives visual form to sounds otherwise lost to both ear and eye.

The phonoscope furnishes for Pound the ocular proof of the cadences he has intuited and proclaimed since the early 1910s. What this chapter will now argue, though, is that the typographical notation of the *Cantos* doesn't effectively record sound; instead, it inscribes impossibly faint inflections of tone that transcend actual recitation. Salvific visions of order, I will claim, are what this typography maps out. The phonograph's styluses inscribe a script finer and more discriminating than that of any other inherited notation, just as de Souza's stepped lines are said to give shape to the full spectrum of the voice:

> And this little machine with its two fine horn-point recording needles, and the scrolls for registering the "*belles vibrations*" offers a very interesting field of research for professors of phonetics, and, I think, considerable support, for those simple discriminations which the better poets have made, without being able to support them by much more than "feel" and "intuition."[53]

The ungainliness of an apparatus that requires tubes to be shoved up the nose of its user is eclipsed here by Pound's evocation of its elegance. Having been dismayed by the graphical ugliness that is a by-product of the genealogy of notation, topsy-turvy type lines and notes like unjust mince pies, Pound discerns in the phonoscope a calligraphic refinement, with its 'fine horn-point' styluses like exquisitely wrought pens and its cheap graph paper elevated to the bibliographic splendour of 'scrolls'. Paradisial visions

---

[52] 'There are z's, strong j's, half unvoiced, nasalized, and nasal sounds that are unvoiced at the beginning. The particular properties of these consonants, which elude the ear and are only revealed by experimentation, have not been notated in writing'; Jean-Pierre Rousselot, *Synthèse Phonétique* (Paris: Publications de la Parole, 1901), 25.

[53] Ezra Pound, 'The Island of Paris: A Letter', *The Dial* (December 1920), 639.

in the early *Cantos* are often textured as a crystallization of sound into a resplendently beautiful score:

> 'as the sculptor sees the form in the air . . .
> 'as glass seen under water,
> 'King Otreus, my father . . .'
> and saw the waves taking form as crystal,
> notes as facets of air,
> and the mind there, before them, moving,
> so that notes needed not move.[54]

Waves function as an ur-rhythm in Pound's aesthetics: a line from the *Iliad*, 'the turn of the wave and the scutter of receding pebbles', emblematizes Grecian onomatopoeia, Homer's accomplishment in making verse resonate with the primal undulations of the sea. Likewise, Virgil is held to be inferior to his Scots translator because Gavin Douglas knew better the sound of the sea and irrigated his poetry with this prosodic wellspring.[55] The waves here, though, do not pulsate with the ebb and flow of some natural rhythm that verse should sound out; rather, they are frozen into glacial formations, their susurrations rendered static. Canto XXV, in its paean to creation infused with love and generative ardour, as opposed to the mercenary dealings of Titian, lionizes art that works in rarefied schematics, graphs sketched in the ether. The sculptor who envisions a 3-D blueprint, 'the in, and the through', is set against the cloddish labour of the stonemasons who, overburdened by the materiality of their craft, entrammeled in the stone pits, confess: '"We have gathered a sieve full of water."'[56] Mauberley, struggling to free himself from an aestheticist morass, ditched the sieve for the seismograph, and the frozen waveforms that emerge here summon up the precise undulations of the phonoscope's scrolls. Artistic creation, when inspirited by erotic and cerebral passion, is figured as a celestially inscribed score, a superfine spatialization, unencumbered by the matter of sound or stone.

[54] Ezra Pound, *A Draft of XXX Cantos* (London: Faber & Faber, 1933), 124.
[55] Ezra Pound, 'Letter to W.H.D. Rouse, 23 May 1935', in *Selected Letters*, 274–75 (p. 274); Ezra Pound, *ABC of Reading* (London: George Routledge and Sons, 1934), 29.
[56] Ezra Pound, *A Draft of XXX Cantos*, 123.

Pound in his darkest hour turned to the solace of notation and the salvific order it promised. Caged in the Disciplinary Training Center in Pisa, where the transmission and preservation of his verse was more precarious than ever, he writes at the close of Canto LXXIV:

> out of hell, the pit
> out of the dust and glare evil
> Zephyrus / Apeliota
> This liquid is certainly a
> property of the mind
> nec accidens est   but an element
> in the mind's make-up
> est agens and functions   dust to a fountain pan otherwise
> Hast'ou seen the rose in the steel dust
> (or swansdown ever?)
> so light is the urging, so ordered the dark petals of iron
> we who have passed over Lethe.

The 'crystal jet' and 'bright ball' of the transcendent *nous*, the neo-Platonic schema that illuminates *The Pisan Cantos*, is dangerously close to being mere corporeal matter—to being 'dust to a fountain pan'. Indeed, this pellucid liquidity in the 'mind's make-up' recalls the malleability of the body and languid personhood Pound decries in Canto XXIX. But what disciplines the mind's steel dust is the magnetic assumption of shape. What emerges 'out of hell' is spatial pattern. Drafts of *The Pisan Cantos* show Pound fine-tuning the alignment with pencil annotations, and then effecting these corrections in later typescripts.[57] This is a method of positioning his broken lines similar to that which he had used, for example, in correcting the page proofs of *Homage to Sextus Propertius* (though his practice in annotating drafts is more revisionary and experimental than his proofing procedures).[58] These

---

[57] Ezra Pound, 'The Pisan Cantos', box 76, folders 3394 and 3400. Ezra Pound Papers, Beinecke Rare Book and Manuscript Library, Yale University. These are Pound's pencil annotations to the typescript produced by his daughter, Mary de Rachewiltz, which is based on the typescript Pound originally typed himself in the DTC in Pisa. Throughout these typescripts, upon which the 1948 New Directions edition is based, Pound makes the margins more uniform with autograph annotations and retouches the typography, such as broken lines.

[58] Ezra Pound, 'Homage to Sextus Propertius', box 126, folders 5201. Ezra Pound Papers, Beinecke Rare Book and Manuscript Library, Yale University. In the proofs for the 1934 Faber edition, for example, Pound repositions successive broken lines in the fifth lyric, so that lines such as 'The primitive ages sang Venus / the last sings of a tumult' now overlap. Phrases like 'I

lines are sharply etched; the scholastic glosses are prised apart from the rest
of the verse line, almost diagrammatically, and the lines are broken by the
qualifications and precisions of the thought. Mental rigour is articulated
in inscriptional exactitude, typography scoring a map of the mind, just as
poets and psychophysicists of the 1910s speculated on the brain itself being
striated like a record. The subsequent canto makes the redeeming grace of
notation even more explicit as from 'Out of Phlegethon!' emerges a musical
score of the sixteenth-century composer Clément Janequin's *Le chant des
oiseaux*, mediated through multiple sources, its presence testifying to the
perdurability of transmission, the minor miracle that these scraps of birdsong Janequin imitated could endure on the page. The tensity of shape in
Janequin's score is ingrained in the fibres of *The Pisan Cantos*, such that
Pound begins to transform the bleak landscape of the DTC into a vision of
order by its assuming the character of notation:

> 4 birds on 3 wires, one bird on one
> the imprint of the intaglio depends
> in part on what is pressed under it
> the mould must hold what is poured into it
> in
> discourse
> what matters is
> to get it across e poi basta
> 5 of 'em now on 2;
> on 3; 7 on 4

These lines echo that wrangling over the possibilities and limits of the
page's notation which Pound had voiced back in 1918: 'Emotions shown
in actual speech poured out under emotion will not go into verse. The
printed page does not transmit them.' At this climactic point in Pound's
cogitations on notation, his wiring of his typography is fastidiously conspicuous, so much so that it inflects the very aesthetic principle these lines
seem to espouse. To say 'in discourse what matters is to get it across e poi
basta' in prose or conventional typography might be a bluntly antiformalist

---

was stupefied', when Propertius sees Cynthia naked in bed, which is hyperbolically disjoined
from the text block, are more decorously repositioned with ink annotations.

statement, that the message trumps the medium, that statements can dispense with style, a line of argument that the politically impatient Pound of the 20s and 30s often gravitates towards, as if exorcizing his former role as verse technician-in-chief. The Pound who tinkered with the minutiae of his 'recording instrument', though, lives on, even in 1945; for the angular bending of the lines, so that 'in' and 'discourse' hang in mid-page, attests to the necessity of shape, of typographical mould and imprint, that getting it across depends on the scrupulousness of notational finesse, just as the *meaning* these birds have for Pound depends on their place on the stave.[59]

This spatialization of sound is adumbrated in Canto XVII, another salvific vision, and one that is positioned immediately after the Hell Cantos. The Hell Cantos had the printed body contract the contagion of linguistic corruption, expunging sound to create lines that are unspeakable, inverting the typographical conventions of censorship to record infamy by blotting out the infamous. Hell, for Pound, is the inverse of a crystalline score; it is a text mutilated by redactions, a text that deletes rather than records. Canto XVII also tries to muffle sound:

> Cave of Nerea,
>   she like a great shell curved,
> And the boat drawn without sound,
> Without odour of ship-work,
> Nor bird-cry, nor any noise of wave moving,
> Nor splash of porpoise, nor any noise of wave moving,
> Within her cave, Nerea,
>   she like a great shell curved.
> In the suavity of the rock,
>   cliff green-gray in the far,
> In the near, the gate-cliffs of amber,
> And the wave
>   green clear, and blue clear,
> And the cave salt-white, and glare-purple
>   cool, porphyry smooth,
>   the rock sea-worn.[60]

[59] Ezra Pound, *The Pisan Cantos* (New York: New Directions, [1948]), 27, 28–29, 63–64.
[60] Ezra Pound, *A Draft of XXX Cantos*, 80.

These lines ring with the insistence of their soundlessness. The curvature of acoustic spaces, hollowed-out rock and the undulations of shells, is meticulously inscribed in these lines, while the apparition of sound is kept at bay. The broken lines mould an overly resonant space: the already conspicuous echo of 'she like a great shell curved' is redoubled by its parallel indentation. Hexameters are evoked by splitting lines into three-beat formations. The ear becomes attuned to infinitesimal nuance: the lines that begin 'And the wave' and 'And the cave' mirror each other's syntax and rhythm with their postposed adjectives and anapaestic opening, but the typography cleaves in the first one, as if we are supposed to hear it differently, discern some minute inflection.

Sound in this canto is transmuted into geological and typographical space, where it can be moulded into shapes foreign to conventional printing. The voice is enjoined to descry intonational contours so subtle that the recitation it graphs borders on the inaudible. It is as if Pound's imagining of a superhuman soundscape impels him to inscribe an 'audition of the phantasmal sea-surge', an ideal score whose notes are too precisely inflected, too rarefied to ever be exactly voiced: sounds only readily apprehended as waveforms of a graph or in the quiddities of typographical experimentation. Pound writes shape and pattern into this verse throughout its composition:

> Marble trunks out of stillness,
> On past the palazzi,
>   in the stillness,
> The light now, not of the sun.
>   Chrysophrase[61]

Stepped lines and dilated spacing pattern the manuscript drafts.[62] While some inflections shift or only emerge in typescript, the typography of lines like the ones directly above are already plotted in pen. As breaks and

[61] Ezra Pound, *A Draft of XXX Cantos*, p. 80.
[62] This is a page from an autograph manuscript of Canto XVII on squared paper, with autograph numbering. Subsequent typescripts [box 71, folder 3176–3177] based on this manuscript contain lexical and typographical corrections by Pound in red crayon and pencil; the latest one in the dossier, as shown in Figure 3, clearly demarcates the typography of the published versions. The majority of the text of the autograph manuscript is retained in the published versions, though with significant additions (the first four lines of the final version are added in typescript, for example), and a few specific typographical features, as mentioned, are preserved throughout the genesis of the text.

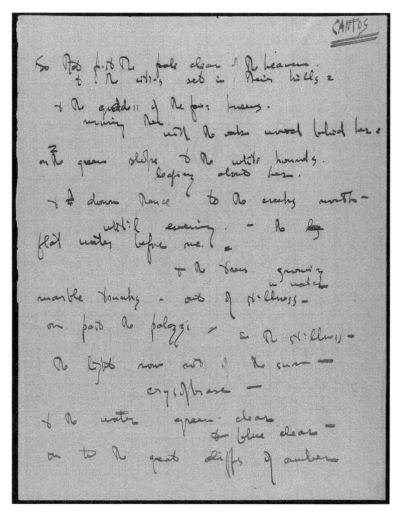

Figure 2. Ezra Pound, 'Canto XVII', box 70, folder 3175. Ezra Pound Papers, Beinecke Rare Book and Manuscript Library, Yale University. New Directions Pub. acting as agent, copyright ©2022 by Mary de Rachewiltz and the Estate of Omar S. Pound. Reprinted by permission of New Directions Publishing Corp.

indents are finessed in the typescripts and assume their final form (the break after 'And the wave' is added in typescript, for example, while the one after 'In the suavity of the rock' is already present in the manuscript) what does not emerge is an easier score to read but a one where spectral precisions

```
                                                                2

Without  odour  of  ship-work ,
Nor  bird-cry ,  nor  any  noise  of  wave  moving ,
Nor  splash  of  porpoise ,  nor  any  noise  of  wave  moving , .
Within  her  cave , Nerea ,
                          she  like  a  great  shell  curved ,
In  the  suavity  of  the  rock ,
                          cliff  green-gray  in  the  far ,
In  the  near ,  the  gate-cliffs  of  amber ,
And  the  wave
                  green  clear ,  and  blue  clear ,
And  the  cave  salt-white ,  and  glare-purple ,
              cool ,  porphyry/smooth ,
              the  rock  sea-worn .
No  gull  cry ,  no  sound  of  porpoise ,
Sand  as  of  malachite ,  and  no  cold  there ,
              the  light  not  of  the  sun.


Zagreus ,  feeding  his  panthers ,
              the  turf  clear  as  on  hills  under  light.

And  under  the  almond  trees ,  gods ,
              with  them ,  choros  nympharum .  Gods ,
Hermes  and  Athene .
                      As  shaft  of  compass ,
Between  them ,  trembled  ---
To  the  left  is  the  place  of  fauns ,
                      sylva  nympharum ;
The  low  wood ,  moor-scrub ,
      the  doe ,  the  young  spotted  deer ,
      leap  up  through  the  broom-plants ,
```

Figure 3. Ezra Pound, 'Canto XVII', box 70, folder 3177. Ezra Pound Papers, Beinecke Rare Book and Manuscript Library, Yale University. New Directions Pub. acting as agent, copyright ©2022 by Mary de Rachewiltz and the Estate of Omar S. Pound. Reprinted by permission of New Directions Publishing Corp.

linger and are retouched, where 'stillness' echoes 'stillness' but with a slight inflection of shape.

Pound at times speaks of music as though it were a mode of pure intellection, an intercourse that might 'serve as communication between intelligent beings', a kind of angelic speech.[63] When the two gods at the centre of Canto XVII converge, they do not utter a sound:

> Hermes and Athene,
>> As shaft of compass,
> Between them, trembled —[64]

Instead, what hangs between Hermes and Athene is a recording needle, an oscillating stylus, incising an abstract thread of sound, as if their speech, circumventing sound, were the undulations of a graph. Looking back at his Parisian years, Pound recollects De Souza's poetry, Wurmser's *chantefable* and Rousselot's phonoscope:

> [. . .] I am called back to an evening when Wörmser was reading something forgotten as far as the subject went, but unforgettable as to the tone. There was in those days still a Parisian research for technique. Spire wrangled as if *vers libre* were a political doctrine. De Souza had what the old Abbé called *une oreille très fine* [. . .] The Abbé was M. Rousselot who had made a machine for measuring the duration of verbal components. A quill or tube held in the nostril, a less shaved quill or other tube in the mouth, and your consonants signed as you spoke them. They return, One and by one, With fear, As half awakened each letter with a double registration of quavering.[65]

Recapitulating the actors of his 1920 article, Pound reimagines the phonoscope as a conduit by which the voice is directly channelled into script. Tone, pitch, and duration are not hazarded to the air, emitted as transient sounds whose notation is uncertain, but are perfectly preserved on the page. Sound is not heard here but instantly becomes script. Through this fantasy of the phonoscope's capabilities, Pound imagines a truly natural writing, the organs of poetry, the lungs of the bard, funnelling breath into a quill, the body's own stylus, both inscribing the voice as an inerrant script, transcribing it into exactly synchronous signs, but also signing it in the sense of authenticating it, guaranteeing the idiosyncrasies of tone by giving them written form, making the page the poet's own signature. It is to this archetype of writing, a script that crystallizes verse into a perdurable shape and carves Pound's prosodic ambition into a lapidary record, where

---

[63] William Atheling, 'Music', *The New Age*, 25 March 1920, 338–39 (p. 338).
[64] Ezra Pound, *A Draft of XXX Cantos*, 81.
[65] Ezra Pound, *Polite Essays* (London: Faber and Faber, 1937), 129.

the printed page and the written score solidify artistic achievement, that his typography aspires.

5. Eye Troubles, Ocular Politics, and the Health of Nations

Rousselot's phonoscope was in part an instrument of auscultation, which served to sound out and diagrammatize irregularities in speech. Pound, though, is not exclusively concerned with the aural health of poetry; nor, despite his phonocentric instincts, does he only conceive of typography as a conduit for sound. Through much of the 1920s and 1930s, it is the optical health of readers and nations about which he is anxious. Typography, I will argue, becomes for Pound an index of intellectual well-being, not only of readers but of civilizations. The rhythm of the reading eye and the speed of the mind become intertwined in Pound's thinking and typographical practice. Reviewing the work of Ralph Cheever Dunning in 1925, Pound makes an alarming diagnosis:

> Dunning, using a language or a verbal system almost identical with the verbal systems of Swinburne, Dowson, or that which Fitzgerald uses in the *Rubaiyat*, and a strophic form like those employed by the "nineties" and the Victorians, has nevertheless composed musical phrases; their freshness and precision are no less remarkable because they are not set out in fancy type, broken lines, hosiery-ad fonts, valentine wreaths or other post-Mallarmé devices. Neither is it possible to improve Mr. Dunning's verse by rewriting it in the style of Mr. Cummings. Note, kindly reader, that this, in the year of affliction 1925, constitutes in itself a distinction.

Contemporary poetry, 'in the year of affliction 1925', is in a state of distemper, brought about by an excess of graphical experiment. Having feted the innovations of the post-Mallarmeans five years earlier, Pound has come to discern a poetic culture that is plagued by typographical aberrations. The gradual inclusion of white space has by now so dilated the membrane of the page as to admit not only 'broken lines' but the typeface of 'hosiery ads', as if the graphical demarcations which reinforce the dignity of poetry, divide it from the vulgarity of commercial mise-en-page, have dissolved. More insidious than the promiscuity of text types, though, what impels Pound to his grandiose claims of a general malaise, is the notion that 'freshness and

precision' have become synonymous with graphical energy. That conces-
sive 'nevertheless' and defensive 'no less remarkable' stave off the implicitly
pervasive assumption that musicality, rather than being independent of the
written text, has come to be seen as co-extensive with typography. Rhythmic élan has come to be equated with typographical verve; the prosody of
Dunning's Victorian strophes judged regressive when put alongside Cummings's mise-en-page. Surveying 'a world (of letters) filled with neo-*Yellow
Book*, neo-Gongorists, rebuses, fans, inverted printing, etc', Pound fears that
the literary world, the republic of letters, of *belles-lettres*, has shrunk to its
etymological roots and become a world of lettering.[66]

   That the epistolary letters of humanism, that ideal of a scholarly exchange
of ideas, have degenerated into an interchange of typography is implicit in
Pound's 'world (of letters)'. But placing 'of letters' in parenthesis, not making
recourse to exclamatory capitals as he so often does, suggests an ambivalence
in Pound's critique: 'letters' are partly subordinated by the punctuation,
partly cordoned off, but they still cling syntactically to the preceding noun,
as if Pound, in the moment of trying to exorcise the unruly graphemes of
'inverted printing' and the like from what the literary world ought to be,
still concedes that the graphic text cannot be extirpated. This ambivalence
pervades the article, for while he figures Dunning's strophes as a refuge
from typographical anarchy, he is at pains to maintain his allegiance to
Cummings's style:

   I am not – no, not in the least – heaving bricks at Mr. Cummings and
   the generation that has succeeded me. Most of our current verse would be
   decidedly improved if Mr. Cummings *would*, with his scintillating talent,
   rewrite it for the struggling authors.

Pound, though, does articulate his misgivings about the style Cummings
epitomizes, electing a term, *Gongorism*, which he will apply to the poet
repeatedly in years to come:

   Having, again quite personally, arrived at the sober years, I happen to find
   a good deal of this newer and younger work analogous in manner to a good
   deal that was written in the time of Montemayor, of Lyly, and of Don Luis
   De Gongora. The brilliant multiplicity of detail seems often to monopolize
   the page, at the expense of main drive or intensity.[67]

---

[66] Ezra Pound, 'Mr. Dunning's Poetry', *Poetry*, 6 (1925), 339–45 (p. 341).
[67] Ezra Pound, 'Mr. Dunning's Poetry', *Poetry*, 6 (1925), 341.

The poets Pound lists all typify styles of overly cultivated rhetoric and excessive neologizing, often glossed as euphuism in English and *culteranismo* in Spanish. These baroque tropes, for Pound, have been reincarnated as the fastidious detail of contemporary typography. As the reader of Góngora or Lyly is waylaid by a congeries of hyperbaton and latinisms, where figures decentralize the authority of themes or ideas, so the reader's apprehension of the text has become atomized by the local energies of type and spacing. The page, the interface of reading, has an innate drive, a focalizing of attention, that is liable to be dissipated in typographical experiment.

Why Pound is so concerned about the reading eye being misdirected by a 'brilliant multiplicity of detail' is that, in both his poetic and medical opinions, seeing and thinking, optical and intellectual health, interpenetrate. Classing Cummings as a satirist, and defining satire as the remedying of a diseased mind, a kind of brain surgery with syringes, Pound affirms:

> The whole Anglo-Saxon world needs satire, more galling and more blistering than Mr. Cummings or I or anyone else is likely to be able to apply to it; and in the end the most galling satirist, tortured for an impractical ideal, is likely to find that he has been using his hypodermics not on a mind at all, but only on unorganized ganglia, incapable of cerebration, and subject only to tropisms.[68]

Characteristic of Pound's uneasy loyalty to Cummings, this passage disallows an easy separation of doctor and patient. For, given the article's central assault on the hypertrophy of print culture and the proliferation of 'fancy type', we would expect 'unorganized ganglia' to be a description of the disarray of neo-Gongorist typography. The mind of the 'Anglo-Saxon world' is paralleled with the 'world (of letters)' in the subsequent sentence. Likewise, tropisms echo the Gongorist tropes of the preceding paragraph. The term usually denotes the inclination of a plant towards external stimuli, though the definition Pound seems to have in mind is that of George M. Gould's neurotropism, defined in his 1905 medical dictionary as the growth of nerve tissues into or out of a substance, the latter being a negative form. This image of a singular mind being replaced by decentralized ganglia, their nerve fibres disconnected from any central cortex, then, realizes Pound's anxiety over graphical aberrations clustering outside of the core ideas of the poem.

Pound's concern over the reading eye being afflicted in 1925 by the excesses of typographical experiment taps into a longstanding worry about

---

[68] Ezra Pound, 'Mr. Dunning's Poetry', *Poetry*, 6 (1925), 342.

optical health and the act of reading and how the motion of the eye regulates body and mind. Following James Joyce's severe episode of glaucoma and synechia in March 1917, Pound offers him advice and relates his own salvation from childhood eye troubles: 'I put on glasses at age of five or six, at about twenty I found (no need to be circumstantial) that an inharmonic astigmatism was supposedly driving toward blindness (probably very remote) and also twisting my spine.' Pound evinces a meticulous interest in the exactitudes of ophthalmology, peppering the letter with decimal measurements, even sketching a diagram of how his astigmatism was corrected. His conviction that slight optical misalignments have grave bodily repercussions is traceable to George M. Gould, the doctor whom Pound credits as saving his sight and to whom he recommends Joyce. Gould was not just an ophthalmologist whose medical skill Pound esteemed; he was also a poet, literary critic, and biographer, who tried to link his two vocations by theorizing the relationship between optical health and literary style as well as probing the optics of reading. In his letter to Joyce, Pound writes:

In the mean time, I will today send on your letters to, or toward, Dr Gould, with a request to forward them to Pyle, if he is unable to tackle it. Just what he did for Lafcadio Hearn I dont [sic] know, but he kept him going a long while and [*insert*: at least] prevented blindness. BUT Hearn, I think, lived with him for some months. I suppose it is out of the question for you either to come here or go to America ?? ?? Unfortunately I have not any of Gould's books here. The last I remember seeing was a pamphlet on a man who could see a whole page of print at a glance, one eye doing the rim and the other the middle of the page.[69]

Gould's 1908 *Concerning Lafcadio Hearn* attempts to comprehend the temperament and style of a writer according to the disposition of their eyes. The month before Joyce's attack of glaucoma, Pound had tried to coax him into a project of literary portraiture, reformulating Joyce's poor eyesight as a virtue of minute observation: 'It has always struck me that you could do a unique series of "portraits" [. . .] God knows where you have been and what you have gazed upon with your [*crossout*: myopic] microscopic [*crossout*: eye], remarkable eye.'[70] Pound's idea of myopia as the physiological root

[69] Ezra Pound, 'Letter to James Joyce, 17 March 1917', in *Pound/Joyce: The Letters of Ezra Pound to James Joyce, with Pound's Essays on Joyce*, ed. Forrest Read (London: Faber and Faber, 1968), 100–3 (pp. 100, 101).
[70] Ezra Pound, 'Letter to James Joyce, 9 February 1917', in *Pound/*Joyce, 91–92 (p. 92).

of a literary virtue recapitulates the terms of Gould's book, which, quoting Maxime du Camp to better enunciate its categories, claims:

> The dependence not only of the literary character and workmanship of a writer, but even his innermost psyche, upon vision, normal or abnormal, is a truth which has been dimly and falteringly felt by several writers [. . .] [quoting from Du Camp:] The literature of imagination may be divided into two distinct schools, that of the myopes and that of the hyperopes. The myopes see minutely, study every line [. . .] They have, as it were, a *microscope* (my emphasis) in their eye which enlarges everything. [. . .] The hyperopes, on the other hand, look at the *ensemble*, in which the details are lost, and form a kind of general harmony.

That Pound the *imagiste*, the theorist of *phanopoeia*, would sympathize with Gould's stress on vision is unsurprising, but, as is evident from his recollection of superhuman eyes that can process whole pages of print, he is pre-eminently drawn to Gould for his thoughts on the reading eye. In Du Camp's formulation, the myopic writer is not shown scrutinizing a landscape or an object but, rather, lines of text, as if the kinetics of how such a subject views the world is miniaturized on the printed page. It is to typography, indeed, that Gould turns at the climax to a passage defending his theory of the optical nature of poetry:

> It is evident that the poet is largely a visualizer, if one may so designate this psychic function, and without sight of the world of reality and beauty, poetry will inevitably lack the charm of the real and the lovely [. . .] All thinking, all intellectual activity, is by means of the image and the picture; all words are the product of imaging, and the very letters of the alphabet are conventionalized pictures.[71]

Gould does not segregate the printed text from 'the world of reality and beauty', such that the optics of reading are continuous with viewing the natural world. Further, bypassing the age-old Aristotelian configuration wherein the written word is the sign of a sign, a phonetic cipher at two removes from thought, Gould envisions visual language as the organon of thought, speaking as though cognition is first concretized in the shapes of words. Intelligence, down to the very letter, is ocular. Thought is inflected and conditioned by the motions of the eye.

---

[71] George M. Gould, *Concerning Lafcadio Hearn* (Philadelphia, PA: George W. Jacobs, 1908), 145, 151.

Pound also believed in a form of ocular intelligence that is active in the process of reading. Writing to Marianne Moore in 1918, Pound interrogates her typographical choices:

> ?Are you quite satisfied with the final cadence and graphic arrangement of same in 'A Graveyard'? The ends of the first two strophes lead into the succeeding strophe, rightly. The ending
>
>

'*it is*

neither with volition nor consciousness'

>
> closes the thing to my ear. Perhaps you will find a more drastic change suits you better. I do not offer an alternative as dogma or as single and definite possibility. Very likely you are after a sound-effect which escapes me [. . .] Hang'd if I now know which I thought better. But I think the eye catches either cadence rather better if you break the line at *is* [. . .] Also when you break words at end of line, DO you insist on caps. at beginning of next line? Greeks didn't, nor does [René] Ghil. Not categorical inhibition, but . . . .

Scrupulously attentive to Moore's 'graphic arrangement', every capital and line break, Pound's eye dominates his apprehension of the poem. Repeatedly apologizing for being too lazy to analyse Moore's metre or not hearing a 'sound-effect', Pound trusts to his ability to see cadences and judge a poem's prosody through sight. Cognizant of the aural difficulties syllabics present to the English reader, Pound envisages a rhythmic identity communicated through shape: 'Syllabic, in stanzas, same shape per stanza'. Indeed, Moore's distinction as a poet is imagined as a print signature, a typographical ID that marks her out in the pages of modernist magazines. Pound speaks of this identification like a sort of racial profiling. Mirrlees in *Paris: A Poem* and Pound in *The Pisan Cantos* both use racialized and derogatory language to describe the typographical blackness of printed music—how such print stands out and strikes their eyes. Pound asks Moore: 'And are you a jet black Ethiopian Othello-hued, or was that line in one of your *Egoist* poems but part of your general elaboration and allegory and designed to differentiate your colour from that of the surrounding menagerie?'[72]

In the radically uncertain sound-world of early modernism, where Pound admits to being unsure as to what he hears in Moore, whether she is

---

[72] Ezra Pound, 'Letter to Marianne Moore, 16 December 1918', in *The Letters of Ezra Pound*, 141–44 (pp. 142, 144, 143).

imitating quantitative metres or the rhythms of French Symbolists, the eye still apprehends poetic value:

> Your stuff holds my eye. Most verse I merely slide off of (God I do ye thank for this automatic selfprotection), BUT my held eye goes forward very slowly, and I know how simple many things appear to me which people of supposed intelligence come to me to have explained.[73]

Moore's poem, which hinges on perspectival displacement, the sea refracting an anthropocentric viewpoint, ('the sea is a collector, quick to return a rapacious look. / There are others besides you who have worn that look –'), is superconscious about the act of looking, and in recounting his apprehension of the poem, and Moore's verse more widely, Pound is sharply aware of the tempo of vision.[74] There is a traction between page and eye in great verse, and Pound locates his faculty of judgement in the attunement of his eye to the pace of Moore's typography. Surveying reams of print, pages of dubious rhythm and aesthetic worth, Pound credits this ocular instinct as discerning the heightened tempi of reading that distinguished poetry enforces. This passage is crucial in articulating Pound's understanding that typography has not just a notative and symbolic valency, but a prosodic one. That is, spaces or line breaking aren't just cues for the voice, nor do they only engage in a textual mimicry as in the correspondence or banking documentation of *The Cantos*; they punctuate the kinesis of reading, the rhythm of the eye.

Just as Pound is buoyed in his search for minute rhythmic quanta by the psychophysical claims of correspondences between affect and vibration, so are his pronouncements on typographical rhythm ballasted by his faith in optical science, mostly derived from Gould. When Dorothy Pound corresponds with Kataue Kitasono about the printing of *The Cantos*, relating Pound's exacting typographical requests 'so the shape of the strophe can be seen by american eye', it is to a national optical norm that she makes reference.[75] American writers like Cummings and James baffle European readers, according to Pound's thesis, because they coin new words and they demand an unusually slow pace of reading.

---

[73] Ezra Pound, 'Letter to Marianne Moore, 16 December 1918', in *The Letters of Ezra Pound*, 143.

[74] Marianne Moore, 'Two Poems', *The Dial* (July 1921), 33–34 (p. 34).

[75] Olga Nikolova, 'Ezra Pound's Cantos De Luxe', *Modernism/modernity*, 1 (2008), 155–77 (p. 166).

In an unpublished document, Pound claims that his nationality bestows upon him the capacity to discern the technical minutiae of the American page. His eyes are primed to intuit the unspoken signatory style of the Founding Fathers. There is a pioneering quest for semantic newness inherent in the neologisms of Thomas Jefferson, which only a fellow countryman discern. This virtue in the American eye, Pound claims, is still as potent in the present day. The *tmesis* and punctuational subdivisions of Cummings's *Eimi*, every graphical detail, registers the exactitude of an American writer's appraisal of Soviet Russia. Pound, using an anti-Semitic slur in tune with the jingoistic nativism of this passage, then recalls a theory of how the eye filters the words on the page, rather than reading all of them.

Advising Cummings on the typography of *Eimi*, Pound gestures to empirical proofs for his recommended measurements:

[A] page two, or three, or two and one half centimetres <u>narrower</u>, at least a column of type that much narrower might solve all the difficulties.

   //
      That has I think been tested optically etc. the normal or average eye sees a certain width without heaving from side to side.
      May be hygienic for it to exercise its wobble . . . . but I dunno that the orfer shd. sacrifice himself on that altar. at any rate I can see

      he adds, unhatting and becombing his raven mane. ==

but I don't see the rest of the line until I <u>look specially at it.</u> multiply that 40 times per page for 400 pages. . . .
   ///
      Mebbe there IZ wide=angle eyes. But chew gotter count on a cert. no. ov yr. readers bein at least as dumb as I am.[76]

Here again the fluency of the eye in negotiating the page is classed as an intellectual faculty. Dumb readers need narrower blocks of text, and Pound speculates on a higher class of eye, like those able to apprehend a whole page of print in Gould's pamphlet. As in reading Moore's verse, Pound exhibits an acute sensitivity to the motion of his eyes, stressing the conscious pull needed to see the end of Cummings's lines. Pound's belief that

---

[76] Ezra Pound, 'Unpublished note', box 130, folder 5436. Ezra Pound Papers, Beinecke Rare Book and Manuscript Library, Yale University; Ezra Pound, 'Letter to E. E. Cummings, 6 April 1933', in *Pound/Cummings: The Correspondence of Ezra Pound and E. E. Cummings*, ed. Barry Ahearn (Ann Arbor: University of Michigan Press, 1996), 23–25 (p. 24).

the reading eye assumes a certain gestalt that may be ruptured or strained, and that there is a synchronicity between ocular and cognitive motion may not be the fanciful pseudoscience it first appears to be. Investigating experimental typography in the work of Geoffrey Hill and Susan Howe in a study of 2013, a team of cognitive scientists and literary scholars attempted to gauge how mise-en-page shapes the apperception of poems through eye-tracking:

> Do we read space – and, if so, how? Experimental evidence from eye movement research provides a model of the reading process, and a claim that such eye movements are directly related to cognitive processes. Specifically, it is assumed that the location of the current eye fixation indicates the content of the current cognitive operations (eye–mind assumption), and that the duration of that fixation reflects the extent of cognitive processing of that word (immediacy assumption).

The study is duly prudent in acknowledging that eye-tracking does not in itself attest to readers' interpretation, but after having participants compare Hill's original typography of 'To the Nieuport Scout' with a version that has the experimental spacing omitted, and then questioning them as to the poem's semantic content, it was concluded that the typographically experimental version 'was both better recalled and better understood'.[77]

Pound's assumption that ocular rhythms pattern comprehension, though, germinates conclusions far more extravagant than those which cognitive linguistics would entertain. In the later 1920s and throughout the 1930s, as Pound increasingly turns his attention to the intellectual health of nations, his typographical notions assume a political urgency. In his pioneering monograph *Ezra Pound, Wyndham Lewis, and Radical Modernism*, Vincent Sherry astutely traces the genealogy of a politics of the eye in the early twentieth century, in particular though Remy de Gourmont, Julien Benda, and José Ortega y Gasset. Political philosophers and modernist writers, Sherry convincingly argues, praised vision as an elite, superior faculty to the demotic emotionality and vulgar passivity of hearing. De Gourmont, in *Le problème du style*, divides writers into the acoustically sensitive '*émotifs*' and the more

---

[77] Andrew Michael Roberts, Jane Stabler, Martin H. Fischer, and Lisa Otty, 'Space and Pattern in Linear and Postlinear Poetry', *European Journal of English Studies*, 1 (2013), 23–40 (pp. 25, 28).

cerebral caste of '*les visuels*', but describes an even more elevated class of artistic visionaries:

> Au lieu qu'au prononcé du mot *océan* une immensité glauque, ou une plage de sable ou des falaises, ou telle vision surgisse devant eux, ils voient, simplification admirable ! le mot même écrit dans l'espace en caractères d'imprimerie, OCÉAN. Plus avancés intellectuellement que les visuels, ces individus privilegiés se groupent au pôle negative de l'aimant dont les artistes occupent le pole positif. Un grand pas a été fait vers la simplification; au monde des choses s'est substitué le monde des signes.[78]

Intellectual acuity and discrimination is imagined by De Gourmont as a typographical faculty: the sharpest minds reduce the world to print. Benda, Sherry suggests, synthesises optical and political elitism in his term *séverité*:

> Writing less than a decade after Gourmont, he joins the ideas of optical privilege and political superiority in a single word. *Séverité*, in an unusually literal but not untrue sense, means 'severance' or 'separation,' and as such describes the twofold condition of visual perception: distance from the objects of sight and discrimination among them. Construed also as 'aloofness' or 'austerity,' moreover, *séverité* describes the virtù of an aristocracy at once inherited and earned – its traditional privileges the reward for percipients gifted with this superior visual faculty.[79]

Benda repeatedly pathologizes what he views as a bourgeois materialism in the Europe of the late 1910s as a musical malady, an aural fallibility shared with *fin-de-siècle* aesthetes. Optics, for Benda, impose distinctions between active subject and passive object, between aristocrat and parvenu.[80] This politics of the eye is most forcefully articulated in the writings of Ortega

---

[78] 'When the word "ocean" is spoken, instead of a glacous expanse or a sandy beach or cliffs or some such vision rising up before their eyes, they see—what a laudable simplification— the word itself written in printed characters: OCEAN. More intellectually advanced than "the visuals", these special individuals are attracted to the negative pole of the magnet, whereas the artists are situated at the positive pole. This is a considerable step in the direction of simplicity; the world of signs has replaced the world of things.' Remy de Gourmont, *Le problème de style* (Paris: Societé du Mercure de France, 1907), 37.

[79] Vincent Sherry, *Wyndham Lewis, Ezra Pound and Radical Modernism* (New York: OUP, 1993), 22.

[80] Julien Benda, *Belphégor: essai sur l'esthétique de la présente société française* (Emile-Paul Freres Editeurs: Paris, 1918), 189–91.

y Gasset. Modernist aesthetics, Ortega argues, has precipitated a political crisis, since avant-garde artworks are alien to the ocular habits of the masses:

A time must come in which society, from politics to art, reorganizes itself into two orders or ranks: the illustrious and the vulgar. That chaotic, shapeless, and undifferentiated state without discipline and social structure in which Europe has lived these hundred and fifty years cannot go on.

The optics of modernist art divide the sheep and the goats, in Ortega's thesis. 'We have here a very simple optical problem. To see a thing we must adjust our visual apparatus in a certain way', he writes, but 'not many people are capable of adjusting their perceptive apparatus to the pane and the transparency that is the work of art.'[81]

Pound's alertness to a visual crisis in the 1920s is no less politically charged, and this politics of the eye takes place in the architectonics of print. His theories of ocular rhythms and readerly comprehension take on geopolitical dimensions. His domestic concern for his friends' eyesight and the legibility of their lines morphs into an obsession with how whole nations scan the page. Pound shares Ortega's belief that the political health of a nation can be diagnosed in its visual orderliness. One of the chief indices of visual orderliness for Pound is typography. Print cultures that passively record a demotic cacophony of opinions, a mass of unfiltered information with no hierarchy of viewpoints, increasingly come under attack as Pound becomes involved in Italian Fascism. Transmissibility, Pound's longstanding preoccupation with communicational speed and getting it across, is far from politically neutral. On the contrary, it symptomatises a far-right anxiety over an equality of communication inherent in democratic societies. An obsession with audiovisual engineering stops being innocuous when you're broadcasting over Radio Rome in the early 1940s. The history of civilizations, for Pound, is discernible in the shapes of their print. Lettering stamps the apex of the Italian Renaissance, and demotic, egalitarian print marks the decline of the West. Only an elite few—and Pound later tries to enlist his fellow modernist poets into this cenacle—possess this superior optics, this typographical discrimination that allows them to read history correctly. It is no coincidence that one of Pound's most elaborate typographical projects, the 1932 Genoa edition of Cavalcanti, a synthesis of mediaeval craft and

---

[81] José Ortega y Gasset, *The Dehumanization of Art and Other Essays on Art, Culture, and Literature* (Princeton, NJ: Princeton University Press), 7, 10, 11.

modernist functionality, looks as though it were produced by the fusion of two vocations beloved of Italian Fascism—the artisan and the engineer. Ordering the page and ordering history for Pound become one and the same.

Advertising his diagnosis in *Poetry*, Pound calculates the advancement of civilizations by their print culture, claiming that America is hobbled by the cost of book production and Germany by its typography:

> Germany—"scholarly Germany"—neglects history, and forgets that the awakening of the Renaissance accompanied, in time and in place, the aban-doning of the gothic type, black-letter, etc. The only discernible causes for the retention of German gothic types are laziness and obstinacy. Tons of eye-sight, and aeons of time, are wasted crumb by crumb in Germany and Austria every year; they have the habit of ploughing slowly through these wiggles and hedges of underbrush, and don't know that they are doing it. It keeps them from seeing clearly what they read.[82]

Those saccades and twitches of the eye Pound measured in Moore's and Cummings's mise-en-page are multiplied to epochal quantities, the span of aeons, just as sight is weighed as a civic resource whose expenditure needs to be rationed. Gould suggests that myopia spreads to other motor functions, and similarly Pound imagines vision as a form of ambulation entrammelled by the thickets of gothic type.[83] Magnifying his scrutiny of the optics of thought to historical proportions, Pound sees the Germans as blind to how their typography filters their cognition—'It keeps them from seeing clearly what they read'—and centuries behind as a consequence.

Pound's alignment of civilizational and typographical progress assumes a cardinal position in *The Cantos*. Poised at the commencement of the Italian Renaissance, closing the medieval gestes of Malatesta and Niccolò d'Este that dominate the *Draft of XXX Cantos*, Canto XXX ends on a seminal juncture of typographical history. An undercurrent of artistic and sexual sterility, stemmed by the Latin love elegist Sulpicia and Cunizza, whom Pound figures as a custodian of Provencal love poetry, erupts in this canto with its juxtaposition of barren unions: Aphrodite yoked to the 'doddering fool' Hephaestus, Pedro I of Portugal's morbid attachment to his dead wife, and the mercenary match of Lucrezia Borgia and Alfonso d'Este. Depicting

---

[82] Ezra Pound, 'Practical Suggestions', *Poetry*, 6 (1929), 327–33 (p. 327).
[83] George M. Gould, *Concerning Lafcadio Hearn*, 162.

the exhumed Inés de Castro on the throne, Pound has one detail jut out
conspicuously on the page, a detail he first sketches in the manuscript drafts:

> Time is the evil.   Evil.
>   A day, and a day
> Walked the young Pedro baffled,
>   a day and a day
> After Ignez was murdered.
>
> Came the Lords in Lisboa
>   a day, and a day
> In homage. Seated there
>   dead eyes,
> Dead hair under the crown,
> The King still young beside her.[84]

The ocular rhythm of the indented refrain beats out the malign accretion
of unobserved time, the 'crumb by crumb' wastage of civilizational decay
that Pound discerns in blackletter Germany. Inés' eyes supplant the refrain's
position on the page, upsetting the typographical rhythm and contracting
the rising triple rhythm of 'a day and a day' to a sudden spondaic density,
an abrupt obtrusion of dead vision. This accumulation of dead time and
dead vision is answered by the narrative of typographical history, necrotic
chronology by the kairotic time of intellectual advancement, as Pound
instantly segues from these sterile marriages to the arrival of innovative
printers in the Italian city of Fano:

> ... and here have I brought cutters of letters
> and printers not vile and vulgar
>   (in Fano Caesaris)
> notable and sufficient compositors
> and a die-cutter for greek fonts and hebrew
> named Messire Francesco da Bologna
> not only of the usual types but he hath excogitated
> a new form called cursive or chancellry letters
> nor was it Aldous nor any other but it was
> this Messire Francesco who hath cut all Aldous his letters

[84] Ezra Pound, *A Draft of XXX Cantos*, 152; Ezra Pound, 'Canto XXX', box 72, folder 3234, Beinecke Rare Book and Manuscript Library, Yale University.

What rejuvenates the dead eyes of senescent civilizations, what occasions 'the awakening of the Renaissance', is the typographical renewal accomplished by the inventor of italics, Aldus, the new typefaces of Francesco da Bologna, and the innovative printing of Hieronymous Soncinus.

> Whence we have carved it in metal
> Here working in Caesar's fane :
>> To the Prince Caesare Borgia
>> Duke of Valent and Aemelia

Stressing the physical force of type creation, letters being cut into metal, Pound erects this typographical shrine (Fano and fane deriving from the Latin *fanum*) to stand against the altar of Madame Hyle, his embodiment of moribund materialism, a few lines earlier, centring '(in Fano Caesaris)' and the eulogy to Borgia on the page like an inscription. Electing the verb 'excogitate' for the devising of new types, which principally means 'to construct in thought', Pound publishes this shift in lettering as an advance in cognition.[85] History is written in the shape of letters.

6. Striking the Eye

Besieged by a contemporary print culture he believes to be moribund, democratic, and congested, Pound typologizes the historical shift from blackletter to Latin fonts as a modernist typographical renaissance. In the 1930s, Pound increasingly trumpets his possession of the printed page and, more broadly, becomes a fervent activist for rebalancing bibliographical power. What this final section will claim is that controlling the printed word and reclaiming graphical space become a matter of political urgency for Pound. To engineer the layout of verse, comprehensively realized in his editing of the *Rime* of Guido Cavalcanti, is to reclaim print culture from the ground up. A few months after publicizing his remedy for the global book trade, where he cited the Aldine Press as a historical exemplar, Pound tries to take matters into his own hands by commissioning a new typeface from Wyndham Lewis:

> Dear W.L. Wd. it in least interest or profit you to make an alphabet; caps. for printer, not tied to any particular text. General style that of yr. late Timon

[85] Ezra Pound, *A Draft of XXX Cantos*, 153.

(after portfolio) or your most latest as you see fit. The late Timon wd. go very well with Caslon. In fact Ed Wad[sworth]. set for Ovid press were quite good but you cd. nacherly do the job better. I dont want to start agitating unless you wd take the job.[86]

Classing his efforts as 'agitating', Pound makes it clear that his ambitions stretch beyond the disposition of a single text or his own work to influencing typographical culture much more broadly. His agitations over printing in the 1930s, faithful to the term's association with activism, are political agitations. Ford Madox Ford's magnanimous attempts to secure Pound a salaried post at a liberal arts school, Olivet College, founder on Pound's insistence that the college ally with him in his print war and become a proxy for his politics: 'Will he [the college president] GET a printing press/ LINO or monotype/ I.E. practical and not fancy hand arty machine for the DISTRIBUTION of knowledge and ideas?' Pound's anti-Semitism catalyses his bibliographical activism, and he later opines that '[u]sury has never endowed a press/ It is time someone burnt the stock exchange and set up a linotype on the ruins.'[87] Standing against the indulgences of fine-press printing, whose 'fancy' mise-en-page is complicit with a credit-enabled materialism, the linotype, with its economical and functional typography, becomes a weapon of war. It is imagined as a DIY machine for a grassroots, far-right upsurge against entrenched bibliographical power. The disposition of the printed page bears the markings of its technological provenance and thereby the stamp of political allegiance.

With the matter of print furnishing a paper trail to the sources of civic power, Pound applies himself to righting the dynamics of literary production. In an article in 1936, which punctuates its paragraphs with the italicized refrain 'The printing press was invented', he writes:

Painting & music are cared for, at least materially, but writers do not even observe the material sabotage of communication inherent in the lack of printing machines at the disposition of writers & in the use whereof the voices of the few men whom we read wd. have at least as much weight

[86] Ezra Pound, 'Letter to Wyndham Lewis, 18 August [1929]', in *Pound/Lewis: The Letters of Ezra Pound and Wyndham Lewis*, ed. Timothy Materer (London: Faber and Faber, 1985), 168.
[87] Ezra Pound, 'Letter to Ford Madox Ford, 21 February 1938' and 'Letter to Ford Madox Ford, 22 March 1938', in *Pound/Ford: The Story of a Literary Friendship*, ed. Brita Lindberg-Seyersted (London: Faber and Faber, 1982), 155; 159–60 (p. 160).

as those of the dominant controllers who demand that we write for monetary profit.

Poets—and Pound goes on to cite Williams, Moore, and Cummings, as well as Eliot, glossing over the fact of his editorship at Faber—are uniquely disenfranchised in the arts by not being at the helm of the publishing industry and thereby being deprived of the very material of their art, a position diametrically opposed to that which he adopts in his 1920 article 'Art and Luxury', where the incorruptibility of poetry is premised on it not being tied to a physical form. Convinced that this usurpation of means is corrupting the 'mental life of their craft & of the nation', Pound begins to see writing surfaces in general as a cartography of power. The dispossession of the writer is juxtaposed with the province of the painter granted wall space for mural-painting by the New Deal's federal art funding: 'Now the New Deal could just as well encourage printing as painting walls. The efforts to get good mural painting in California are praiseworthy, but they in no way rule out the effort to have much needed books PRINTED.'[88] Pound also makes this comparison in his attempts to commission a new typeface from Lewis in 1929:

As one can't get architecture or even mural stuff DONE one retreats to printed page . . . . (or not as case may be.) At any rate a chance to see something done right in a chaotic environment. Nor worth interrupting anything else for.etc. Possibly useful in breaking up a state of mind; something O.K. but unfamilar strikin the eye. etc.[89]

Pound speaks of the page space here as if it were contiguous with the civic spaces of frescos and buildings in a map of cultural control. *The Cantos* are interspersed with signage, inscriptions, and public notices, and here typographical space is envisaged as a miniaturized polis where the poet, powerless to govern 'the chaotic environment' that borders the text, can bring about textual order.

In his essay 'Medievalism', which forms the introduction to his translation of Guido Cavalcanti's 'Donna mi prega', Pound again elides walls and pages, graduating from a discussion of Guido's verse lines to the outlines of Byzantine ornament, duly flattened to bring it closer to the two-dimensional text: 'Byzantium gives us perhaps the best architecture, or at least the best inner structure, that we know, I mean for proportions, for ornament flat on the

[88]   Ezra Pound, 'The Printing Press Was Invented', *Poetry*, 1 (1936), 55.
[89]   Ezra Pound, 'Letter to Wyndham Lewis, 5 September [1929]', in *Pound/Lewis*, p. 168.

walls, and not bulging and bumping and indulging in bulbous excrescence.' This is not the only echo of his letter to Lewis. Justifying the experimental typography of the 'Donna mi prega', Pound reformulates his phrase 'striking the eye': 'I trust I have managed to print the Donna mi Prega in such a way that its articulations strike the eye without need of a rhyme table.'[90] Pound speaks here as if he were operating the printing press himself, and this is not altogether a deception. For the production of the 'Donna mi prega', above all in the 1932 Genoa edition, which he prints at his own expense, sees Pound consciously trying to exert total bibliographical mastery, to seize the material means of literary production which he regards as having been wrested from the rightful hands of poets. With the 1932 Genoa edition, Pound assumes the composite role of scholar, editor, translator, and designer, sourcing original manuscripts and overseeing the printing process on site to ensure his typography is precisely realized. Without any editorial precedent, he relineates the Italian text and plots the innovative graphics of his own English translation. Writing to Zukofsky at the time, Pound stresses the toll of his hegemonic role and the manual labour of typesetting: 'Have had a hard day settin' on the printin' press in genova.'[91]

As David Anderson notes, Pound had experimented with the layout of Cavalcanti since the 1912 *Sonnets and Ballate*, and the 'Donna mi Prega', which first appeared in *The Dial* in 1928, is the centrepiece of Pound's 1932 Genoa edition, and it has its mise-en-page, phrasing, and rhythm reworked to form Canto XXXVI in 1934. Given this sustained work on its layout and Pound's intimacy with every stage of its printing, the 'Donna mi prega' manifests his idea of an eye rhythm and thereby gives a vital insight into his typographical practice more generally. Pound elsewhere uses typographical experiment to better convey the stylistic quiddities in the canzone of Arnaut Daniel or Confucius's *Classic Anthology*, but no other translation does Pound publish so conspicuously as a project of reengineering the reader's comprehension through reordering the printed page. The proofs of the edition show Pound not only correcting the typography of his innovative translations but also engineering the mise-en-page of the book as a whole, designing title pages, and even plotting the font and placement of the critical

[90] Guido Cavalcanti, *Rime* (Genova: Edizioni Marsano, [1931/1932]), 2, 22. Bibliographical records for this edition, whose colophon cites the Italian Fascist calendar, tend to mention both 1931 and 1932 as dates. I use the latter date for ease. Please note that I refer to the pagination of the section 'Frammenti dell'edizione bilingue'.

[91] Ezra Pound, 'Letter to Louis Zukofsky, 22 December 1931', in *Pound/Zukofsky: Selected Letters of Ezra Pound and Louis Zukofsky*, ed. Barry Ahearn (London: Faber and Faber, 1987), 122–24 (p. 122).

apparatus. Directions in Italian such as 'più alto' are appended to scholarly marginalia, as are careful alternations of roman and cursive lettering.[92] As such the 'Donna mi prega' and its experimental layout crowns an edition exhaustively designed to pattern scholarly communication through typographical planning. In an unpublished 'Apologia', Pound apologizes for the Genoa edition being 'presented all hindside before and out of the order' by suggesting that the reader further reorient how they process the text by reading backwards:

> Any peruser earnestly desiring the sensation of contact with a truly learned, scholastic work may attain same by the simple process of commencing at the last page (or anywhere he likes among the indices) and reading thence toward the front of the volume. Any other departures from habitual typography or order are intended to emphasize my reason for issuing the edition at all, namely that ten or a dozen of these poems of Guido's are as important as anything we possess, by which I include Sappho's fragments, the verses of Catullus, Bion on the death of Adonis or any other poetry whatsoever.[93]

In this formulation, 'the sensation of contact' with Cavalcanti's poem is felt by redirecting the flow of reading. In an essay for an abortive complete works of Cavalcanti with the Aquila Press, Pound defends his inclusion of photographs of the original manuscripts by arguing that '[i]n the present state of textual scholarship and the present efficiency of photographic process, it is offensive to give descriptions of manuscripts, etc., never satisfactory, a weariness to the eye, wholly unconvincing to the beholder.'[94] Resurrecting the 'mental content' of Cavalcanti and his Tuscan audience is pre-eminently achieved through reanimating 'the weariness of the eye' by eschewing the normative habits of reading.

'Mental content', though—the term Pound employed back in 1912 to describe what his 'traductions' of Cavalcanti try to carry over (*trans-ducere*)—is something of a misnomer, since Pound does not cherish Guido's canzone for any kind of propositional content, a set of precepts or notions, but rather its defining of an intellectual transformation induced by love, as Ronald Bush convincingly demonstrates through excavating Pound's

[92] Ezra Pound, 'Cavalcanti's Rime', box 81, folder 3583 and box 236, folder 37, Beinecke Rare Book and Manuscript Library, Yale University.

[93] David Anderson, *Pound's Cavalcanti: An Edition of the Translations, Notes, and Essays* (Princeton, NJ: Princeton University Press, 1983), xv, 6.

[94] David Anderson, *Pound's Cavalcanti*, xxi, 285.

reading of scholastic philosophy.[95] Its value to Pound is *how* it perceives, not *what* it perceives. Consequently, Pound's efforts to micromanage the reader's perception of the canzone stem from the poem being predicated on definitional and perceptual clarity: '[I]f ever poem seemed to me a struggle for clear definition, that poem is the Donna mi Prega. Nor do I see where a code cypher could be slipped into it.'[96] No 'code cypher', no exegetical paraphrase suffices—the poem's way of seeing is what needs to be contracted. In his preamble to the poem, Pound expounds that the modern reader is alienated from Cavalcanti's poetry at the physiological level of their faculties. The 'Tuscan aesthetic', that term carrying the original Greek connotation of sensory, not just artistic, perception, has been dulled by Christian asceticism and 'European Hindoos'. In the dilated faculties of Cavalcanti's poem, perception is telescopically expanded: 'The senses at first seem to project for a few yards beyond the body.'[97] It is such a sensory shift that Pound's typography asks of the reader in the 'Donna mi prega'. In the disposition of the Italian, sound is to be seen; Guido's byzantine internal rhymes are transmuted into fracturing line breaks.

> Donna mi priegha
> > > perch'i volglio dire
> > D'un accidente
> > > > che sovente
> > > > > > é fero
> > > Ed é si altero
> > > > c'é chiamato amore[98]

This requires considerable ocular dexterity, for the eye is expected not only to apprehend proximate rhymes like 'accidente' and 'sovente' but also delayed pairings; 'priegha' and 'dire' are only answered in the following strophe, so that what we must be primed for are homologies in the shape of strophes. In his English rendering, Pound strains against the paucity of potential rhymes compared with their superabundance in Italian by mimicking Cavalcanti's internal rhymes:

---

[95] Guido Cavalcanti, *Sonnets and Ballate*, 2; Ronald Bush, 'La filosofica famiglia: Cavalcanti, Avicenna, and the "Form" of Ezra Pound's Pisan Cantos', *Textual Practice*, 4 (2010), 669–705. 673.

[96] Guido Cavalcanti and Ezra Pound, *Rime*, 29.

[97] Guido Cavalcanti and Ezra Pound, *Rime*, 3.

[98] 'A lady asks me so I wish to speak of an effect that is often fierce and is so haughty that it is known as love.'

> I for the nonce to them that know it call,
> Having no hope at all
>   that man who is base in heart
> Can bear his part of wit
>   into the light of it,[99]

As the erotically enlightened speaker vaunts his superior comprehension, Pound expands the dimensions of the English by graphing his own rhymes in broken lines, working beyond the remit of the pedagogical requirement of visualizing rhymes for 'the linguistically lazy reader' who cannot be trusted to hear the Italian. (There is, of course, no need to show English rhymes to an English reader, particularly when this version is reprinted in *Make It New* in 1934.)[100] Indeed, as the poem proceeds, the typographical translation of rhyme is supplanted by an even more acrobatic perceptual shift:

> Hom seghue merto
>   spirito che punto
> E Non si puó chonosciere per lo viso
> Chompriso
>   biancho in tale obbietto chade

Lines directly translated as follows:

> To follow a noble spirit,
>   edge, that is, and point to the dart,
> Though from her face indiscernible;
> He, caught, falleth
>   plumb on to the spike of the targe

There are no internal rhymes in the English, but Pound breaks up the lines nevertheless. Here, the sound of the Cavalcanti is translated into shape, and it is this shape, rather than any kind of rhyme, which Pound carries into the English. At the expense of exacerbating the already jolting qualifications of the syntax, Pound breaks up the lines on the page so that their shape replicates that of the Italian. 'Hom seghue merto' becomes 'To follow a noble spirit' and 'Chompriso' becomes 'He, caught, falleth', exactly disposed so

---

[99] Guido Cavalcanti and Ezra Pound, *Rime*, 16, 6.
[100] cf Ezra Pound, 'Donna Mi Prega', in Ezra Pound, *Make It New* (London: Faber and Faber, 1934), 353–55.

that the split line/full line/split line pattern is maintained even at the level of sentence structure. Labouring to define the peculiar cognition of Guido's poem, its resistance to a compartmentalization of faculties, Pound seizes upon a protean quality that is not limited to any sense, which he terms the 'interactive force: *virtu* in short', and goes on to specify, with scholastic nomenclature: 'The force is arrested, but there is never any question about its latency, about the force being essential, and the rest "accidental" in the philosophic technical sense. The shape occurs.' Morphing from Italian rhyme to English rhyme to purely strophic shape, it is through the malleability of typography, its readiness to assume whatever shape it is pressed, that Pound fashions a poetic material susceptible to the interactive perception of the 'Donna mi prega'.[101]

Retranslating the canzone to form the bulk of Canto XXXVI, the sounds of Guido's poem are almost entirely suppressed. Only one rhyme, between 'season' and 'reason' in the first strophe, is revealed by the mise-en-page. Once again, though, shape persists. Many of the broken lines of the earlier translation are omitted in Canto XXXVI as Pound communicates a streamlined form through enlarged capitals, just as the earlier version contains fewer split lines as the English lacked the sonic intricacy of the Italian. Nevertheless, certain of those split-line formations in the mise-en-page of the Italian are preserved:

> Donna mi priegha
> perch'i volglio dire
>
> A lady asks me
> I speak in season
> [...]
> In quella parte
> dove sta memoria
>
> Where memory liveth,
> it takes its state

'[P]riegha' and 'parte' once jutted out to visualize their rhymes with 'negha' and 'Marte', but here they are not even typographically paired with 'denys' and 'Mars', both contained in normative lineation. Thus, for the reader of Canto XXXVI, bereft of the facing translations and complex sonic cartography of earlier versions, their contours on the page are all that

[101] Guido Cavalcanti and Ezra Pound, *Rime*, 20, 10, 3–4.

remain, a palimpsestic vestige of Pound's successive rethinking of the poem. In this canto, Pound credits typography with an extravagant capacity for communication.

> Never adorned with rest Moveth he changing colour
> [...]
> Yet shall ye see of him That he is most often[102]

These lines manifest an audacious functionalizing of the conventions of medieval manuscripts, the seeming paradox of an illuminated codex pressed into communicational efficiency. The enlarged decorative lettering that shows the strophic divisions of the canzone, whilst maintaining the calligraphic elegance of illuminated texts, has been jammed into the middle of the verse line. Rather than being ornamental embellishments, the font-size of these decorated capitals is schematized according to a systematic hierarchy. A draft typescript of this canto includes a typographical legend with single, double, and triple underlining of the capitals in pen denoting 14-, 16- and 18-points, respectively (see Figure 4).

In this scrupulous rationalizing of scribal ornament, gradations of font become the load-bearers of a formal hierarchy buried by successive translations.[103] Against the grain of the page, against any inherited sense of typographical etiquette, against any notational function for the voice, Pound subordinates all other considerations to transmitting the key articulations of Guido's canzone. With no explanatory preamble or scholarly apparatus, Pound exhorts us to see the cognitive outlines in these fractured typographical patterns. Shape, the implication is, needs no footnotes. Our reading eye ought to adapt. Pound's discussion of the strophic shapes of the canzone is telling:

> I trust I have managed to print the *Donna mi Prega* in such a way that its articulations strike the eye without need of a rhyme table. The strophe is here seen to consist of four parts, the second lobe equal to the first as required by the rules of the canzone; and the fourth happening to equal the third, which is not required by the rules as Dante explains them.

---

[102] Ezra Pound, *Eleven New Cantos XXXI–XLI* (New York: Farrar and Rinehart, 1934), 27, 28.

[103] There are two other extant typescripts of Canto XXXVI [box 73, folders 3262 and 3263]. The first of these, like that shown in Figure 4, indicates the lineation of the published versions but not the enlarged capitals. The typescript in Figure 4 [box 73, folder 3284], however, indicates both the lineation and the point size of the capitals that emerged in published versions.

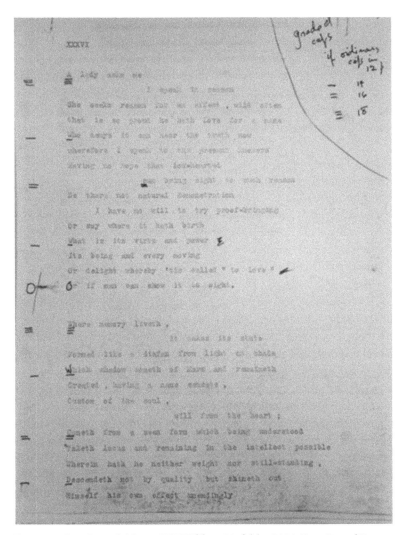

Figure 4. Ezra Pound, 'Canto XXXVI', box 73, folder 3284. Ezra Pound Papers, Beinecke Rare Book and Manuscript Library, Yale University. New Directions Pub. acting as agent, copyright ©2022 by Mary de Rachewiltz and the Estate of Omar S. Pound. Reprinted by permission of New Directions Publishing Corp.

Pound only really speaks of rhymes in passing here; it is really the more abstract 'articulations' which he apprehends, articulations which he goes on to gloss as 'lobes'. Lobes, despite being the soft, pendulous part of the ear, have little to do with hearing. Pound's habitually technological phraseology might guide us to see them as a portion of radiation pattern, when the transmissions of aerials are diagrammed, a usage first recorded in 1926, a reading encouraged by the way the canzone diagrammatizes its own sound. But in his wide-ranging cogitation of the term *virtù* in his introduction to Cavalcanti, Pound makes a dramatic attempt to fuse neuroscience, plant biology, and art, all held together by shape, by a 'persistent notion of pattern':

> Even Bose with his plant experiments seems intent on the plants [sic] capacity to feel—not on the plant idea, for the plant brain is obviously filled with, or is one idea, an *idée fixe*, a persistent notion of pattern from which only cataclysm or a Burbank can shake it. Or possibly this will fall under the eye of a contemporary scientist of genius who will answer: But, damn you, that is exactly what we do feel; or under the eye of a painter who will answer: Confound you, you *ought* to find just that in my painting.[104]

Lobes can connote both an unusually foliate part of the cerebellum and the divisions of a leaf; they are thus the perfect term to crystallize this concept of a thought pattern, common to the brains of plants or the painter's canvas. Pound had espoused a version of this idea of transcendental patterns, common to biology and cognition, in an article on Louis Berman's physiology a few years earlier: 'The brain-cell holds also an image; a generalisation may be considered as a superposition of such images.'[105] Believing shape to be an ur-language, ingrained in the body and mind, Pound's typography in the 'Donna mi prega' appeals to this ocular intelligence. Convinced that moribund ways of thinking inflect the very motions of the reading eye, it is in the plasticity of the printed page, its homology with his model of cognition, that Pound believes perception can be rejuvenated and inveterate patterns of thought broken apart.

---

[104] Guido Cavalcanti and Ezra Pound, *Rime*, 22, 5.
[105] Ezra Pound, 'The New Therapy', *The New Age*, 16 March 1922, in *Contributions to Periodicals*, IV, 222–23 (p. 222).

2

Cummings's Typewriter Language

1. Typewriter Language and Linotype-ese

What does a typewriter bestow upon a poet of the twentieth century, and what does it take away? To answer such a question, we need first to ascertain why it is adopted; whose needs does it serve? In Martin Heidegger's formulation, the advent of the typewriter conspires in a usurpation of human presence in writing:

> This mechanism of setting and pressing and 'printing' is the preliminary form of the typewriter. In the typewriter we find the irruption of the mechanism in the realm of the word. The typewriter leads again to the typesetting machine. The press becomes the rotary press. In rotation, the triumph of the machine comes to the fore. Indeed, at first, book printing and then machine type offer advantages and conveniences, and these then unwittingly steer preferences and needs to this kind of written communication.[1]

The typewriter here is eminently an agent of the machinery of publishing; it is not a possession that the individual writer deploys, but an annexing of the once organic province of the written word, the scribal hand being 'the essential distinguishing mark of man'.[2] Worse yet, in this post-lapsarian narrative, the typewriter's influence is so insidious that it morphs from an ancillary role, easing the passage from composition to publication, to rewiring the 'preferences and needs' of the writer, to reconfiguring their aesthetic predilections.

But Heidegger's claim that the typewriter conspires with the printing press to encroach upon the organic freedom of the writer is questionable because it does not get to grips with their differing material affordances and practical usages. Machines do not all belong to one homogeneous presence

---

[1] Martin Heidegger, *Parmenides*, trans. Andre Schuwer and Richard Rojcewicz (Bloomington: Indiana University Press 1992), 85.
[2] Martin Heidegger, *Parmenides*, 84.

The Graphics of Verse. Daniel Matore, Oxford University Press. © Daniel Matore (2023).
DOI: 10.1093/oso/9780192857217.003.0003

of the Mechanical. In reading an account of processing typescripts for publication, as in the one E. E. Cummings provides in his dealings with the
Golden Eagle Press for his 1935 volume *No Thanks*, we can see how Heidegger's figuring of the typewriter belies editorial procedures taking place
only eight years prior to his lecture:

Dear Aunt Jane

∗ ∗ ∗ am fighting – forwarded & backed by a corps of loyal assistants – to
retranslate 71 poems out of typewriter language into linotype-ese. This is
not so easy as one might think;consider,if you dare,that whenever a typewriter "key" is "struck" the "carriage" moves a given amount and the "line"
advances recklessly or individualistically. Then consider that the linotype
(being a gadget)inflicts a preestablished whole – the type "line" – on every
smallest part;so that words,letters,punctuation marks &(most important of
all)spaces-between-these various elements,awake to find themselves rear-
ranged automatically"for the benefit of the community" as politicians say.
Oddly,this malforming or standardizing process is technically called "justify"ing:thanks to it,the righthand margin of any printed page which has
been "set" on a linotype has a neat artificial evenness – which the socalled
world-at-socalled-large considers indispensable forsooth.[3]

Typescript here does not kowtow to a culture of pristine, automated profes-
sionalism.[4] Nor does the typewriter grease the cogs of book production as it
does not smoothly '[lead] again to the typesetting machine', but rather dis-
sents from default justifying.[5] Not calibrated so as to order and regularize the
typography of the page, not instrumentalized in a fixed teleology of publishing, Cummings's typewriter behaves spontaneously and unpredictably like
those irrepressible individuals he hymns throughout his career. Machines
can be co-opted for unfettered self-expression: in the third of his Norton
lectures, trying to exemplify the generation with which he identifies himself, Cummings offers the anecdote of a young man who repeatedly rides an

[3] Martin Heidegger, *Parmenides*, p. xiii; E. E. Cummings, 'Letter to Jane Cummings, 11
March 1935', in *Selected Letters of E. E. Cummings*, ed. F. W. Dupee and George Stade (London:
Andre Deutsch, 1972), 140–41 (p. 140). Here and throughout I transcribe as faithfully as possible Cummings's unorthodox typography in both his poetry and his prose as well as in titles
of works.
[4] Wilfred A. Beeching, *The Century of the Typewriter* (Bournemouth: British Typewriter
Museum Publishing, 1990), 36.
[5] E. E. Cummings, 'Letter to Jane Cummings, 11 March 1935', in *Selected Letters*, 140.

unconnected elevator that careers down a building simply for the fun of it.[6] The typewriter here is the plenipotentiary of the poet's subjectivity and an avatar of Cummings's libertarian politics.

Following Cummings's careful nomenclature, a Heideggerian 'irruption of the mechanism' is experienced here, but only on the floor of the printing press. Cummings domesticates his typewriter as a pianistic instrument— 'a typewriter "key" is struck'—in tune with the sexist advertising rhetoric that tried to market the typewriter to women on the basis of their presumed skills as accompanists.[7] By contrast to this familiar *tool*, the linotype machine is, with technophobic aversion, labelled as a 'gadget'—something not concordant with subjectivity but mindlessly automatic. The linotype would unnerve Cummings on several levels. Its inherent justification of text and efficiency makes it suitable for the mass production of newsprint, rather than the precision of book design and the typography of modernist poetry; even in the realm of journalism, Hugh Kenner illustrates the machine's lack of subtlety in recalling how botched lines of newsprint were stuffed with the letters ETAOIN SHRDLU, as the operator ran his or her fingers down the leftmost column of lettering.[8] Furthermore, since '[the] linotype had been especially bold in straddling two domains: of the foundry (hot lead) and of the fingers (mats, slugs), so combining founder's sweat with compositor's dexterity', the linotype evokes a conveyor-belt industrialism.[9] Cummings, with patrician naivety, will later define slavery as 'service without love'; and the linotype operator, 'the Slave of the Linotype', embodies this type of joyless collective activity that eschews an ideal of loving vocation.[10]

When he complains about the homogenizing obduracy of the linotype operator, Cummings implies that the typesetter's politics mould their freeness with print—'(like all "operators",or all I've met, this bird is a communist)'—as though there were a crypto-Bolshevist plot to iron out American poetry.[11] But just as Heidegger's assertion that typewriting necessarily produces machinic texts is reductive, so too the politics of typography are more chameleonic than Cummings's swipe at his linotype operator

---

[6] E. E. Cummings, *I: Six Nonlectures* (Cambridge, MA: Harvard University Press, 1953), 44.

[7] E. E. Cummings, 'Letter to Jane Cummings, 11 March 1935', in *Selected Letters*, 140; Darren Wershler-Henry, *The Iron Whim: A Fragmented History of Typewriting* (Ithaca, NY: Cornell University Press, 2007), 56.

[8] Hugh Kenner, *The Mechanic Muse* (New York: Oxford University Press, 1987), 5.

[9] Hugh Kenner, *The Mechanic Muse*, 7.

[10] E. E. Cummings, *I: Six Nonlectures*, 26; E. E. Cummings, 'Letter to Jane Cummings, 11 March 1935', in *Selected Letters*, 140.

[11] E. E. Cummings, 'Letter to Jane Cummings, 11 March 1935', in *Selected Letters*, 141.

suggests. By 1953 Cummings has moved sufficiently to the right that he can write of his support for Senator MacCarthy's attempt to root out alleged communists in the US State Department, framing it as a counterweight to what he views as Democratic support for Bolshevism under the Roosevelts:

> As a possibly not quite nonintelligent human being,I'm aware that socalled Macarthyism didn't drop unmotivated from the sky – that(on the contrary)it came as a direct result of exactly what it decries:namely, procommunist-&-how-activities throughout the USA,sponsored by Mrs FD Roosevelt & her messianicallyminded partner plus a conglomeration of worthy pals[12]

But finding reds under the bed is tricky in typography and government. Soviet or communist typography—much like American or capitalist typography—is a mercurial quantity. Margit Rowell, in her chapter in *The Russian Avant-Garde Book 1910–1934*, insists on the bifurcation between an anarchistic, individualist Russian Futurism of the 1910s and a political and communitarian Soviet Constructivism of the 1920s and 1930s, but she also chronicles how figures like El Lissitzky move between the two while maintaining a graphical identity and continuity. She writes of the Soviet typographical experiments of the 1920s that

> [t]he end result was a revolution in graphic design that was among the earliest and most radical in the Western world. However, it is important to stress that this expression of modernism may be seen virtually as a by-product of the Soviet purpose. The primary objective was the dissemination of the Utopian promise of social transformation and a collective culture. A comparison of Soviet graphic design with contemporaneous movements emerging in Europe and the United States shows that whereas the basic vocabulary—space, color, typography—and a will to rationalize visual culture were identical, the context was entirely different.[13]

Context, varying political imperatives, might shine a different light on the page in question, but the colours often had a disarming similarity. An iron

---

[12] E. E. Cummings, 'Letter to Elizabeth Cummings, 27 March 1953', in *Selected Letters*, 222–23.
[13] Margit Rowell, 'Constructivist Book Design: Shaping the Proletarian Conscience', in *The Russian Avant Garde Book 1910–1934*, ed. Margit Rowell and Deborah Wye (New York: MOMA, 2017), 51.

curtain between Western and Soviet typography is hard to maintain if the two antagonists shared a visual fabric. The Cummings who is writing *Tulips & Chimneys* writes to his father on 7 November 1919 of his mutual celebration with the 'N.Y. radicals' of the two-year anniversary of the October Revolution and reaffirms in 1923 as that debut volume is being published that 'As usual, I admire Russia'.[14] But the Cummings who publishes *No Thanks* in 1935, four years after his odyssey through Soviet Russia as recorded in *Eimi*, a journey which cements his view of Russia as 'the subhuman communist superstate,where men are shadows & women are nonmen', does not denounce the typography of his radical youth as Bolshevist propaganda.[15] Experimental typography in this sense is like a double-agent, unnervingly adaptable to opposing political programmes. What abides in Cummings's politics, through his pro- and anti-communism periods, is an inextirpable individualism and libertarianism, an impulse which, as I will argue in the final part of this chapter, will manifest as a mania for poetic smallness. And what irks Cummings most about his nemesis the linotype operator is that he doesn't see an operator as an individual artist or artisan. Most crucially of all, the linotype might summon up the criticism of a mutual degeneration in poetic and editorial standards. For the linotype, irreconcilable with the artisanal values of the fine-press printing Jerome McGann claims as a well spring of modernist book production and aesthetics, rendered much skilled workmanship redundant; as Kenner observes, the linotype's mechanical accuracy 'bypassed all the skill with hairline spaces for which master compositors had earned respect.'[16] A dismissive review of Cummings's play 'Him', released partly as a pamphlet, sneered that 'This new poetry is going to make life much easier for the printer's apprentice. He shuts his eyes and dips into caps or lower case as he wills, or rather as he lists.'[17] Sensing this closely woven bond between his professional standards and Cummings's worth as a poet, Cummings's first typographer, Samuel Jacobs, responded to his critic with a telling parallelism:

> The typography of Cummings is not a matter of shutting the eyes and dipping into the caps or lower case. There are definite reasons for everything

[14] E. E. Cummings, 'Letter to Edward Cummings, 7 November 1919' and 'Letter to Edward Cummings, 18 September 1923', in *Selected Letters*, 62, 104.

[15] E. E. Cummings, 'Sketch for a Preface', in *Eimi* (New York: Liveright, 2007), n.p..

[16] Jerome McGann, *Black Riders: The Visible Language of Modernism* (Princeton: Princeton University Press, 1993), 20; Hugh Kenner, *The Mechanic Muse*, 8.

[17] Charles Egleston, *Dictionary of Literary Biography Volume 288: The House of Boni & Liveright, 1917–1933: A Documentary Volume* (Detroit; London: Gale, 2004), 250.

he does with special values on the page, and there is a concomitant result in that remote and underlying field of aesthetic phenomena – the kinaesthetic.[18]

A typographical arbitrariness in composition being seen to license typographical sloppiness in production, Jacobs counters by asserting a shared physicality between his and Cummings's workings, an artisanal precision and exactitude.

If the linotype unsettles Cummings with its aura of industrial production and its usurpation of individual craftsmanship, what especially fires Cummings's imagination is that the linotype with its default setting of justification, of imposing 'a neat artificial evenness', arrogates a prosodic agency away from the poet: corralling the reckless page rhythms of the typescript, there is the 'type "line"' of the linotype.[19] Michel Foucault, considering whether the blandest linguistic or mathematical expressions, like the tabulation of random numbers in statistics, can still constitute a statement, concludes that the layout of the French typewriter, once written out, does indeed constitute the expression of institutionalized preferences, and is indeed an 'énoncé'.[20] For Cummings, too, the default settings of the mechanisms of publishing are not innocuous. The justification of text by the linotype encodes the homogenizing of mass communication and collective politics that postulates a falsely uniform community—'the socalled world-at-socalled-large'—in order to validate its typographical regularity.[21] Though he calls for a renewed attention to the page space in modernism, George Bornstein erects an interpretative dichotomy by imploring us to 'recognize that the literary text consists not only of words (its linguistic code) but also of the semantic features of its material instantiations (its bibliographic code)', noting that '[s]uch bibliographic codes might include cover design, page layout, or spacing, among other factors.'[22]

This ontology of the literary text, though, should be inflected, since typography doesn't just belong to singular material instantiations. Modernist poets designed mise-en-page to transcend any given edition. Typography in much modernist poetry, and especially in Cummings, is not in the domain of

[18] Charles Egleston, *Dictionary of Literary Biography*, 250.
[19] E. E. Cummings, 'Letter to Jane Cummings, 11 March 1935', in *Selected Letters*, 141.
[20] Michel Foucault, *L'archéologie du savoir* (Paris: Gallimard, 1969), 116-8.
[21] E. E. Cummings, 'Letter to Jane Cummings, 11 March 1935', in *Selected Letters*, 141.
[22] George Bornstein, *Material Modernism: The Politics of the Page* (Cambridge: Cambridge University Press, 2001), 6.

book production but of composition. In 'arguing for two and a half hours(or some such)over the distance between the last letter of a certain word and the comma apparently following that letter', Cummings is doggedly claiming compositional ownership over his typography: it is not a feature of bibliographic code that confers superadded meaning to particular 'material instantiations' and is thereby able to be delegated to competent publishers; rather, it is a part of the linguistic code, an inherent aspect of the text, such that to alter it is not to produce a different edition, but a different version.[23]

The clash between the typewriter and the machinery of printing in this formulation is not just some technical hitch to be ironed out. Rather than the typewriter facilitating the preset functions of the typesetting machine as Heidegger would have it, its reckless advances on the page articulate a typography that strains against being co-opted into a house style or a prevailing culture of printed neatness, that cannot be comfortably absorbed into a mechanism of mass production. But this friction between the two machines must make audible some poetic thinking for Heidegger's objections to the typewriter to be soundly rebutted. Heidegger is at pains to show that he is not some reactionary Luddite. Vindicating the apparent irrelevance of his assault on the typewriter during a lecture on pre-Socratic philosophy, Heidegger clarifies that it is the typewriter as a concretion of man's alienation from written language that must be brought to light, that it manifests the Greek concept of λήθη (concealment and forgetting), where the word is no longer indivisible from being, rather than it being the nuts and bolts of the mechanism he objects to.[24] Developing this seed seven years later, Heidegger unfolds a rich and sophisticated critique of technology in his 1953 lecture, where he explains that it the unquestioned, entangling classifications of technological thinking that we must be on guard against, and it is only insofar as they manifest such cognitive entrapment that the material appendages are to be denounced. He goes on to remind us that '[o]nce there was a time when the bringing-forth of the true into the beautiful was called *technē*. The *poiēsis* of the fine arts was also called *technē*', implying that true technological thinking ought to keep us in touch with the rudiments of articulation.[25]

But the typewriter does indeed return Cummings to the roots of poetic expression. Cummings's 'type "line"' gestures to a theory of typography as

---

[23] E. E. Cummings, 'Letter to Jane Cummings, 11 March 1935', in *Selected Letters*, 141.

[24] Martin Heidegger, *Parmenides*, 87.

[25] Martin Heidegger, *Basic Writings*, ed. David Farrell Krell (London: Routledge and Kegan Paul, 1978), 309, 315.

a prosodic constituent in the poem, a structural element as fundamental as the verse line. Even stronger is the honorific categorizing of the typescript as 'typewriter language', as a unique and irreproducible province of expression (as opposed to the pejorative implication of jargon in the suffix -*ese* appended to the linotype), such that whatever typographical adaptation may be imposed upon a poem in the process of publication incurs the violence, the potential loss of meaning, that may be undergone in translation. But the typewriter as a tutelary guardian of expressive freedom is in many ways a counter-intuitive position. Jerome McGann in *Black Riders* exemplifies Heidegger's 'triumph of the mechanism' in recent critical thinking by arguing that Emily Dickinson's manuscripts have been misread and misjudged by being taken as preparatory materials for an eventual printing, specifically by her unusual line breaks being read as something that would be cancelled out in print:

> Dickinson's scripts cannot be read as if they were 'printer's copy' manuscripts, or as if they were composed with an eye toward some state beyond their handcrafted textual condition. Her surviving manuscript texts urge us to take them at face value, to treat all her scriptural forms as potentially significant *at the aesthetic or expressive level.*[26]

McGann brilliantly pinpoints how the superabundance of signs and graphical richness of manuscript is impoverished if we think of it as merely a rough sketch for printing; in so doing he exposes the relative poverty of the printed page. This visual simplification is even more apparent if we think of precisely what typographical paradigms early typewriters relied upon; Darren Wershler-Henry summarizes this as 'Typewriting places an invisible grid onto the blank page: one character or space per cell, no more, no less [. . .]'.[27] That is, the typewriter constructs a typography that is retiform, quantifiable, and fixed; it cannot register any of the fluid graphological nuance of pen upon paper. Moreover, the kind of interpretative approach that Nina Nørgaard employs in her article 'The Semiotics of Typography in Literary Texts: A Multimodal Approach', a study of the nuances of variations of font in contemporary novels, can only be practised upon texts that vary their typeface, something not compositionally possible for the set lettering of the typewriter.[28]

---

[26] Jerome McGann, *Black Riders*, 38.
[27] Darren Wershler-Henry, *The Iron Whim*, 136.
[28] Nina Nørgaard, 'The Semiotics of Typography: A Multimodal Approach', *Orbis Litterarum*, 2 (2009), 141–60.

These sacrifices for a poet who deals in typescripts and who presents typescripts to a publisher open up a decisive strategic gain in the overall genesis of the printed book. For the fluid imprecision of manuscript is exactly what makes it problematic as a blueprint for rendering the typography of a book. By virtue of the quantifiability of typescript, the poet has access to a notational precision that is legible for the typesetter; that is, they can now engineer the typographical body of the printed text. Typography can become a property of the text's composition, not something delegated to the prerogative of the typesetter or book designer. Walter Benjamin fears that the reproducibility of a work of art erodes its historical singularity, but in being savvy enough to anticipate the process of reproduction, Cummings, though not ringing it with the kind of one-off aura Benjamin imagines, safeguards a durable visual singularity and wrests one facet of homogenization from mechanical reproduction.[29] Though losing the immeasurable verve of manuscript, in reckoning with the question of the visual legibility of his work—the practical question of what can reproduced by the typesetter—a poet like Cummings can lay claim to typography as an in-built expressive aspect of his poetry.

To unlock a new dimension in poetic expression, though, is not to guarantee an expansion in the semantic and ideational transfer from conception to publication. Cummings falls short of claiming that the typewriter embodies his own voice and, importantly, that he has full control over it. First, if Cummings is exact in his terminology, then a 'retranslation' of 'typewriter language into linotype-ese' suggests that the original typing up was itself a translation from some originary conception—either written or imagined—of the poem. Second, Cummings's claim that the typewriter 'advances recklessly or individualistically' is laced with ambiguity: does Cummings mean that the typewriter is less finely calibrated than the linotype and entails a measure of typographical imprecision, or is he being figurative in casting the typewriter as vibrantly individual in its typographical range?[30] For on this question hinges a key dilemma in reading both Cummings's and other poets' typographical experimentation. Does the typewriter facilitate an intentionalist extension of self-expression, an addition to the vocal repertoire of rhythm and rhyme, or does it let loose a second self, a typewriter language, not depersonalized and mechanized, but beyond the remit of the

---

[29] Walter Benjamin, *Illuminations*, ed. Hannah Arendt, trans. Harry Zorn, (London: Pimlico, 1999), 215.
[30] E. E. Cummings, 'Letter to Jane Cummings, 11 March 1935', in *Selected Letters*, 141.

poet's careful mastery, an influx of typographical and spatial characters that cannot be encompassed in a secure web of signification?

This vexed question of expressive freedom, expressive control, and the self typography incarnates is central to the practice, theory, and criticism of experimental mise-en-page. Two of the most eminent and trenchant expositions of the possibilities of typography in poetry, Stéphane Mallarmé's 'Préface' to *Un coup de dés* and Charles Olson's essay 'Projective Verse', are wracked by the degree of control and uncertainty the typewriter confers. At one point Olson envisages an unprecedented notational control because of the quantifiable exactitude of typescript; not because the poet can fend off the typographical incursions of printing like the linotype, as in the formulation above, but because of his faith in the semiotic clarity of the page:

> It is the advantage of the typewriter that, due to its rigidity and its space precisions, it can, for a poet, indicate exactly the breath, the pauses, the suspensions even of syllables, the juxtapositions even of parts of phrases, which he intends. For the first time the poet has the stave and the bar a musician has had. For the first time he can, without the convention of rime and meter, record the listening he has done to his own speech and by that one act indicate how he would want any reader, silently or otherwise, to voice his work.[31]

Olson's typewriter is not in the least reckless: it is a trustworthy instrument of perfect self-replication, crystallizing the poet's voice on the page. Mallarmé likewise speaks of his mise-en-page as a musical score, 'une partition', though denoting oscillations in intonation rather than Olson's pauses and phrasing.[32] Yet, contrary to this confident intentionalism, both poets admit a drastic loss of creative governance. Both speak of poetic typography assuming autonomy: Olson claims that in projective verse, '[the poet] can go by no track other than the one the poem under hand declares, for itself'; Mallarmé speaks of visual and typographical images acting of their own volition—'Le papier intervient chaque fois qu'une image, d'elle-même, cesse ou rentre [. . .]'.[33] Moreover, in the reception of *Un coup de dés*, it is

---

[31] Charles Olson, *Human Universe and Other Essays*, ed. Donald Allen (San Francisco: The Auerhahn Society, 1965), 57.

[32] Stéphane Mallarmé, *Un coup de dés jamais n'abolira le hasard* (Paris: Gallimard, 1914), n.p.

[33] 'The paper intervenes each time that an image of its own accord ceases or resumes'; Charles Olson, *Human Universe*, 52; Stéphane Mallarmé, *Un coup de dés*, n.p.

the abnegation of poetic mastery that is often admired. Maurice Blanchot is dazzled that Mallarmé, a poet 'fasciné par le désir de maîtrise', can erect a 'constellation du doute' as his final utterance; and for Roland Barthes typographical experimentation is Mallarmé's final resort in a career dedicated to destabilizing the authority of the poet over language, achieved only through the agraphia that typographical blanks diagnose, 'l'agraphie typographique'.[34]

Cummings's work, though, cannot be accounted for by the apologias of other poets. The avowed impersonality that impels Olson and Mallarmé towards typographical experimentation—Olson's 'Objectism', 'the getting rid of the lyrical interference of the individual as ego, of the "subject" and his soul' or the supersession of a governing self by autonomous poetic constituents in Mallarmé—is not concordant with the dedicated egocentricity of Cummings.[35] What this chapter aims to do, then, is to argue for an ingrained and unique typographical thinking in the work of Cummings, a corpus alive to the expressive freedom and control that mise-en-page offers. Further, I wish to argue that it is a failure to embrace this dynamic of freedom and control that has held back criticism of experimental typography to date. What is needed is an exploration of typographical experimentation as an in-built and organic constituent of Cummings's poetics, responding to the poet's own vision of a self-sufficient 'typewriter language'.[36] By not explicating its motivations or capacities in advance, the riskiness of typographical experimentation, its place in a tradition of wrestling with poetic mastery, and the perils of unintelligibility need to be confronted rather than eschewed. Such volatility is central to understanding the poetry of the twentieth century because, as Olson reminds us in seeing a unified correlation in the sight and sound of Pound, Cummings, and Williams, and as Mallarmé implies in asserting that his typography participates in the aims of free verse, prosodic progress was often predicated on typographical expansion.[37]

---

[34] 'enthralled by the desire for mastery'; 'typographical agraphia'; Maurice Blanchot, *L'espace littéraire* (Paris: Gallimard, 1955), 119; Roland Barthes, *Le degré zéro de l'écriture* (Paris: Éditions du Seuil, 1972), 59.

[35] Stéphane Mallarmé, *Un coup de dés*, n.p.; Charles Olson, *Human Universe*, 59.

[36] Norman Friedman, *E. E. Cummings: The Art of his Poetry* (London: Oxford University Press; Baltimore, MD: The John Hopkins Press, 1960).

[37] Charles Olson, *Human Universe*, 53; Stéphane Mallarmé, *Un coup de dés*, n.p.

2. Typographical *faits* and the Body of the Text

The ambit in which typography is allowed to expand, though, determines the nature and breadth of its semantic capacities. Mallarmé and Olson adopt distinctly similar metaphors for the shape of experimental mise-en-page which are telling not only about how they visualize the page, but also about their sense of it. Olson's chosen figuration for 'Projective Verse' is not strictly projective at all, for projection, implying a casting forth from a fixed point of departure, is eclipsed by the multiple plotting of possible loci in 'FIELD COMPOSITION'. Analogous is the image of 'UNE CONSTELLATION' from *Un coup de dés*, a potentially self-reflexive symbol for the poem's mise-en-page that Blanchot adopts as an icon for the poem as a whole.[38] While we should refrain from claiming that human figures have been erased from the page, given that Olson and Mallarmé's poetic spaces are traversed by the poet and 'LE MAÎTRE' respectively, both gravitate towards a schematizing of the printed page as an open space, be it an agrarian one or a cosmic one.[39] In the absence of the cohesive text block, the schema of the decentred plane emerges.

Cummings, too, is drawn to such a schema as he embarks upon his early experiments with typography in 1916 and 1917. Of the ten unpublished poems that George Firmage first released in *Etcetera*, and whose isolation as a distinct sequence by the editor is validated by their radical, formal innovations, three, all audacious in their spacing, foreground the emblem of the sky, another of these expansive planes.[40] But as much as these poems lay the groundwork for Cummings's evolving technique, they are as important for signalling what Cummings will omit from his typographical repertoire. The successive indentation of chunks of text in 'VII' and 'VIII', text blocks in a stepped sequence, is a rudiment of Olson's visual idiolect, as Eleanor Berry notes in her scrupulous taxonomizing of his page space, but will be avoided by Cummings in published volumes to come.[41] What Cummings did glean from these propaedeutic essays can be deduced by comparing the

[38] Stéphane Mallarmé, *Un coup de dés*, n.p.; Blanchot, *L'Espace Littéraire*, p. 119.
[39] Charles Olson, *Human Universe*, p. 58; Stéphane Mallarmé, *Un coup de dés*, n.p.
[40] E. E. Cummings, *Etcetera: The Unpublished Poems of E. E. Cummings*, ed. George James Firmage and Richard S. Kennedy (New York: Liveright, 1983).
[41] Eleanor Berry, 'The Emergence of Charles Olson's Prosody of the Page Space', *Journal of English Linguistics*, 1 (2002), 51–72 (p. 66).

original version of 'the sky' to the revised version in the 1922 manuscript, later published in *XLI Poems*:

```
            the sky
      was           can dy
       lu                 mi
            nous              ed
                              i
            ble
               spry    pinks
               shy              lem
            ons
                                   greens
         cool
         choco                 lates
              un                          der
       a    lo
            co
            mo                 tive              s pout
                                ing
                  vi
          o                    lets
```

Cummings's poem in this its original plotting is visionary in its extreme decentralization and disorientation of the trajectory of reading.[42] In its vertical clustering of rhyming syllables and words such as 'lo/co/mo', even against the grain of the actual word order as in 'dy' and 'mi', 'spry' and 'shy'—and distantly as in 'lates' and 'lets', and in its minute alignment of graphemes despite their sonic variation in the 'c's and 'o's of 'cool', 'choco', and the 'co' in 'locomotive'—Cummings engineers an all-pervading synaesthetic diffusion. Truly a 'COMPOSITION BY FIELD', local sonic and graphic energies are granted a decisive autonomy in warping the texture of the poem; syllables and even letters are points of gravity here, pulling homologous linguistic particles into their varying orbits on the page.[43] Contrast the second version:

---

[42] E. E. Cummings, 'the sky was', bMS Am 1823.5 (359). E. E. Cummings Papers, Houghton Library, Harvard University.
[43] Charles Olson, *Human Universe*, 52.

```
the
    sky
        was
can  dy  lu
minous
            edible
spry
    pinks shy
lemons
greens    coo  l choc
olate
s.


    un    der,
    a   lo
co
mo
        tive        s   pout
                        ing
                            vi
                            o
                            lets
```

This is by no stretch of the imagination typographically conservative, and
the poem represents one of the manuscript's most distinctive examples of
mise-en-page, yet the proliferating dimensions of the poem's prototype have
been decisively curtailed. Most of those vertical rhyming strands have been
cut, and verbal identity is more delicately prised apart. That zigzagging final
'vi-o-lets' now is neatly formatted and no longer visually maps a disorientat-
ing correlation with the final syllable of 'chocolates'. Crucially, this version
of the poem is held upright with the paginal backbone of a mostly stable
left-hand margin, bar the faint indentation of 'un der' and 'a lo'.[44] That is to
say that those words and syllables that hover towards the right-hand side of
the page are still readable as subdivisions of lines that begin at the left-hand

[44] E. E. Cummings, *XLI Poems* (New York: The Dial Press, 1925), 9.

margin. These subdivisions are still oriented in relation to the springboard of the margin, whereas in the previous version the left-hand margin veers further and further to the left four times after the first two lines. Relations between the constituents of the first version have a dizzying openness; much of its spacing in a given line is so broad as to dispel even the ghost of some direct vocal notation. Globally, then, the shift between the two poems is from the atomized constellation of the first to the much tauter, though still flexible, arc of the second. Cummings's tempering of this early impulse, then, is vital in comprehending the idiosyncrasy of his typography. Confronting the extreme mise-en-page of late-twentieth–century poets like Susan Howe, Marjorie Perloff sees a decisive break with lineated free-verse:

> What can be said, however, is that the 'free verse' aesthetic, which has dominated our century, is no longer operative[.] Take a seemingly minor feature of free verse like enjambment. To run over a line means that the line is a limit, even as the caesura can only exist within line limits. To do away with that limit is to reorganize sound configurations according to different principles.[45]

In those sound clusters of the first version of 'the sky was', there is already a radical rerouting of the sonic network of verse. Perloff is astute in highlighting a trend of recent poetry that is nonlinear, though how much early modernism adumbrates such poetics ought to be acknowledged. In poems with such sprawling mise-en-page as Cummings's early forays, the unit of the line—even a poetic line broken by indentation and atypical spacing, in terms of formal categorization and readerly experience—evaporates. In thus warding off a topography of the page, Cummings preserves a discernible, albeit elastic and volatile, linearity.

'the sky was can dy' is exceptional in being the only one of Cummings's 1916–17 experiments to survive into print. But, though intended for publication in the 1923 volume *Tulips and Chimneys*, it first appears in print in *XLI Poems*, a collection in which Cummings intended to include all of the poems rejected by the publisher Thomas Seltzer, but which suffered further truncation at the hands of Lincoln MacVeagh.[46] Its appearance in the 1922

---

[45] Marjorie Perloff, 'After Free Verse: The New Nonlinear Poetries' in *Close Listening: Poetry and the Performed Word*, ed. Charles Bernstein (New York: Oxford University Press, 1998), 86–110 (p. 106).

[46] E. E. Cummings, *Tulips & Chimneys: The Original 1922 Manuscript with the 34 Additional Poems from &*, ed. George James Firmage (New York: Liveright, 1976), ix.

manuscript is crucial because that document, which provides the basis for the 1937 archetype edition of *Tulips & Chimneys*, is one that Cummings has already self-censored and revised since at least 1919.[47] It is difficult to definitively discount the possibility that Cummings revised the poem with a view to its reception by publishers, and the manuscript had been rejected by other publishers before Seltzer accepted it, but Cummings's dealings with publishers and editorial temperament show a clear preference for outright omission over revision from external pressure.[48] Cummings's intransigence when faced with even modest editorial incursions is attested to by his repeated refusal to comply with the format of a 1954 radio program on New England poets, with the result that the program was never broadcast in his lifetime.[49] Furthermore, this chapter will follow the editorial practice of the Firmage editions and that of The Golden Eagle Press's archetype edition in referring primarily to the 1922 manuscript of *Tulips & Chimneys*, given that Cummings conceived of this as having an independent and superior status to the 1923 first edition. References are therefore normally to the earliest publication of a given poem as poems excised from the 1923 *Tulips and Chimneys* but belonging to the 1922 manuscript often appeared in later volumes like the 1925 *XLI Poems* or the archetype edition of *Tulips & Chimneys* in 1937. Disappointed by the omissions of Thomas Seltzer and then the Dial Press, Cummings notes sardonically in 1924: 'When my beard is white with dotage, etc. [. . .] the entire *Tulips & Chimneys* may possibly have made an appearance per 71 different selective passages conducted by 407 publishers.'[50]

The revised version of 'the sky' takes pride of place as the very first poem in *XLI Poems*, and what this revision typifies is a divergence from a species of visual poetry that Cummings formulated in 1916 and 1917, a series of unpublished typographical experiments engineered according to often hermetic principles of versification. In the poetry Cummings is best known for, that of his debut volume *Tulips and Chimneys* (1923), the inherited concept of a verse line is still a meaningful term. Narrow, undulating verse paragraphs, comparable to those of William Carlos Williams's *Spring and All*, published in the same year, and a plethora of sonnets dominate the published collection. These poems refract, augment, and syncopate, by means

[47] E. E. Cummings, *Tulips & Chimneys* (The Golden Eagle Press: Mount Vernon, NY, 1937); Christopher Sawyer-Lauçanno, *E.E. Cummings: A Biography* (London: Methuen, 2005), 158, 241.
[48] Christopher Sawyer-Lauçanno, *E.E. Cummings: A Biography*, p. 200.
[49] E. E. Cummings, 'Freedom, Joy & Indignation: Letters from E. E. Cummings', *The Massachusetts Review*, 4 (1963), 497–528.
[50] E. E. Cummings, *Tulips & Chimneys: The Original 1922 Manuscript*, p. ix.

of a dilated typographical vocabulary, past and contemporary verse forms. It is chiefly by this repertoire of styles that fellow modernists like Williams, Pound, Zukofsky, and Olson identified Cummings's typographical poetics. 'The sky was can dy' of 1916, though, forms part of a series of ur-versions and wholly unpublished poems sufficiently distinct and *sui generis* that Cummings gave them a title all of their own, naming them *faits*. The particular salience of these experiments for the history of modernist poetics is largely, but not wholly, negative. They incarnate the revolutionary spirit of typographical experiment, its presumed virtue to reboot poetics, a utopian vision that enthralled poets throughout the last century; yet, conversely, they obey a stylistic dogmatism which Anglo-American modernists will ultimately steer clear of. For in these experiments Cummings so destabilized the category of verse with the catalyst of mise-en-page that it transmuted poetry into something that seems of a different aesthetic species. To deploy the term *fait* is to suggest that the term *poem* no longer fits. Though Cummings acknowledges the hand of a conscious artist in their making by referring to a *faiteur*, the word is palpably impersonal. The substantive is shadowed by the past participle, stressing that this 'deed' or 'fact' is also a 'thing done', imperviously final and complete in itself. This connotation is borne out in the predetermined mechanics of these *faits*. A recurrent principle of organization is that the occurrence of a vowel sound governs the alignment of all subsequent iterations of that vowel sound in the poem, such that the typography of these poems in a sense forms itself autonomously.

The alienating thinghood of these *faits* resides in the way they operate outside of the bounds of creative control, of established frontiers of genre, and of conventional communication. What the impersonality of these poems seems first to consist in, though, is a type of naturalistic reportage; poems in which the voice of the poet retires and ambient conversation—quotidian, unpoetic chatter—irradiates the page. What is deficient about conventional typography under this viewpoint is that the printed page does not represent speech—especially demotic speech—in all its suprasegmental complexity. In a *fait* like 'logeorge', a putative transcription of a telephone call about a 'jilted suitor' as Milton A Cohen puts it, speech might be said to assume its proper dimensions (see Figure 5).[51]

Ironically, though, the attempt to map speech more accurately onto the space of the page exposes the incommensurability between sound and

---

[51] Milton A. Cohen, *Poet and Painter: The Aesthetics of E. E. Cummings's Early Work* (Detroit: Wayne State University Press, 1987), 222.

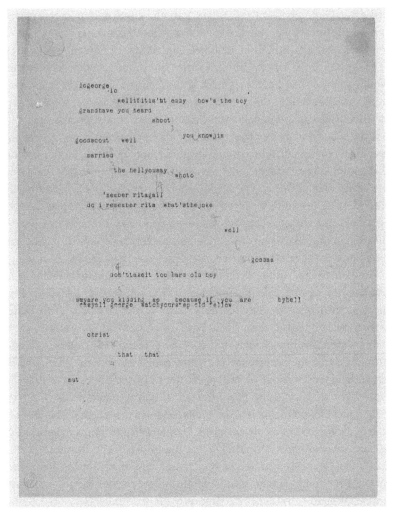

Figure 5. E. E. Cummings, 'logeorge', 1823.7 (21), from Cummings Collection at Houghton Library, Harvard University, by E. E. Cummings. Copyright by the Trustees for the E. E. Cummings Trust. Used by permission of Liveright Publishing Corporation.

print.[52] Cummings carefully pencils in numerals like '4' and '5' between blocks of text, but the futility of trying to voice a four-line or a five-line

---

[52] This is a typescript of 'logeorge', a poem unpublished in Cummings's lifetime. The typography is faithfully rendered in its printing in the 1994 Firmage edition.

pause, given the absence of a metric by which the reader might measure this, is unmistakeable. Superscribed numbers do not transmute alphabetic script into a quantifiable time-bound notation.[53]

Rather than mathematical exactitude, what the typography of 'logeorge' retains is a productive suggestiveness closer to symbols like ellipses or the cues of a playscript. Taut indignation followed by airy disbelief, the contours of this exchange, is legible in the concertina contractions and dilations of the text. What the poem expresses is a translation of objectified sound—a phone call overheard without its sounds being ascribed to specific speakers, a nebula of syllables and compounded words—into objectified space, a typographical plane of lines, blocks, and lacunae. The objective, even alien, autonomy of the typographical *fait* illuminates the objective autonomy of sound unconstrained by orthographical and visual convention: sound returned to its natural state. All this would suggest, though, that Cummings is closer to the modernist topos that inherited versification is incommensurate with the brio of natural, especially American, speech than he is fact is. Like Mallarmé, Pound, and Olson, Cummings is drawn to the paradigm of the musical score as a model for typographical experiment, but in his theorizations of his *faits*, the poet extracts classes and forms native to musicology and stitches together an aesthetic species quite foreign to the biology of counterpoint or harmony.

That typographical experiment was to transcend the function of recording the human voice or inscribing sound with greater precision is discernible in the genesis of the *fait* 'two brass buttons'. By equating pitch with vowel sounds, Cummings confects a homology between the substance of poetry and the substance of music. With assonance rarely being codified in theories of versification, vowel sounds are treated as disposable cells, unbound by traditional metrics, which the poet can arrange into structures calqued from musical forms. Syllables, in the first version of 'two brass buttons', are duly arrayed as though on a stave, with a column of full stops in the left-hand margin indicating the horizontal alignment (see Figure 6).

Despite the disparities, that the five lines of the musical stave do not map onto the horizontal rows of the typescript, a stave whose lines in fact oscillate according to the local gamut of vowel sounds, it is with a blinkered literalism that poetry is worked into the shape of musical notation here.[54]

---

[53] Milton A. Cohen, *Poet and Painter*, 187.
[54] There are two typescript versions of 'two brass buttons' shown in Figures 6 and 7. There are no extant autograph manuscripts, and neither has been published.

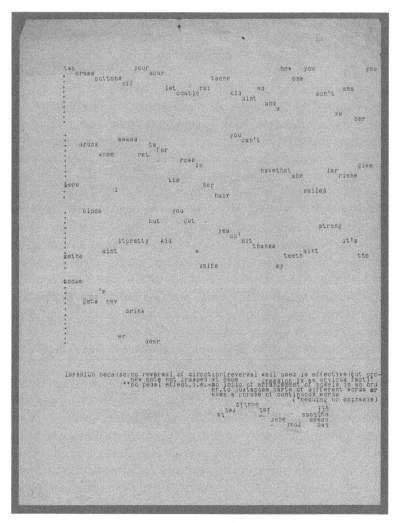

Figure 6. E. E. Cummings, 'two brass buttons', 1823.7 (23), from Cummings Collection at Houghton Library, Harvard University, by E. E. Cummings. Copyright by the Trustees for the E. E. Cummings Trust. Used by permission of Liveright Publishing Corporation.

To this typescript Cummings appends his own critical evaluation, deeming the poem 'INFERIOR' on the basis that it has no 'reversal of direction', an allusion to the reverse typing of some other early experiments, and that it has no 'pedal effect'. In an unpublished essay on the *faits* entitled 'The

Poetry of Silence', Cummings says of his typographical poetics that 'the new poem is conceived as a whole, every part of which is a motif, significant not only in itself but toward the entirety of fused motives, by which is meant the sensation to the perceiver of the completed poem'.[55] Mimicking musical notation so inflexibly thwarts this desired holism, since these horizontal staves have to be recurrently re-erected once the right-hand margin is met so that, despite the relation of pitches, long 'o' sounds placed over short 'a' sounds in each stave, these motivic alignments are local; the whole isn't fused together. Redrafting this poem, Cummings forgoes the horizontality of the musical stave for a vertical arrangement based on the same principle of typographically aligning vowel sounds (see Figure 7).

'Poetry is [. . .] a disruption of the easiest order, i mean of conversation', Cummings opines, and, in dispensing with the contours of the musical stave in this version, the optics of reading are scrambled. Despite the zigzagging fluctuations, the linearity of the stave preserves the linearity of print in the previous version; the eye can follow the wave of the sentence like a melodic line. The exactions of this typographical scheme demand acrobatic agility of the reading eye; they have it rove over an atomized plane, its conditioned vectors upended, so that the word 'remember' is read backwards, downwards, and right-to-left. It is apposite that the verb 'remember' should be so strained in this poem, since the memory of the 'perceiver' of this poem must dilate. Distant rhymes that otherwise might not be registered are forced on the eye. This is the 'pedal effect' whose absence Cummings lamented in the anterior version. As the eye might easily read up and down, against the flow of the sense, these tabular columns of vowel sounds, so is assonance hyperextended in this typographical frame, so that in the drawing out of the syllables of 'scar let' its note of libertinage and violence suffuses the whole poem. In this schematic the ambit of sense memory is augmented; we are to see things whose subtlety would escape the ear; the knowing finality of 'dear' is that it strikes a new, unheard note, its isolation in the column stressing the previously unheard diphthong.

Such straining of the ear and the eye betrays how far this typographical experimentation is from a familiar sense of notation; how it impedes much more than transmits the human voice. Musical notation was often held up by modernists as a superior system for transcribing sound, but the accompanying critical note to this second version of 'two brass buttons' suggests

[55] E. E. Cummings, 'The Poetry of Silence', MS Am 1892.6 (94). E. E. Cummings Papers, Houghton Library, Harvard University.

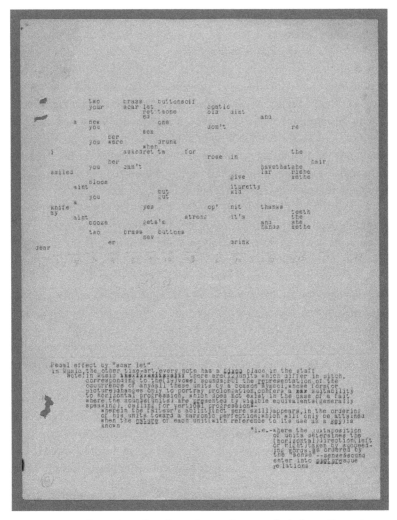

Figure 7. E. E. Cummings, 'two brass buttons', 1823.7 (23), from Cummings Collection at Houghton Library, Harvard University, by E. E. Cummings. Copyright by the Trustees for the E. E. Cummings Trust. Used by permission of Liveright Publishing Corporation.

the extent to which Cummings dissented from this commonplace and how heterodox his concept of notation was. Directly beneath the poem he writes:

Pedal effect by "scar let" in Music, the other time-art, every note has a <u>fixed</u> place in the staff Note: in Music there are (12)units which differ in pitch, corresponding to the (19) vowel sounds; BUT the <u>rep</u>resentation of the occurrence of any&all these units by a common symbol,whose form(or picture)changes only to portray prolongation,confers a suitability to horizontal progression, which does not exist in the case of a fait where the sounds(units) are <u>pre</u>sented by visible equivalents(generally speaking), calling for vertical progression∗- wherein the faiteur's ability(not mere skill)appears, in the ordering of his units toward a harmonic perfection; which will only be attained when the <u>nature</u> of each unit(with reference to its use as a <u>key</u>)is known ∗i.e.-where the juxtaposition of units determines the (horizontal) direction(left or right)taken by succeeding words, as ordered by the "sense"– sense&sound enter into <u>pictures</u>que relations[56]

Far from all arts aspiring to the condition of music, Cummings holds that its notational system is inherently limited. Alphabetic script is commonly chastized for the strictures of its symbology, but, for Cummings it is the 'common symbol[s]' of music which are intransigent, the fact that a B-flat is always positioned at the same latitude on a stave in a given clef, its shape only shifting according to its 'prolongation' as a crotchet or minim or so forth; whereas the placement of a sound in one of the *faits* is determined by the inner logic of the poem. The word 'bloom' appears at a particular locus on the page in 'two brass buttons' because of the poem's peculiar network of assonance, unique to it. Its notation, then, or visualization, is individualistic, particular to it, graphically unique. Counterintuititively, then, what Cummings is critiquing is not the communicational competency, its efficacy for performance and transmission, but its visual uniformity. A B-flat quaver with some given articulation or ornamentation always looks the same whether in a score of Beethoven or of Brahms. The scores of the *faits*, by contrast, are autonomous, one-off typographical constellations formed by their own transitory laws.

'[S]ense&sound enter into <u>pictures</u>que relations' as syllables and words fall into places where columns of assonance and linear syntax contingently intersect. It is telling that Cummings abandons the model of the score altogether at the end of this passage because the nature typography is to assume is quite unlike that of musical notation. For the primacy of sound is displaced in these aesthetic formulations. The bedrock of music and poetry is not sound, which is only one element among many. Contra Lessing and

[56] E. E. Cummings, 'two brass buttons', MS Am 1823.7 (21). E. E. Cummings, Houghton Library, Harvard University.

the famous discrimination between temporal and spatial arts in *Laocoön*, Cummings argues for a convergence between music, painting, poetry and sculpture:

> Never believe the distinction of time and space arts is anything but elementary prattle: no painting capable of appreciating but partakes of the quality of time art, just as much as music does – and this is as true of sculpture (v. Gaudier-Brjeska) if sculpture can be said to exist. So music is dimensional, extensional, moving in depth as well as merely progressing horizontally and vertically, as truly as ever painting. The German's idiotic hypothesis is based at bottom on a distinction of notation; but here again the barriers are transparent: the ideas remain.[57]

All arts notate, Cummings reasons. Brushstrokes and similes are as much notation as crotchets and minims. What they notate is not sound but ideas. For all their borrowings from and imitations of musical notation, the abiding shape of Cummings's early experiments is not that of a score but a grid. *Quadrillage* abounds in the drafts, and manuscripts and typescripts are divided up into numbered rows and columns; syllables and even phonemes are appointed linguistic coordinates. The 'picturesque' in 'picturesque relations' needs to be cleansed of its scenic geniality, its bucolic complacency, for if the word originally denoted an optical familiarity derived from the harmonies found in the landscapes of Lorrain or Poussin, the eye of these poems is to refocus on a thoroughly unnatural vantage. To say that sense and sound enter into picturesque relations is to sketch a territory that is native to neither; to uproot linear syntax and deracinate the notation of sound. Arranged in these retiform patterns, sound and sense are exploited for their geometrical possibilities. The ease of syntactical comprehension and phonetic transcription are sacrificed by a typography that intellectualizes sense and assonance, constellating them in a cerebral schematic beyond the normal capacities of the eye or the ear. Though these poems putatively relate gritty, bodily Americana, drunken barroom exchanges and demotic speech, the *quadrillage* of the typography sieves this raw material for particles of sound and sense to arrange in a disembodied visual net, a geometry of the mind.

---

[57] Gotthold Ephraim Lessing, *Laocoön, Nathan the Wise and Minna von Barnhelm* (London: Dent, 1930); E. E. Cummings, 'two brass buttons', MS Am 1823.7 (21). E. E. Cummings Papers, Houghton Library, Harvard University.

3. Seeing Bodies: The Typographical Eye and the Sexual Gaze

Far from a rarefied transcendence of sensory capacities, what emerges from the atelier of these *faits* is a sense of the physicality of typography and a closer intimacy with the eye and the ear of the reader. *Tulips & Chimneys* emerges out of and digests a pregnant mass of bodily encounters. Cummings's escapades in Boston as a Harvard postgraduate and his encounters with French prostitutes during his time in the American Ambulance Corps provide bountiful material for the volume. Moreover, its publishing history and status as a bibliographical object constantly negotiate bodily issues, both in terms of Cummings's designing of the book and how it is interpreted and managed by his editors. Though, as I argued earlier, the 1922 manuscript is key for understanding the full range of Cummings's typographical creativity and poetic intentions, the publishing history of the 1923 *Tulips and Chimneys* is revelatory about how sexuality and style interlock. Accepted by Thomas Seltzer in 1922, the same year the publisher was embroiled in a censorship case over his publishing of explicit literature, including D. H. Lawrence's *Women in Love*, the 1922 manuscript was published the following year, but only after Seltzer excised over half of the original poems, with an eye to suppressing the most sexually explicit.[58]

There is an alliance between typographical and bodily assertion in the saga of *Tulips and Chimneys*'s publishing history that incarnates the vexed issue of the poet's control over the bibliographical object. For Cummings's title stamps the book with a sigil of sexual liberation, albeit a half-concealed one: in the poet's own words, 'Tulips= Two Lips Chimneys= Penises'. This title exhibits an intimacy between sign, symbol, and body: its latent sexuality is shaped through its homophonic and metaphoric form. But the title also stakes its governance over the book by being recapitulated at the beginning and midpoint of the volume, splitting it into 'Tulips' and 'Chimneys', as if each poem were a discrete corporeal object, and, furthermore, subtly but conspicuously emblematizing the poet's authority in the book's layout beyond the arena of the individual lyric, an experimental typography that stations itself at the border of the publisher's domain. But the most controversial and prized item is the ampersand in Cummings's original manuscript that, despite the poet's insistence on it being kept ('On this I am portland cement and carrara'), is substituted for the conventional 'and'.

[58] Christopher Sawyer-Lauçanno, *E.E. Cummings: A Biography*, 68–69, 110, 220, 225.

This contexture between graphical signs and graphic bodies is most conspicuous in the epilogue to the genesis of *Tulips and Chimneys*, where, at
Cummings's express behest, a volume of some of the poems previously omitted was released as a privately printed book, free of censorship laws, under
the title *&*.[59]

Cummings's method of having *&* published is practically and perfor-
matively expressive of the belief that typography ought to be free of the
incursions of editorial design. Bypassing the career publisher or even the
small-scale vanity press, it is to the typographer Samuel Jacobs that Cummings addresses himself in 1925:

> I was ever so pleased to discover that my most personal work had been
> carefully omitted by both Thomas&Lincoln. I hope that you will publish
> this under your coatofarms. Nobody else in the world can set what I like
> best of my own poems.[60]

Though we should not reject the pragmatic motivation of flattering Jacobs
into accepting the commission, this interchange also imagines an ideal distillation of the procedure of publication, where the poet's visual imagination
can be fostered by the artisanal care of a composite typographer-publisher.
Moreover, Cummings's ambivalent phrasing, reducible neither to 'nobody
else can best set my poems' nor to 'nobody else can set the poems I like best',
enmeshes the exceptional mise-en-page of the poems with their exceptional
personality and explicitness. Furthermore, that heraldic eye for Jacobs's
personal seal, his 'coatofarms', again reveals Cummings's sensitivity to bibliographical authority and the symbolic weight of labels and imprints: *&*, in its
alphabetic transcription, is staggered over the three sections of the volume,
'A', 'N', and 'D', such that far more emphatically than *Tulips and Chimneys*,
the title of the book, that locus of definition and ownership, is brought
under the aegis of Cummings and Jacobs's radical typography, a dynamic of
typographical energy beginning to annex the realm of the bibliographical.

If a struggle over bodily and typographical freedom animates the publishing and afterlife of *Tulips and Chimneys*, how do bodies figure in reading
the mise-en-page of individual poems? A working hypothesis from surveying the publication history might be that Cummings saw the exposure
of the body as coextensive with an unfolding visuality of the page. But in

[59] Christopher Sawyer-Lauçanno, *E.E. Cummings: A Biography*, 158, 220, 241.
[60] Christopher Sawyer-Lauçanno, *E.E. Cummings: A Biography*, 241.

Cummings's first Norton lecture, it is oral self-explication that he refers to as 'aesthetic striptease'.[61] He proposes didactic, impersonal lecturing as decent clothing, but a more obvious way in which Cummings covers himself up might be the trappings of visual form in his poems, that the sumptuary weight of typography cloaks bare meaning. How to see the body of Cummings's texts, and whether one sees the shapes of bodies in them, has exercised the poet's critics from the outset. Edmund Wilson, writing in 1924, is convinced that the visuality of Cummings's page masks a kernel of conventional sentiment, but he is even more repulsed by the physicality of these poems: 'His poems are hideous on the page [. . .]'.[62] Marianne Moore astutely propounds a notational theory of Cummings's spacing, her focus on the accentual ictus electing a suprasegmental feature that is different from both Mallarmé's intonation and Olson's pauses, and wisely discounts the pictorial association with the 'typographic wine-glasses' of the Elizabethans on account of their moribund literality. Yet even Moore is most enchanted by the graphical beauty of Cummings's page:

> We have, not a replica of the title [as in Elizabethan picture poetry], but a more potent thing, a replica of the rhythm – a kind of second tempo, uninterfering like a shadow, in the manner of the author's beautiful if somewhat self-centred, gigantic filiform ampersand of symbolical 'and by itself plus itself with itself'. The physique of these poems recalls the corkscrew twists, the infinitude of dots, the sumptuous perpendicular appearance of Kufic script [. . .][63]

Moore's account of typography is bracing because, so rare amongst the descriptions of mise-en-page, she opts for superabundance over reductionism. Moore rightly notes how Cummings's ampersand accrues a talismanic resonance, a signature of his visual élan, embracing that 'second tempo' of the typography as whole. But Moore does entangle herself in her 'filiform' argument, for to say that Cummings's typography is 'a replica of the rhythm' is to say that it replicates a pre-existent vocal rhythm; but if Cummings is 'determining the pauses slowly, with glides and tightrope acrobatics, ensuring the ictus by a space instead of a period', then the mise-en-page is not a

---

[61] E. E. Cummings, *I: Six Nonlectures*, p. 3.

[62] Edmund Wilson, 'Wallace Stevens and E. E. Cummings', in *Critical Essays on E. E. Cummings*, ed. Guy Rotella, (Boston: G.K. Hall, 1984), 43–46 (p. 45).

[63] Marianne Moore, 'People Stare Carefully', in *Critical Essays on E. E. Cummings*, ed. Guy Rotella, 46–49 (p. 46).

shadow of the reciting voice but formative of it.[64] Moore's 'second tempo' is on the cusp of voicing the radical possibility of a visual prosody that is not phonocentric but veers off into a conception that is much more traditional and that embodies the flip side of Wilson's impression of typographical ugliness. This being a review specifically of *XLI Poems* and *&*, not of *Tulips and Chimneys*, Moore's symbolic ampersand is alive to a bibliographical significance of the sign as a hallmark of Cummings's idiosyncrasy. But it gravitates away from emblematizing the energy of typography to the fluency of calligraphy. Moore is not quite harking back to the cult of typographical beauty of William Morris and fine-press printing, as the appearance of an exotic, non-Western script would more ally Cummings with Ezra Pound, Ernest Fenollosa, and Paul Claudel.[65] However, having banished pictorial shapes from Cummings's texts, her suggestion detracts from those prosodic apprehensions of the page she has signalled by gesturing to an equally surface-level appreciation of scriptural form. An apprehension of beauty and ugliness ought not to be cleansed from our reading of Cummings entirely, but I wish to argue that Moore's sense of prosodic shaping is a much better guide to how *Tulips & Chimneys* engages with a typographical body.

Pictorial poetry does not interest Moore because it is too quickly seen, unlike the arabesques she traces in Cummings's pages. Cummings's poems, though, can be alert to the force of instantaneous visual judgements. The twelfth sonnet of the 'REALITIES' sequence, according to Cummings's intended sequencing, is alive to the speed of apprehending body and character, summing up its subject in the first line as:

"kitty". sixteen, 5' 1", white, prostitute.

The graphical character of this line, its aloof quotation marks and numerical measurements, has the summative concision of a police profile. Further, the spacing of the poem interacts with the familiar unit of the decasyllabic line to expose the dimensions of 'kitty'. The elongated spaces in the repeated profiling of the eighth line—'Kitty.   a whore.   Sixteen'—lay bare the rhythmic make-up of the line and strip it of its organic cohesion by visually isolating each two-syllable unit, as if to rob metre of its spontaneity and

---

[64] Marianne Moore, 'People Stare Carefully', in *Critical Essays*, 46.
[65] Ernest Fenollosa, *The Chinese Written Character as a Medium for Poetry*, ed. Ezra Pound (San Francisco: City Lights Books, 1964); Paul Claudel, *Cent phrases pour éventails* (Paris: Gallimard, 1942).

depth. Similarly, in the fourth line, 'skilled in quick softness.   Unsponta-neous. cute', those spaces and full stops punctuate a contraction of epithets and a graduated belittling as if the typographical eye of the poem cuts 'kitty' down to size.

> The babybreasted broad "kitty" twice eight
>
> —beer nothing, the lady'll have a whiskey-sour—
>
> whose least amazing smile is the most great
> common divisor of unequal souls.[66]

These final lines ring hollow in their conciliation, not least because lauding 'kitty' as a shared factor recalls the forms of callous enumeration the rest of the poem has enacted, flattening out her dimensions to the numerical labels of age and height. In the final sonnet of this sequence, 'life boosts herself rapidly at me', there is similarly incisive focalization of the page's gaze:

> life boosts herself rapidly at me
>
> through sagging debris of exploded day
> the hulking perpendicular mammal
>   a
> grim epitome of chuckling flesh. [. . .]
> gums skidding on slippery udders
>
>   she
> lifts an impertinent puerperal face
> and with astute fatuous swallowed eyes
> smiles,
>   one grin very distinctly wobbles

Those late indentations of monosyllables accentuate the hypertrophic mass of this 'friendless dingy female frenzy'.[67] The indefinite article and personal pronoun are made to look incommensurate with the bulbous flesh of the textual body, as if the grammar of human singularity does not fit. By contrast,

[66] E. E. Cummings, *Tulips and Chimneys* (New York: Thomas Seltzer, 1923), p.113.
[67] E. E. Cummings, *Tulips & Chimneys* (The Golden Eagle Press: Mount Vernon, NY, 1937), 183.

the implicitly male 'me' is not disjoined by such indentation, not under the lens of such visual exposure.

There is a robust argument, then, that Cummings's typographical nuances have an unsettling flair for taxonomizing and flattening out female bodies; for sounding out their dimensions on the page. Further, it seems such objectification is enmeshed in the scrupulousness of Cummings's visual poetics: for to read Cummings's typography carefully is precisely to scrutinize with renewed incision. Those indentations and spaces in these poems apply a critical pressure to the familiar forms of metre and grammar to single out banalities and inadequacies with a surgical wit. This interpenetration of visual creation and objectification is especially explicit in the fifth poem of *Portraits*:

> Babylon slim
> -ness of
> evenslicing
> eyes are chisels
>
> scarlet Goes
> with her
> whitehot
> face,gashed[68]

Chiselling eyes co-opt a topos of the poet as an artisanal stonemason (one that echoes from Théophile Gautier's exhortation to 'Sculpte, lime, cisèle' in 'L'Art' to Basil Bunting's poetic craftsman in *Briggflatts*) into the scope of typography.[69] Cummings venerates the eye of Picasso in his homage to the artist precisely because it is honed for truncation and excision—Picasso is a 'Lumberman of The Distinct', forming 'bodies lopped / of every / prettiness'. Though the reference to 'Trees of Ego' might suggest a work like the 1919 'Landscape with Dead and Live Trees', those unpretty bodies also conjure up the geometrically sculpted female forms of 'Les Demoiselles d'Avignon'.[70] In Maurice Merleau-Ponty's conception in *La phénoménologie de la perception*,

---

[68] E. E. Cummings, *Tulips & Chimneys* (The Golden Eagle Press: Mount Vernon, NY, 1937), 106.

[69] 'Sculpt, file, chisel'; Théophile Gautier, *Émaux et camées* (Paris: Gallimard, 1981), 150; Basil Bunting, *Complete Poems* (Tarset: Bloodaxe, 2000), 61.

[70] E. E. Cummings, *Tulips & Chimneys* (The Golden Eagle Press: Mount Vernon, NY, 1937), 144; cf Gerald N. Izenberg, *Modernism and Masculinity: Mann, Wedekind, Kandinsky through World War I* (Chicago: The University of Chicago Press, 2000), 2.

the normative human gaze is inhabited by the pressures of sexuality and cannot be neutral:

> Chez le normal, un corps n'est pas seulement perçu comme un objet quelconque, cette perception objective est habitée par une perception plus secrète : le corps est sous-tendu par un schéma sexuel, strictement individuel, qui accentue les zones érogènes, dessine une physionomie sexuelle et appelle les gestes du corps masculin lui-même intégré à cette totalité affective.[71]

Vision encodes a creative individuality where sexuality shapes the physiognomy of the bodies it encounters. Creativity and sexuality are interwoven in this conception of vision, and Merleau-Ponty goes on to describe the sexual imagination using the verb 'ébaucher', which, in addition to its more habitual usage as 'to sketch', can mean to 'rough-hew', cognate with the noun 'ébauchoir', designating a sculptor's paring chisel.[72] The body of the published poem emerged from a rough-hewing of the typography. In an act of compositional violence, Cummings splits the lines of the manuscript drafts in two with an abrupt stroke of the pencil to form this corsetted textual shape. Adjacent to the text in an early typescript of the poem, Cummings dashes off an ink squib of the female persona, a spindly half-undressed figure who holds up her left arm so awkwardly that she seems to do so against her volition.[73] This imagined figure, not based on any actual sitting in Cummings's atelier, exudes the unnatural stasis of a model transfixed by the artist's gaze. Cummings's typographical eye seems wired with this impulse to shape the desired body of the text and the desired female body in a seeing where aesthetic and erotic urges are indistinguishable.

This is by no means to extirpate the strands of misogyny in some of Cummings's visions by declaring objectification a healthy, normative response in contradistinction to the pathologically asexual gaze of Merleau-Ponty's patient Schneider. Quite the contrary, it is to show that Cummings's sexual

---

[71] 'In the case of the normal subject, a body is not perceived merely as any object; this objective perception has within it a more intimate perception: the visible body is subtended by a sexual schema, which is strictly individual, emphasizing the erogenous areas, outlining a sexual physiognomy, and eliciting the gestures of the masculine body which is itself integrated into this emotional totality'; Maurice Merleau-Ponty, *The Phenomenology of Perception*, trans. Colin Smith (London; New York: Routledge, 2002), 180.

[72] Maurice Merleau-Ponty, *Œuvres*, ed. Claude Lefort (Paris: Gallimard, 2010), 841.

[73] E. E. Cummings, 'Babylon slim', MS Am 1823.5 (38) and MS Am 1823.7 (23). E. E. Cummings Papers, Houghton Library, Harvard University.

ethics cannot be divided from his visual poetics. But I say 'some of Cummings's visions' because the volume equally contains some moments of a heightened self-awareness, wherein the ethics of seeing are more bracingly ambivalent. Redrafting the poem, Cummings may have more forcefully etched its typographic body, but he conversely blurred the woman's syntactical form. Displaced from its original position at the head of the poem, 'scarlet' sounds less like a named figure and more like an adjective, and there are no unequivocal subjects to moor the drifting grammar. Agency is elusive, and those chiselling eyes may very well be those of the female subject. The visual constriction of the text with its unspaced compounding and lines sapped of accentual weight—the second and sixth line consisting of two unstressed syllables as if only having typographical substance rather than a rhythmic one—could rather connote a self-objectification, an auto-erotic shaping. Such self-objectification, though, could still suggest a male gaze, prompting such self-examination. Merleau-Ponty refines and bifurcates his concept of the sexual gaze later on in the chapter 'Le Corps Comme Être Sexué': 'La pudeur et l'impudeur prennent donc place dans une dialectique du moi et d'autrui qui est celle du maître et de l'esclave [. . .].'[74] In the vertiginous power relations of a Hegelian master/slave dialectic, not only is the masterful gaze potentially objectified in turn, the seer seen, but to wish to be mastered by another's erotic gaze is futile as the attracted gaze is no longer dominant but impotently entranced. In poems like 'Babylon slim', the eyes are frozen in a stalemate where the formative gaze of the viewer is being seen and formed in turn, the refractions of mise-en-page registering this tangle of glances.

4. 'Evident invisibles': Typography as Prosody

To comprehend typography as prosody requires a radical break with fixity. It is not to discern pictorial shapes in print, the wine glasses and other replicas Moore carefully dismisses. That interplay of glances involves Cummings's poems not in a simple polarity of viewer and object, but a subtler critique of the act of viewing. At such a point the physical fixity of the body becomes a problematic analogue for viewing the poems. Cummings's sonnet

[74] Maurice Merleau-Ponty, *Œuvres*, 853; 'Shame and immodesty, then, take their place in a dialectic of the self and the other which is that of master and slave.' Maurice Merleau-Ponty, *The Phenomenology of Perception*, trans. Colin Smith (London; New York: Routledge, 2002), 193.

sequences contain not only 'REALITIES' and 'ACTUALITIES' but 'UNRE-ALITIES'. *Tulips & Chimneys* in its expressionistic fecundity, especially in relation to the female body, inherits the legacy of Baudelaire, Mallarmé, and Valéry. But these poets also know how to exhaust the body. So embedded in the imagination of the fin-de-siècle is a hyper-sensualized female body that Mallarmé can experience the thrill of only glancing off it, skirting it:

> La chevelure vol d'une flamme à l'extrême
> Occident de désirs pour la tout déployer
> Se pose (Je dirais mourir un diadème)
> Vers le front couronné son ancien foyer[75]

This queenly splendour is not visible in some cloying bodily presence but rather sublimed into the glint of a reflect. Beauty is glimpsed not in a cluster of jewels but the light of a dying diadem. Cummings, whose oeuvre recurrently alludes to the celestial hierarchy of the *Paradiso*, which he studied at Harvard, also learned from Dante of bodies transformed into pyrotechnic elements.[76] Such sublimations of solid, sensory mass occur in Cummings too, though not always with a Dantescan or Mallarméan radiance:

> nearer:breath of my breath:take not thy tingling
> limbs from me:make my pain their crazy meal
> letting thy tigers of smooth sweetness steal
> slowly in dumb blossoms of new mingling:

After eleven lines of sensual and imaginative saturation, the poem concludes:

> Querying greys between mouthed houses curl
>
> thirstily. Dead stars stink. dawn. Inane,
>
> the poetic carcass of a girl[77]

---

[75] Stéphane Mallarmé, *Les poésies* (Bruxelles: Edmond Deman, 1899), 71; Stéphane Mallarmé, *Collected Poems and Other Verse*, trans. E. H. and A. M. Blackmore (New York: Oxford University Press, 2006), 46–47: 'The hair flight of a flame to the extreme / west of desire if it should all unlace / settles (a diadem dying it would seem) / near the crowned brow its former fireplace'

[76] Richard S. Kennedy, *Dreams in the Mirror: A Biography of E. E. Cummings* (New York: Liveright, 1994) 61.

[77] E. E. Cummings, *Tulips & Chimneys* (The Golden Eagle Press: Mount Vernon, NY, 1937), 171. I have altered some small aspects of spacing here based on E. E. Cummings, *Complete*

In the amplified span of the volume's typography, the suspension of line spacing, elongated word spacing, or indentation is suffocating in its density. *Tulips & Chimneys* recalibrates the reader's eye such that 'normative' typography is not normative in Cummings, but a marked linguistic feature. In this post-coital aubade, spacing is synchronized with an evacuation of sensual and poetic substance. There is a disturbingly necrophilic weight to that word 'carcass' that recalls Baudelaire's 'Une charogne' and anticipates the *danse macabre* of Yves Bonnefoy's *Du mouvement et de l'immobilité de Douve*, though this poem is also interested in the body as a site for the schematic of desire and in stripping bare the thick daubing of lust. Once drained of the language of sexual frenzy—synaesthetic expressionism—it is in the stark spacing of the page that the poem encounters the barren skeleton of desire.

This sonnet is a powerful corrective to the notion that typography is inherently involved in the physical body and the material text. Yra Van Dijk compellingly associates typographical blanks with a late nineteenth- and early twentieth-century obsession with nullity, though her argument focuses on the margins of the page in free-verse poetry, a paginal blankness that is present in non-experimental mise-en-page and not confined to the period she identifies.[78] Experimental mise-en-page is difficult to comprehend and to see as a substantive addition to poetry because it is so much an art of absences. Olson's theoretical solution to this unsettling lack is to fill it with quantifiable mass, to not have immeasurable spaces, but ones which have the notational substance of a crotchet rest in music.[79] Richard Cureton, in his incisive article on Cummings's morphology, also tries to make the currents of negativity in Cummings positive by ascribing his negating prefixes to a Manichean division between a lifeless world he denounces as opposed to the vital one he exults in.[80] Cummings's agrammatical negative nouns are not always pejorative, however; in the thirteenth sonnet of 'UNREALITIES', 'unwisdom' is part of a fabric of transcendent nothingness:

> when learned darkness from our searched world
>
> wrestest the rare unwisdom of thy eyes

Poems: 1904—1962, ed. George J. Firmage (New York: Liveright Publishing Corporation, 2016), 135, which is likely to represent Cummings's original intentions.

[78] Yra Van Dijk, 'Reading the Form: The Function of Typographic Blanks in Modern Poetry', *Word & Image*, 4 (2011), 407–15.

[79] Charles Olson, *Human Universe*, p. 58.

[80] Richard D. Cureton, 'E. E. Cummings: A Study of the Poetic Use of Deviant Morphology', *Poetics Today*, 1 (1979), 213–44 (p. 222).

A poem that concludes:

> if god should send the morning; and before
> my doubting window leaves softly to stir,
> of thoughtful trees whom night hath pondered o'er
> —and frailties of dimension to occur
>
> about us
>   and birds known,scarcely to sing
>
> (heart, shalt thou bear the marvel of this thing?)[81]

The negative doubt implicit in typographical blanks, their frailty of dimension, is what their prosodic value is predicated upon. Prosody is a current that is not reducible to any single type of sonic or visual content; intonation, pitch, accent, or quantity become prosodic by assuming meaningful contours, but prosody itself transcends these given incarnations of it. To speak of a prosodic typography as more than bodily is to ward off the role that the body takes in a naive dualism, where it is a machine of organic matter governed by an immaterial soul or self; for criticism falls short when it treats typography as a physical matter to be vivified by a sound or sense that remains detached from it. Prosody is negative in the sense that selfhood is, in that it is articulated in the body but more vital than an anatomy of fleshy parts. His pages riddled with blanks, Cummings's mise-en-page, when it explicitly confronts its kinship with negativity, announces itself as a true species of prosody. His experimental typography has the elasticity to deconstruct and reshape syntax, metre, or rhyme, and indeed to exist as a rhythm independent of these. Cummings's typography can electrify the bodily trysts and twinings of *Tulips & Chimneys*, but it refuses to be reduced to simply an ongoing metaphor for the physical body. The fixity on the page of mise-en-page can lead us into a category error. For it is only if these blanks have a set semiotic function that they are semantically fixed. As prosody, they move.

---

[81] E. E. Cummings, *Tulips & Chimneys* (The Golden Eagle Press: Mount Vernon, NY, 1937), p. 196.

5. 'A Pure Optical G': Hope Mirrlees, E. E. Cummings, and Graphical Minima

Illegitimating or repressing certain aspects of the visuality of writing is a recurrent feature of even quite radical appreciations of literary language. Quoting from Rousseau's *Profession de foi*, Jacques Derrida argues that a distinction between legitimate and illegitimate writing is at the heart of the phonocentric tradition: 'Il y a donc une bonne et une mauvaise écriture: la bonne et naturelle, l'inscription divine dans le cœur et l'âme; la perverse et l'artificieuse, la technique, exilée dans l'extériorité du corps.'[82] Typographical experimentation, since it oversteps a Saussurean documentation of speech, is liable to be seen as perverse, artificial, and marginalized when measured against such phonocentric standards. But often the visuality of reading cannot be expunged even from appraisals which lack the terms to express it or fear to confront it directly. Williams's 1932 essay on Marianne Moore is exemplary in what it sees but cannot say:

> There must be edges. This casts some light I think on the simplicity of design in much of Miss Moore's work. There must be recognizable edges around the ground which cannot, as she might desire it, be left entirely white. Prose would be all black, a complete black painted or etched over, but solid.

It is impossible not to see Moore's jagged, diagonal margins alluded to in these 'edges', yet the bisections throughout Williams's essay have been cast in such insistently geometrical, ideational, or metaphorical terms that we cannot but hesitate in assigning a typographical reading to this passage.[83] It is as if a typographical apprehension of Moore's poetry is repressed, only to resurface as the analogue for Williams's whole perception of Moore's philosophy and aesthetics. Margins can be thought but not seen.

Under reigning conditions that cannot process or articulate it, the dominance of a phonocentric prosody and a phonocentric linguistics, the visual aspect of a text which is insubordinate to sound becomes taboo. Assessing Cummings's poetry in 1954, Williams, still circumspect about confronting

---

[82] 'Therefore there is good and bad writing: the good and natural one, which is a divine inscribing in the heart and soul; and the abnormal and artificial one, a device, which is exiled to the exteriority of the body'; Jacques Derrida, *De la grammatologie* (Paris: Éditions de Minuit, 1967), 30.

[83] William Carlos Williams, *The Williams Carlos Williams Reader*, 391, 389.

typography head on, is alive to the fact that a graphical poetics is still almost unspeakable; painting Cummings as a fugitive from 'the whole accepted modus of english', he is uneasy about his own conclusion: 'I don't see how you can avoid speaking of cummings in this way, dangerous as it surely is [...]'.[84] Cummings, though, was aware and willing to broach the penumbra of the mute apprehension of the page from very early on. In one of his 1916–17 experiments, Cummings depicts mr. smith 'reading / his letter / by the fire- / light':

> no type bold o's
>   d's gloat
>   droll l's twine
>   r's rove
>
>   haha
>
>   sweet-hearts
>   part   fellow
>   like   darl- write
>   i dream my   try ned   ma
>   thinks
>   right thing   will be still
>   till death
>   thine[85]

Cummings here tries to transcribe the very experience of reading. First, in the rapid graphological survey, he delineates the affective idiosyncrasies attached to the shape of letters, but then, with greater audacity, he tries to articulate the cognition of writing as an experience: through those fragmented phrases and typographical blanks, Cummings attempts to find a script to record the uneven and elliptical manner in which the eye filters and recognizes the written text.

Cummings's experiment, however, was never published in his lifetime. Poems like '"let's start a magazine' and 'o prgress' may be disdainful of the way in which typographical stability is predicated upon a suppression of the latent expressive capacities of the written text, but such satire does not in itself construct a liberated typography. How can Cummings intelligibly

---

[84] William Carlos Williams, *The William Carlos Williams Reader*, 403, 405.
[85] E. E. Cummings, 'mr. smith', bMS Am 1823.7 (23). E. E. Cummings Papers, Houghton Library, Harvard University.

tap into the visual kinetics of silent reading that his 'mr. smith' experiment identifies? Barthes, likewise apprised of writing's untapped potential, writes:

> Si l'orthographie était libre – libre d'être simplifiée ou non, selon l'envie du sujet –, elle pourrait constituer une pratique très positive d'expression; la physionomie écrite du mot pourrait acquérir une valeur proprement poétique, dans la mesure où elle surgirait de la fantasmatique du scripteur [. . .][86]

Barthes may be willing to afford the writer the liberty to indulge their graphical imagination, but if such a language is constructed by private, hermetic associations, how can this be other than a freedom pleasurable to the writer? Cummings may know that there is an unspoken dynamism in reading and posit a utopian typography 'mobile, vide (apte à prendre n'importe quels contours)' that could do it justice, but how can this energy be realized if it is subconscious?[87]

Cummings is able to realize such energy because even graphical conventions are, when closely observed, inherently unstable. *No Thanks*, published in 1935, is especially unorthodox in its punctuation, and punctuation, even in typographically normative writers, is a point in the written text where convention is fringed with visual liberty. In the conclusion to his history of punctuation, M. B. Parkes follows the safe evaluation that local punctuational effects spring from existing conventions with the more bracing insight that 'such exploitation could extend the range of usage too, since it also depend[s] on a fundamental characteristic of punctuation in general: that, apart from registering a degree of disjunction, few punctuation symbols have a precise value or exclusive specifying function.'[88] Punctuation is especially susceptible to experimental usage because of its inherent semantic liquidity: it does not provide definitions but pliant points of disjunction. John Lennard embraces such looseness, plotting both entrenched convention and local effect in his pioneering study of the parenthesis. In Lennard's account, Eliot's lunulae (a term the author adopts to refer to the graphical

---

[86] 'If spelling were free – free to be simplified or not, according to the wish of the individual – it could form a very positive and substantial mode of expression; the written physiognomy of the word could assume a truly poetic value, insofar as it would arise from the imagination of the writer [. . .]'
[87] 'moveable, empty (able to assume whatever shape)'. Roland Barthes, *Oeuvres complètes*, IV, 925, 221.
[88] M. B. Parkes, *Pause and Effect: An Introduction to the History of Punctuation in the West* (Aldershot: Scolar Press, 1992), 114.

shape) span from visual echos of seashells on Margate beach to Prufrock's digression to the poet's philosophy of time. Cummings, by contrast, cannot move beyond one-off 'typographical tricks': 'Each of cummings' exploitations has its charm and local validity, but neither contributes beyond itself, and both shade towards the meretricious.'[89]

Cummings's one-off graphical correlations, though, do participate in a persistent engagement with the value and capacity of punctuation:

> emptied.hills.listen.
> ,not,alive,trees,dream (
> ev:ery:wheres:ex:tend:ing:hush
>
>)
> anddark
> IshbusY
> ing-roundly-dis
>
> tinct;chuck
> lings,laced
> ar:e.by (
>
> fleet&panelike&frailties
> !throughwhich!brittlest!whitewhom!
> f
> l o a t ?)
>   r
>   h y t h m s[90]

This is more than a local experimenting with a one-off punctuational effect. In methodically apportioning different punctuation marks to each line, full stops followed by commas followed by colons, Cummings makes these symbols and their usage relative to each other as conspicuous as possible. Such a tabulation of dashes and colons deliberately interrogates the weight of punctuation in general. Adorno's reading of punctuation marks, even whilst prescribing them as 'marks of oral delivery', recurrently exceeds such definitions. Though he claims that punctuation functions analogously to musical language and concludes that cautious punctuating 'pays homage to the sound it suppresses', visual apprehension infiltrates this phonocentric

---

[89] John Lennard, *But I Digress: The Exploitation of Parentheses in English Printed Verse* (Oxford: Clarendon Press, 1991), 182, 184, 212, 233.
[90] E. E. Cummings, *No Thanks*, n.p. [poem 33].

position so that Proust's brackets are a 'bull's eye lantern' that interrupts 'the graphic image' and Theodor Storm's dashes are 'wrinkles on the brow of his text'. Furthermore, Proust's brackets are said to perforate the fabric of a Bergsonian *durée* and Storm's dashes to voice his sense of fatalism. Punctuation thus far transcends 'oral delivery' in Adorno's essay through his avowed 'physiognomic' apprehension of the text and his sense that punctuation can be attuned to the rhythms of the writer's thought.[91] Cummings's poem plots a transcendence of oral function. The full stops in the first line separate three distinct stress units, but in the second line the commas isolate the unstressed 'not', unsettling this musical pattern, though otherwise maintaining it. The colons in the third line separate syllables, but if enunciated as pauses, they would warp normal speech patterns. By the final verse paragraph, that three-beat rhythm reappears, but it is punctuated by marks that do not have a disjunctive function—ampersands and exclamation marks.[92] Adorno, though we should bear in mind that he is writing principally about prose, insists that punctuation marks ought to remain inconspicuous.[93] Cummings, though, by rooting them in a poem about 'fleet&panelike&frailties', makes punctuation as conspicuous and self-aware as he can. Punctuating with the full gamut of visual ciphers, he refuses to allocate disjunction and interruption to any one demarcated set of graphical signs. By exacting such microscopic attention to the joins of the text, Cummings makes disjunction itself the only constant element in the poem.

These points of intersection are immediately reprised in the adjacent poem:

snow)says!Says
over un
    graves
        der,speaking
(says.word
Less)ly(goes

fold?folds)cold
stones(o-l-d)names
aren'ts[94]

[91] Theodor W. Adorno, 'Punctuation Marks', *The Antioch Review*, 3 (1990), 300–305 (pp. 300, 305, 304, 301, 302).
[92] E. E. Cummings, *No Thanks*, n.p. [poem 33].
[93] Theodor W. Adorno, 'Punctuation Marks', 305.
[94] E. E. Cummings, *No Thanks*, n.p. [poem 34].

Snow, intersecting and erasing the texture of landscape and the solid inscription of gravestones, manifests Cummings's fascination with the eloquence of 'bodiless presences' in the text: his own typographical language of spaces, capitals, and brackets.[95] Verbs being recurrently bereft of objects, the insistent acts of speech in this poem proclaim a communication that occurs between and beyond the solidity of names. This is a linguistic affirmation of faith; Cummings exults in the superabundance of visual cognition.

There is a desired aphasia in the halting repetitions of 'says' in this laboured transcription of an act of reading, as though the 'bodiless presences' of visual rhythms could only be discerned by approaching a state of illiteracy. *No Thanks* is a difficult book of poems to read in that it sabotages script; it effortfully impedes the recognition of words. Degrees of illiteracy, in Cummings's aesthetic ruminations, cast light on the penumbra of linguistic communication, substrates of language beneath sound and sense. In an unpublished typescript, Cummings theorizes what he terms an 'Optical G':

An Optical G occurs in the case of a written language which i cannot read.

When i am confronted with a written language whose alphabet i do not recognise(e.g. Syrian) an optical G occurs a Pure Optical G occurs.

When i am confronted with a written language whose alphabet is identical with the English(which alphabet is consequently familiar to my eye,permitting that I recognise words as such) supposing that i am ignorant of what the words mean(e.g. German) an impure Optical G occurs.

When i read a written language which, though not my own,i understand [superscript: perfectly] (e.g. French), there is no G.[96]

Literacy is an erasure of script; to learn a language is to not see the letters. It is, by translation into sound or sense, to delete their graphical presence, hence why the text effectively vanishes at the end of this passage: 'there is no G.' An afterthought, that 'an Impure Optical G occurs helped by the capitalization of nouns', hints that this state of pure optical apprehension might be induced by typographical manipulation. This luminous aphasia not only emerges in reading a Syrian newspaper; as Cummings probes the concept

[95] Theodor W. Adorno, 'Punctuation Marks', 300.
[96] E. E. Cummings, 'Notes on reading', MS Am 1823.7 (25). E. E. Cummings Papers, Houghton Library, Harvard University.

further, he sees it as resident in one's own native tongue, in English. For-mulating blueprints for a new poetics, Cummings is recurrently drawn to a demotic geometry, just as those early essays in typographical experiment were undergirded by grids and *quadrillage*. Eyeing words with the gaze of a geometer, they can be redeemed from fungible counters in the exchange of signification, converted back into pure shapes: 'a word is an optically discrete unit made up of curves and straight lines (letters) preceded and followed by a space(blank)'. To see words like this, though, seems to require the reader to be in a dissociative trance, a perverse state of unlearning alpha-betism, an alien injunction that recalls Spinoza's proposition in his *Ethics* to see human actions in terms of lines, spaces and planes.[97] Cummings, though, maintains that such optics inhabit other acts of reading, substituting this geometrical phantasmagoria for a conceivable, if exorbitant, totting up of figures:

> Suppose the eye be confronted by figures
> I.
>> 345,600,000,000,000,000,000,000,000,000,000,000 [. . .]
> but which the writer expresses
> III.
>> three hundred and forty-five billion and six hundred millions of thousands of millions of millions of billions[98]

This scenario for Cummings is a parable for aesthetics. This quantity is seized upon because, both in its numerical and alphabetic form, it is too great to be processed. The slight contours of a single grapheme, an optical g, may be erased by the literate reader, but this word is too ponderous for the eye to distil into signification. Such figures jam the mechanism of reading:

> We have said that [the figure] "occurs as a homogeneous picture, or suffi-cient graphic entity, or optically unfacoable [sic] whole, to the eye inhibited as to thought." In such a statement at least there can be nothing ambiguous. The eye's virgin look from left to right does not give us a [superscript: defi-nite] number, does not give us a [superscript: precise] quantity but it does give us [a] "distinct feeling". The word "distinct" has been carefully cho-sen. It is the adjective which, in our opinion, most nearly escapes (when

---

[97] Benedict de Spinoza, *Ethics*, ed. and trans. Edwin Curley (London: Penguin, 1996), 69.
[98] E. E. Cummings, 'Notes on reading', MS Am 1823.7 (27). E. E. Cummings Papers, Houghton Library, Harvard University.

coupled with "feeling") from the prison of symbol into the dimension of Being.[99]

This outlying case on the peripheries of reading furnishes a theoretical underpinning for Cummings's typographical poetics. Trapped in the 'prison of symbol', typography is read as efficacious code to be processed into phonetic or lexical values, expedient tokens unimpressed by feeling or form. But such elephantine quantities resist conversion into sound or sense; they stubbornly remain graphic entities or word pictures. In '[t]he eye's virgin look' at the shape of such words and the impression they elicit, Cummings descries an affective residuum, a 'distinct feeling' cleansed from normative reading habits.

Yet it is not in inflated visual quantities that Cummings's verse seeks such quiddities of feeling. In a cognate set of notes on linguistics, he refers to a 'holophrastic g', a theoretical cousin to the 'pure optical g'. This is a heterodox use of the term, for holophrasis commonly refers to the condensing of meaning that would normally extend to a whole phrase into a single word; for example, a baby exclaiming 'ball' to signify 'I want the ball'. Graphical minima similarly animated Hope Mirrlees. Even though Mirrlees abandoned typographical experiment after her long poem of 1920, and there is little evidence that Cummings had read her work, *Paris: A Poem* anticipates the quest for atomicity that exercises Cummings's later lyrics, giving the lie to any claims that American verse is simply ahead of British verse in visual audacity. Casting her eye over the slogans and ads of the Métro, Mirrlees begins her 1920 *Paris: A Poem* with the assertion 'I want a holophrase', and her typography probes how consumer desires have been written into miniaturised graphics, until her verse splits into single words at a commodified vision of the Jardin des Tuileries. Typography often brings poetry uncomfortably close to advertising, and Mirrlees's poem is acutely cognizant of how commerce shapes vision. The opening line, 'I want a holophrase', is disturbingly anonymous, despite the orientation of the first-person pronoun, because it is unclear who the speaker is, and individuality is soon lost in a crowd of third-person utterances. Sandeep Parmar has argued that Mirrlees was influenced by Anna de Noailles and her depictions of the turn-of-the-century *flâneuse*, whilst Julia Briggs has suggested Mirrlees might have had in mind the nomenclature of her mentor and partner, the classicist Jane

[99] E. E. Cummings, 'Notes on reading', MS Am 1823.7 (27). E. E. Cummings Papers, Houghton Library, Harvard University.

Harrison, who in her 1912 *Themis* defined holophrases as 'utterances of a relation in which the subject and object have not yet got their heads above water but are submerged in a situation'.[100] A rootless commercial desire, an amorphous libido, inheres in that opening line. Mirrlees's poem is entranced by the holophrastic power of advertising, how it miniaturises the language of desire; how it condenses thinking from 'I want to buy a bottle of Dubonnet' to simply 'DUBONNET'. Holophrases emblazon the typography of *Paris*:

> I want a holophrase
>
> NORD-SUD
>
> ZIG-ZAG
> LION NOIR
> CACAO BLOOKER
>
> Black-figured vases in Etruscan tombs
>
> RUE DU BAC (DUBONNET)
> SOLFERINO (DUBONNET)
> CHAMBRE DES DEPUTES
>
> Brekekekek coax coax we are passing under the Seine
>
> DUBONNET
>
> The Scarlet Woman shouting BYRRH and deafening
> St. John at Patmos

Mirrlees charts the geography of Paris as a succession of graphical monads: metro signs like 'NORD-SUD' or brands of cigarettes or shoe polish like 'ZIG-ZAG' or 'LION NOIR'.[101] In this regard, Mirrlees's mise-en-page is in dialogue with the 'Chant du Paveur' from Jean Cocteau's 1919 *Le Cap de Bonne-Espérance*, a passage that displays some of the same brands of alcohol as Mirrlees's poem as it maps the terrestrial and aerial scope of contemporary

---

[100] Sandeep Parmar, 'Introduction', in Hope Mirrlees, *Collected Poems* (Manchester: Carcanet, 2011), xxxvii, xl.
[101] Hope Mirrlees, *Paris: A Poem* (London: Hogarth Press, 1920), 3. The colophon erroneously lists the date of publication as 1919.

commerce.[102] This cellular typography diagrammatizes how slogans are impressed upon the urban environment, that parenthetical '(DUBONNET)' implying that the modern *flâneur* or *flâneuse* cannot see rue du Bac without also seeing vermouth. Mirrlees's typography bears witness to how the visuals of commerce infiltrated the sacred precincts of literature. The scarlet woman of an advertisement for Byrrh fortified wine forces herself into conversation with the evangelist, splicing capitalized slogans with holy writ. Elsewhere it's hard to distinguish commerce and poetry:

AU

BON MARCHE

ACTUELLEMENT

TOILETTES

PRINTANIERES

The jeunesse dorée of the sycamores.

The proximity of lines like 'The jeunesse dorée of the sycamores' with fragmented slogans compromises their literariness, or, more bracingly, expands the category of literariness altogether. The gilded youth of the sycamores starts to sound as prettifying and tokenistic as an ad jingle. Mirrlees is compelled by how atomistic the cityscape of 1910s Paris is, how it is formed of 'Cell on cell / Experience', and the dilations, expansions, and contractions of her form dissipate tone and subject. Typography and psyche '[s]corn the laws of solid geometry'.[103] The spindliness of Cummings's later typography, evident most famously in the two-letter lines of 'a leaf falls' from *95 Poems*, is already present in the one-letter lines spelling 'There is no lily of the valley' in Mirrlees's poem:

[102] Jean Cocteau, *Le Cap de Bonne-Espérance* (Paris: Gallimard, 1967) 83–91.
[103] Hope Mirrlees, *Paris: A Poem*, 7, 13, 5, 11.

The first of May
T
h
e
r
e
i
s
n
o
l
i
l
y
o
f
t
h
e
v
a
l
l
e
y

Adumbrating novels of the 1920s, Mirrlees contracts the span of her long poem to a single day, but she has far more scope to miniaturize than a novelist has. Just as Cummings manipulates the junctures of the printed page to seek out bodiless presences in poems 33 and 34 of *No Thanks*, Mirrlees strains the technical possibilities of verse to distill ever smaller units of meaning. The day of Mirrlees's poem isn't just a microcosm of the life of Paris; rather, to see Paris properly is to display a febrile atomicity only intelligible by splitting lines into letters. As the poem shrinks, the final line of Mirrlees's work is articulated in units less substantial than letters: a constellation of asterisks spell out Ursa Minor, as though these *corpora caeca* were the smallest possible script.

Cummings inherits Mirrlees's search for the language of holophrasis. To propose that holophrasis can occur at the diminished scale of the letter is to assert one's faith in very small quanta of linguistic meaning. Experimental typography in Cummings's verse exposes the eye not to grossly inflated figures, like the multiple billions of his optical theory, but radically small bits of language. Cummings's eye is preternaturally sensitive to typographical nuance, as attested by the galley proofs of *Poems 1923–1954*, which he reviewed and annotated prior to that volume's publication, and which show him correcting fractional misalignments of lines and conscious of the visual minima of hairline spaces.[104] Daniel Albright claims that a search for fundamental particles, a language inherited from physics, exerted a compelling force on modernist aesthetics, noting that 'poets started to become seriously engrossed in the nomenclature of elementary poetical particles [. . .] Many of the Modernists liked the scientific notion of a minimum unit – atom or quantum.'[105] Cummings had begun to formulate elementary linguistic quantities from his years at Harvard: '[T]he amount between two objects (nouns) is homogeneous with the nouns and they with it, the whole constituting a verb, and being apprehended by the child in terms of mobility or by the apparatus (mechanism, subjective) of motion.'[106] Key to this theory is the equal valency between the solid units that nouns constitute and the intersections between them. By the time he wrote *No Thanks*, Cummings's demotion of the phenomenological and linguistic primacy of nouns and his scrutiny of the liminal points of language had intensified radically:

go(perpe)go

(tu)to(al
adve

nturin
g p
article

s of s
ini
sterd[107]

[104] E. E. Cummings, 'Poems 1923–1954', bMS Am 1823.4 (114). E. E. Cummings Papers, Houghton Library, Harvard University.
[105] Daniel Albright, *Quantum Poetics: Yeats, Pound, Eliot, and the Science of Modernism* (Cambridge: Cambridge University Press, 1997), 7.
[106] Milton A. Cohen, *Poet and Painter*, 152.
[107] E. E. Cummings, *No Thanks*, n.p. [poem 20].

In this portrait of an anteater, which will only come into focus in the final word of the poem, Cummings engineers the typography of the poem such that the thresholds between words, couplings of letters, are forced into focus, often forming graphical symmetries like 's of s'. To say that these ephemeral formations are nonsensical is only a half-truth. Cummings knows from the transcription of silent reading in his 'mr. smith' poem that the process of reading is not the logical conversion of correctly spelled words into meaning, but an uneven and mobile visual cognition that compresses, slices up, and roves over the graphical body of the text. As such, in that hovering pair of letters—'g p'—there is still an iota of the apprehension of 'adventuring' and 'particles'. In his aesthetic scribbling at Harvard, Cummings conceives of an 'eye-mind' that perceives motion, as if vision were simultaneous with intellection.[108] Testing this hypothesis under the most extreme conditions, Cummings is thus trying to distil the smallest particle of the graphical experience of poetry, to isolate what is felt and thought in the collision of two graphemes from adjacent words.

Mobility and microscopic size converge in the term at the heart of this poem: 'motilities', a word that denotes the capacity for movement of a thing, particularly of a part of an organic entity such as an organelle or cell. Morphemes, progressive suffixes, are typographically isolated as if motors of linguistic motion could be liberated from their lexical stems:

> alingwaysing)
> go to the ant thou go
> (inging)

Cummings's snapshot of a bird in flight, 'a-motion-upo-nmotio-n', pinpoints the phonemic blur between words through dashes and crystallizes movement in this centre of the page:

>)Swi
>
> mming
>
> (w-a)s
> bIr
>
> d,[109]

[108] Milton A. Cohen, *Poet and Painter*, 152.
[109] E. E. Cummings, *No Thanks*, n.p. [poems 20 and 46].

This quest to isolate these tiny particles of motion is generated by Cummings's theory of perception, which he expresses as a vibrant atomicity: 'The idea of Life is a multiplication of successive Incidents [. . .] an instantaneous [and simultaneous] quilt-of-sensation composed of various moments [. . .]'.[110] Restless typographical experimentation does not pervert the natural motion of reading and confect warped experiences, but rather faithfully records the volatility native to human perception, to fashion a language worthy of it. In this estimation, it is the graphical stasis of normative typography that is perverse in its attempt to petrify what ought to be mobile. This is why Cummings bases his sketch of visual apprehension on a child's perspective: because it is to this prelinguistic inclusivity, before vision solidifies into nouns and correct spelling, that Cummings appeals. Beyond this phenomenological fidelity, though, Cummings's quest for minuscule typographical nuance is driven by an ethical imperative. The mystical journey of poem 51 concludes with this vision:

> at the Ending of this road,
> a candle in a shrine
> its puniest flame persists
> shaken by the sea

So, too, the final poem of *No Thanks* sees its guiding star—the 'morsel miraculous and meaningless' and 'isful beckoningly fabulous crumb'—in terms of a beatific smallness on the cusp of non-existence. Individuality, that virtue Cummings praises time and again, is etymologically that which cannot be divided—the atomic. Casting off that 'guaranteed birthproof safetysuit of nondestructible selflessness', doggedly sloughing off all forms of collectivism, ultimately leads to a valorization of tininess.[111] This faith in singular, reckless selves sustains Cummings in his faith in the cellular distinctions of his mise-en-page. Cummings's typography sifts the page for these quarks of distinct irreducible experience, their preciousness predicated on their puniness.

---

[110] Milton A. Cohen, *Poet and Painter*, 155.
[111] E. E. Cummings, *No Thanks*, n.p. [poems 51 and 71]; E. E. Cummings, 'Introduction', in *Collected Poems* (New York: Harcourt, Brace and Company, 1938) n.p.

3

Olson Among the Letterers

1. The New Ear, Breath Stops, and the Beats

By ear, he sd.

With this terse response Charles Olson began his verse epic *The Maximus Poems*. This is the opening that is retained in the first collected edition, comprising Letters 1–10, which Jonathan Williams published in Stuttgart in 1953, a book whose cover is emblazoned with Olson's surname fashioned in faux-Chinese calligraphy, as if bequeathing a stamp of officialdom.[1] Despite the marks of authority that collection bears, its bibliographical pedigree enhanced by its typeface, layout, and page size setting a model for editions to come, Olson appears to have revised this opening in the very same month it was composed, May 1950, relegating it to a much less prominent place halfway through the verse-letter.[2] The line sounds like a response not only because that is the most expedient way to resolve its narratological incompletion, but because it is one of the abiding answers Olson proffers in his 1950 essay 'Projective Verse', where he tasks himself with formulating how '[v]erse now, 1950 […] is to go ahead'.[3]

Cognizant as we now are of the poem that this line would germinate, one of the most visually audacious texts of the last century, Olson's displacement of it seems prescient, as though he knew his poetry would outgrow the claims of this one organ. 'By ear, he sd' seems like a false start for a poet who discerns a canon of typographical experiment in the verse of the preceding half-century, and who exhorts his peers to pick the 'fruits' of this heritage in order that their own work thrive.[4] Yet the line is irresistibly timely, and an appraisal of it, its hasty relocation and belated re-emergence, involves

---

[1] Charles Olson, *The Maximus Poems 1–10* (Stuttgart: Jonathan Williams, 1953), 1.
[2] George M. Butterick, *A Guide to the Maximus Poems of Charles Olson* (Berkeley: University of California Press, 1978), 5.
[3] Charles Olson, *Collected Prose*, ed. Donald Allen and Benjamin Friedlander (Berkley, CA: University of California Press, 1997), 239.
[4] Charles Olson, *Collected Prose*, 245.

The Graphics of Verse. Daniel Matore, Oxford University Press. © Daniel Matore (2023).
DOI: 10.1093/oso/9780192857217.003.0004

rudimentary judgments about how Olson's lines, and those of his contemporaries, ought to be read—and how they might be read aloud. For Allen Ginsberg, writing in 1966, the whole history of verse could be storied as the desuetude, death, and resuscitation of the ear:

> This new ear is not dead because it's not only for eye-page, it's connected with a voice improvising, with hesitancies aloud, a living musician's ear. The old library poets had lost their voices; natural voice was rediscovered; and now natural song for physical voice. Oddly this fits Pound's paradigm tracing the degeneration of poetry from the Greek dance-foot chorus thru minstrel song thru 1900 abstract voiceless page.

Modern poets since Pound owe their vitality to abandoning the paper edifice of the library and emulating musicians, and Ginsberg allies postwar poets with the 'new minstrels' of Bob Dylan, Donovan, and the Rolling Stones. In a fable of the senses, Ginsberg rejects the eye like foreign tissue, transplanting it onto a half-organic object, the 'eye-page', disconnected from the poet's body.[5] Olson had set the two organs against one another sixteen years earlier to plot a similar drama. Modernism's advent is aural, springing from '[t]he revolution of the ear, 1910'. And even though he has just offered a definition of the line-break as 'that time [...] it takes the eye – that hair of time suspended – to pick up the next line', that faculty is supplanted in the conclusion to the first part of the essay, only a paragraph later:

> Already [contemporary poets] are composing as though verse was to have the reading its writing involved, as though not the eye but the ear was to be its measurer, as though the intervals of its composition could be so carefully put down as to be precisely the intervals of its registration. For the ear, which once had the burden of memory to quicken it (rime & regular cadence were its aids and have merely lived on in print after the oral necessities were ended) can now again, that the poet has his means, be the threshold of projective verse.[6]

What underwrites this polemic is a vitalism where the natural physiology of the poet is menaced by the alien life of print. Olson's essay is coloured by a distaste for the foreign parturition of the page: 'that verse which print

[5] Allen Ginsberg, *Deliberate Prose: Selected Essays 1952–1995*, ed. Bill Morgan (London: Penguin, 2000), 259.
[6] Charles Olson, *Collected Prose*, 246.

bred'. His attack on Miltonic blank verse summons up Samuel Johnson's dismissal that Milton only wrote poetry for the eye, but Olson does not critique Milton for having abandoned the 'jingling sound of like endings'.[7] Likewise, he does not inveigh against any avowed modern adherent of poetry for the eye, like Apollinaire or Marinetti, nor any element of experimental typography. Rather, it is the sound effects of 'rime & regular cadence', which, cut off from their mnemonic function in the body, 'have lived on in print', maintaining a parasitic second life on the page.[8] The stanza and the verse line, those constituents of typographical normativity in poetry, are what sustain the senescent music of verse. The 'eye-page' Olson and Ginsberg oppose is not the one Pound diagnosed in 1925 with its 'fancy type, broken lines, hosiery-ad fonts, valentine wreaths or other post-Mallarmé devices'; it is the survival of pre-modernist typography in postwar verse.[9]

Though Olson and Ginsberg, along with contemporaries such as Denise Levertov and Robert Creeley, embrace the pioneering typography of Cummings, Pound, and Williams and begin to dissertate on its capacities far more explicitly than their immediate forebears, this visual language seems *prima facie* inimical to a poetics that so prizes the ear and fashions print as its enemy. Furthermore, the reception of 'Projective Verse' by Ginsberg and the Beat poets often produces a drastically simple explanation for Olson's lineation and for their own. Throughout much of Ginsberg's critical work, the act of writing is secondary, ancillary, even journalistic: 'a matter of transcription in visual shorthand' or 'some very crude and rapid method of notation'. This devaluation of writing is the natural corollary of the precedence aurality assumes in Beat poetics. Ginsberg's vatic figuring of poetic composition, his kinship with Smart, Blake, and Whitman, leads him to a perfect marriage of phonocentrism and logocentrism, where the mind breathes and thought becomes commensurate with exhalation. Dictated by the 'thought-voice', each line becomes 'one single mental breath'. Though he initially applies this principle to his own poetry, opining that '[i]deally each line of *Howl* is a single breath unit', taxonomizing the lineation of the preceding decades in 1977, Ginsberg uses it to group Olson, Creeley, and Williams, exempting himself: '4. Breath stop (Creeley, Olson, Williams) (new breath, new line) (pause)'.[10] If the eye-page spooled out lines generated

---

[7] John Milton, *Paradise Lost* (London: Penguin, 2000), 1.

[8] Charles Olson, *Collected Prose*, 239.

[9] Ezra Pound, 'Mr. Dunning's Poetry', *Poetry*, 6 (1925), 339–45 (p. 341).

[10] Allen Ginsberg, *Deliberate Prose*, 254, 256, 257, 260.

by the inherited quanta of print, this tenet, expressed like an algorithmic gobbet, forces lines into a complete identification with 'the elastic of breath'.

Ginsberg's list of ten principles of 'open' lineation admits of much greater variety in modernist typography as a whole, though it is telling that he does not wish his own verse to be associated with a principle he had earlier espoused. The reason is surely that it deadens the dialectic between the eye and the ear in poetry. There is no artfulness to lineation if you simply begin a new line each time you run out of lung capacity. Nowhere in Olson's critical writings does he license this account of his own typography, but the pneumatic enthusiasm of 'Projective Verse' is complicit in it. The 'space precisions' of the typewriter are supposed to 'indicate exactly the breath, the pauses, the suspensions even of syllables' the poet originally enounced. Breath as a prosodic category is adopted so wholeheartedly by Olson because its gaseous palpability gives substance to the energy, otherwise immaterial and abstract, the poem is supposed to be fuelled by: 'A poem is energy transferred from where the poet got it (he will have some several causations), by way of the poem itself to, all the way over to, the reader.' The 'acquisitions of [the poet's] ear' are vital, but ears do not labour with the same physicality as lungs: 'If I hammer, if I recall in, and keep calling in, the breath'. Inhalation here is in time with the hammer's stroke, and breath has the solidity of iron.[11] Ginsberg, who boasts about his lung capacity, even recounts his poetic formation as strenuous, physical conditioning, until his voice achieves a mineral hardness:

> Subsequent experience in Benares with mantra chanting (short magic formulae sung or repeated aloud as invocation to inner divinity) and in Kyoto with Zen belly-breathing delivered my accustomed voice (and center of self) from upper chest and throat to solar plexus and lower abdomen. The timbre, range and feeling-quality of the physical voice was thus physiologically deepened, till it actually approximated what I'd youthfully imagined to be the voice of rock.[12]

What breath prosody, what a pneumatic poetics realizes, then, is the possibility of a truly somatic poetry, where to talk of the '*kinetics* of the thing' is not metaphorical bluster but an authentic relation of the poem's genesis.

An originary performance, its inhalations and exhalations, its stutters and pauses, shaped by the poet's vocal apparatus, is to be preserved; the breath

[11] Charles Olson, *Collected Prose*, 245, 240, 241.
[12] Allen Ginsberg, *Deliberate Prose*, 257.

contained lest it disperse. The This poetics is tubed together like a bivalvular respiratory system:

> the HEAD, by way of the EAR, to the SYLLABLE
> the HEART, by way of the BREATH, to the LINE

In the purest form of this figuration, the printed page can only be an unwelcome blockage in the flow of ventilation:

> What we have suffered from, is manuscript, press, the removal of verse producer and its reproducer, the voice, a removal by one, by two removes from its place of origin *and* its destination. For the breath has a double meaning which latin had not yet lost.[13]

The 'double meaning' Latin conserves is in *spiritus*, meaning both breath and soul, and Olson is resuscitating a pneumatic poetics that is two millennia old, where Apollo *inspires* the poem by breathing it directly into the *vates*.[14] This was and is a myth, a bardic fantasy of airborne verse unsullied by paper or press. Olson is drawn to origin myths and will exhibit such atavism in his linguistics and historiography. But such a myth jars with the averred anti-subjectivism of 'Projective Verse'. The weakness of Heidegger's ontology, which Adorno seizes upon in *Negative Dialectics*, is its obfuscatory faith in mystical roots and origins, a faith that in disallowing mediation and reflection is authoritarian: 'The category of the root, the origin, is a category of dominion. It confirms that a man ranks first because he was there first; it confirms the autochthon against the newcomer, the settler against the migrant. The origin—seductive because it will not be appeased by the derivative, by ideology—is itself an ideological principle.'[15] The origin myth of breath poetics is inherently domineering. Olson's version of vatic inspiration elevates the poet to the godhead since it is they, not Apollo, who breathe into the reader. And while a reader styled as a 'reproducer' might elsewhere suggest creative fecundity, paired with producer, it evokes a passive replicator, like an audio output device.

This vocal loop, though, is interrupted by manuscript and press. This *cor ad cor loquitur* is mediated by the matter of typography. Olson knew

---

[13] Charles Olson, *Collected Prose*, 242, 245.

[14] Charles T. Lewis and Charles Short, *A Latin Dictionary* (Oxford: Clarendon Press, 1879), 1743, 1960.

[15] Theodor W. Adorno, *Negative Dialectics*, trans. E. B. Ashton (London: Routledge and Kegan Paul, 1973), 155.

that the voice was not the sole producer in poetic labour and that verse was not an auratic utterance that emerged like Minerva from the head of Jove. As Mark Byers has recently observed, Olson, along with avant-garde composers such as Morton Feldman, banish the myth of a self-certain act of creation by admitting the voice's dependence on paper: 'Both Olson and Feldman wanted to abandon conventional kinds of inscription in order to realize the new and egoless soundworld of postwar modernism [. . .]'.[16] This is not speculative theory but Olson's compositional practice. Olson completes his early lyric 'Conqueror' on 9 January 1948, according to his dating of the typescript. This is the version of the poem that is first published, untitled, after the author's death and without his editorial oversight in *The Antioch Review* in 1970.[17] Atypically, since he is often attached to the early form of his poetry's mise-en-page, Olson later revises the typography of the lyric. The ambiguity as to which text has pre-eminence, since the former has the stamp of posthumous publication but the latter is closer to a 'final intention', prompts George Butterick to present it in two versions in his authoritative 1987 edition.[18] It originally begins:

Gulls on the grass / and the odor of live worms / and worms dead on the walk
Nature deranged
(mine as well)
feeding irregularly.

The brackets are a later addition in pen, and Olson adds autograph revisions to the typography, carefully notating '2sp.' to widen the line spacing at the end of the poem. Months later, Olson returns to the poem to reshape the layout:

Gulls on the grass   and the odor of live worms   and worms dead on the walk
Nature deranged   mine as well   feeding irregularly

The eponymous conqueror is far from sure-footed, but proceeds with hesitant self-awareness. The poem already looks back on itself, as if presaging

[16] Mark Byers, 'Egocentric Predicaments: Charles Olson and the New York School of Music', *Journal of Modern Literature*, 4 (2014), 54–69 (p. 63).
[17] Charles Olson, 'Untitled Poem [Conqueror]', *The Antioch Review*, 3/4 (1970), 356–57 (p. 356).
[18] Charles Olson, *The Collected Poems of Charles Olson: Excluding the Maximus Poems*, ed. George F. Butterick (Berkeley: University of California Press, 1987), 72–73. See also George F. Butterick and Albert Glover, *A Bibliography of the Works by Charles Olson* (New York: Phoenix Book Shop, 1967).

its own revision: 'His motion will be less clear, at least double in direction, himself ahead / and backward as he goes.'[19] This revision belies the notion of an infallible, one-off vocalization. Virgules, which Olson equates with 'a pause so light it hardly separates the words', are replaced with the prolonged pauses of elongated spaces. Where the human subject was at first segmented by parentheses and had a line to itself, the revised typography allots to man, gull, and nature homologous units of space. Ginsberg, for all his glamorizing of the 'first thought, best thought' of immediate vocalizing, once spoke of a much more uncertain mode of composition: 'And how can we watch ourselves think and notate that? I'm not sure what happens; generally I pause at the beginning of a new line, having short circuited my visual processes by the constant stop to notate [...] In the course of this notation I finally get out beyond what I'd anticipated and discover what it is that's underlying my whole mind and soul at the moment—and find the course of that discovery now transcribed in the composition just finished.'[20]

Notating is not an activity that passively records the voice—the poem already fully formed in sound—but a stop-and-start process of self-reflection; a looking back on oneself that hopes for self-revelation. *The Maximus Poems* recurrently dramatize out-of-body experiences, visions where Olson beholds a naked and exposed doppelganger, and the poem's identity is split by the mirroring of the persona 'Maximus' and the poet Olson.[21] Revising the typography of 'Conqueror' months later, Olson sees a voice that is no longer quite his own and no longer quite sure of itself— a voice that has become an object to be realigned and reshaped. 'What is "objective": the fact that I sit here, forced to this typewriter and this paper', Robert Creeley writes to Olson in 1950, as if to face the printed page is a necessary trial. 'Conqueror' announces its own maxim: 'If a man is a matter of what consequence in consequence he is an object.' It is through the

[19] Charles Olson, 'Conqueror', MS 14:449. Charles Olson Research Collection, Thomas J. Dodd Research Center, University of Connecticut Libraries.

[20] Allen Ginsberg, *Deliberate Prose*, 256.

[21] Charles Olson, *The Maximus Poems* (London: Cape Goliard Press, 1960), n.p. As the first edition to which I refer and quote is unpaginated, I have also included citations in square brackets throughout the chapter from a more recent edition for ease of reference: [cf Charles Olson, *The Maximus Poems*, ed. George F. Butterick (Berkeley: University of California Press, 1983), 111].

doubtful self-examination of notating and lineating the voice in the 'eye-page' that this principle comes to life.[22]

'Eyes have a major place in this work as anyone familiar with it will know [...]', Creeley writes of *The Maximus Poems* in 1962.[23] Despite the pleas for the new ear to be free from 'eye-logic' that Creeley exchanges with Olson in 1950, as poet rather than critic Olson surrenders aural autonomy from the beginning:

By ear, he sd.
But that which matters, that which insists, that which will last,
that! o my people, where shall you find it, how, where, where shall you listen
when all is become billboards, when, all, even silence, is spray-gunned?

when even our bird, my roofs,
cannot be heard

when even you, when sound itself is neoned in?

The soundscape of *The Maximus Poems* is coterminous with a graphical landscape. Typography matters to Olson even in his earliest writings because sound and sight interpenetrate; poetic rhythm is exposed to the blare of neon billboards. The first letter recurrently evokes a Grecian idyll of lyric song only to violate it. Birdsong is interrupted by the 'twitter' of 'street-cars, and under 'pejorocracy' music becomes 'mu-sick'.[24] Politics, advertising, and industry have their own rhythms, in Olson's dilated sense of what prosody encompasses, and these infringe upon poetic song. Song, then, as lyric self-sufficiency, obsolesces. To sing is to block one's ears. The lone singer in 'Projective Verse' is a figure both self-absorbed and itinerant, mouthing the 'artificial forms' of traditional balladry, unable to gain purchase on his environment, however he 'sprawls'.[25] Creeley opines that '[w]e are so far from song at this point, that it is usually impossible to make use of a pattern such as the Provencal poets / used, etc, the lyricists. It took /

[22] Robert Creeley, 'Letter to Charles Olson, 18 May 1950', in Charles Olson and Robert Creeley, *Charles Olson and Robert Creeley: The Complete Correspondence*, ed. George F. Butterick, 10 vols (Santa Barbara, CA: Black Sparrow Press, 1980), I, 29–34 (p. 31).
[23] Robert Creeley, *The Collected Essays of Robert Creeley* (Berkeley: University of California Press, 1989), 111.
[24] Charles Olson, *The Maximus Poems*, n.p. [cf Charles Olson, *The Maximus Poems* (Berkeley, CA, 1983), 6–7].
[25] Charles Olson, *Collected Prose*, 247.

a background, constant, of "song" to make such possible.'[26] The backdrop of 1950s America is too graphical for song to subsist. When songs appear in *Maximus*, they often seem to lament their own anachronism. 'SONG 1' from the *The Songs of Maximus* begins:

> colored pictures
> of all things to eat: dirty
> postcards
> And words, words, words
> all over everything

'SONG 2' almost deletes itself by rhyming immediately with 'all/ wrong'. Song is not wholly dispensed with by Olson, but its tones are plangent with lack and loss, disenfranchised by the *copia* of visual culture:

> SONG 6
>
> you sing, you
>
> who also
>
> wants

Even as he seems to defend an untrammelled aurality, ears mutate into texts. In a typed note to his fellow poet, Olson writes:

> HAVING SAID TO ED DORN THAT THE WORD AS THING DOES
> SORT ITSELF
> that is, what basket does one carry it in, if it isn't by ear
>
> P.S. I'd still think the word is scoring-paper, that is, how the words lie can register quantity (i-s – in fact that 'basket' is what's left of meaning (that one does run-out of the interest in what one did start to say, like? and thereby achieve whatever 'form'

By figuring them as receptacles for durational quanta, Olson knits together ears as baskets, as latticed wicker bundles. Following the metaphoric thread, it is as if this retiform fabric unfurls into the *quadrillage* of 'scoring-paper', the criss-cross lining of the page, so that, in his poetic imaginary, Olson sees the organ of hearing as a crumpled page, a 'basket' waiting to be folded out into a text. Accordingly, when Olson exhorts his 'Gloucester-man' to resist

---

[26] Robert Creeley, 'Letter to Charles Olson, 25 June 1950', in Charles Olson and Robert Creeley, *Charles Olson and Robert Creeley: The Complete Correspondence*, II: 13–16 (p. 14).

the world of the ad-men and the hegemony of the billboard, he does not
invite him to sing but

> braid
> with others like you, such
> extricable surface
> as faun and oral,
> satyr lesbos vase
>
> o kill kill kill kill kill
> those
> who advertise you
> out)[27]

The rhapsode, the archetypal bard, is not a singer here but a weaver. Tracing the etymology of the Greek ῥαψῳδία, Olson writes to Creeley, with
surprised delight, that 'rhapsode: was (how abt that: (the sound, I mean):
meant, to sew together!'[28] Text comes from the Latin verb *texo*, meaning
to weave, plait, or carefully fashion, and Olson flattens the voice until it is
seamlessly textual.[29] Oral has its adjectival quality stripped from it, to be
juxtaposed with the concrete noun 'faun', just as 'lesbos' has its majuscule
cropped so that it can be stitched together with 'satyr' and 'vase'. Rendering orality as a patch in a neo-Classical *textus*, Olson imagines the voice
as materially dependent on the flat 'extricable surface' of print. It is audible that the pejorative tone that taints 'page' in 'Projective Verse' does not
persist in *The Maximus Poems* or Olson's later criticism. Billboards, post-
cards, and neon signage may be decried, but these compromised graphics
are not resisted by retreating to the supposed immateriality of the voice.
Material texts, free from inherited typographical etiquette, modelled after
the handiwork of the Gloucester men, are to be fashioned. Olson could never
have called his poems cantos as Pound did, for Olson styles his poems as
material documents in a culture of material exchange. Almost every original draft by Olson is signed and dated, and the presiding, but not universal,
analogue is the letter. As Ralph Maud notes: 'Charles Olson believed in letter

---

[27] Charles Olson, 'HAVING SAID TO ED DORN', MS 22:1012. Charles Olson Research
Collection, Thomas J. Dodd Research Center, University of Connecticut Libraries; Charles
Olson, *The Maximus Poems*, n.p. [cf Charles Olson, *The Maximus Poems* (Berkeley, CA, 1983),
17, 20, 8].

[28] George M. Butterick, *A Guide to the Maximus Poems*, 102; cf the definition of the cognate
ῥαψῳδός or rhapsode as 'properly *one who stitches or strings songs together*' from the verb ῥάπτω,
meaning '*to sew or stitch together*' in *A Lexicon Abridged from Liddell and Scott's Greek-English
Lexicon* (Oxford: Clarendon Press, 1891), 622–23.

[29] Charles T. Lewis and Charles Short, *A Latin Dictionary*, 1865.

writing. It was honest communication. He believed in it as a true political act that might create a polis, if anything could [...] The *Maximus* poems [sic] were, he always insisted, literally letters.'[30] The letters of Cummings, Pound, and Olson show them at their most typographically uninhibited. But Olson is the only one of the three to see letter and poem as interchangeable, often suggesting correspondents use spare letters as poems in periodicals and publications. For such reasons Robert von Hallberg has argued that Olson's mission statement as a writer is anti-poetic, but a different formulation might be anti-lyric, where lyric stands for the artifice of song.[31] For Olson does not give up on poetry, but disabuses poetry of a cantabile repertoire of traditional forms. According to Olson, Pound's *Pisan Cantos* lapse into irrelevance when they indulge the faux-literariness of paeans and choric hymns. They 'score', Olson says, playing on the sense of both 'to succeed' and 'to notate', where they realize their music depends on writing.[32] As letters, Olson's poems are part of the graphic fabric of society, of contemporary advertising and documentary history, able to hold their own in wars of print. His poems lose their innocence by becoming aware of their own typography.

2. 'A full graphics-knowing man': Black Mountain College and Ben Shahn's Print Shop

Typography, for Olson as poet and as pedagogue, was instrumental in national re-education. So insidious were 'radio, the movies, the magazines, and national advertising, the 4 Plagues of our time' that even Pound had succumbed to their siren song:

> (o Statue,
> o Republic, o
> Tell-A-Vision, the best
> is soap. The true troubadours
> are CBS. Melopoeia
>
>   is for Cokes by Cokes out of
>
>   Pause

---

[30] Charles Olson, *Selected Letters*, ed. Ralph Maud (Berkeley: University of California Press, 2000), xv.
[31] Robert Von Hallberg, *Charles Olson: The Scholar's Art* (Cambridge, MA: Harvard University Press, 1978), 2-3.
[32] Charles Olson, 'Letter to Robert Creeley, 9 June 1950', in *Selected Letters*, 109–12 (p. 110).

OLSON AMONG THE LETTERERS   153

What this section will argue is that Olson figures the study of typography as a means of resisting a print culture corrupted by commerce and advertising, and that Black Mountain College, under the tutelage of the designer Ben Shahn, could form the centre of this educational programme. Pound had declared to Olson face-to-face, suggests George Butterick, that 'radio commercials are the best verse being now writ'.[33] Not just infecting the airwaves, ad culture is polymorphous, shifting between sight and sound. Television has engendered a hybrid faculty where vision is told. Olson registers this corruption with a disarming philological shift, holding up John Smith's 1630 'ADVERTISEMENTS' as a countersign. Smith's advertisements are accounts of first-hand experience with the New World; he is advertising in the sense of forewarning the 'unexperienced Planters / of *New-England*, or anywhere' about the lay of the land.[34] Olson also sets Smith contra Pound in his essay 'Captain John Smith', in which Olson goes so far as to cast the poet as a commercial huckster, whose 'own act is now ad-writing'. Smith is the true advertiser, with a newness in his prose quite apart from the copywriter's skill in rejuvenating old commodities with fresh sloganeering: 'Why I sing John Smith is this, that the *geographic*, the sudden *land* of the place is in there, not described, not local, not represented—like all advertisements, all the shit now pours out, the American Road, the filthiness, of graphic words, Mo-dess ...'[35]

Smith is *sung* here, of course, and bard and pioneer seem to be ranged against the obscenity of graphical language. This wilderness of roadside signage, where the Edenic interplay of place and prose that occurs in Smith's newfound vistas has become lettering stamped on desolate highways, is echoed by another purveyor of graphical language, one that Olson much admired:

In the casual roadside signs I spoke of earlier, which are the work of amateurs (they might be called 'the unlettered letters'), one can see the violation of every rule, every principle, every law of form or taste that may have required centuries of formulation. This material is exiled from the domain of true lettering; it is anathema to letterers. [...] It is cacophonous and utterly unacceptable.[36]

---

[33] George M. Butterick, *A Guide to the Maximus Poems*, 107; Charles Olson, *The Maximus Poems*, n.p. [cf Charles Olson, *The Maximus Poems* (Berkeley, CA, 1998), 75].
[34] George M. Butterick, *A Guide to the Maximus Poems*, 102.
[35] Charles Olson, *Collected Prose*, 319.
[36] Ben Shahn, *Ben Shahn*, ed. John D. Morse (London: Secker and Warburg, 1972), 162.

These are the words of Ben Shahn, painter, typographer, and lithographer, who was Olson's friend and colleague at Black Mountain College. Shahn, in fact, has a cameo in Book V of Williams's *Paterson*, where he appears in a not dissimilar setting as an itinerant artist on 'the American Road', plotting it with the steady hand of a draughtsman.[37] Shahn is attuned to a typographical imaginary where perjorocracy most readily takes form in 'the filthiness, of graphic words' menacing highways and byways. His figuration, like Olson's, is territorial, but he preserves a graphical sanctuary, 'the domain of true lettering', a polis from which true letterers can exile philistine amateurs.

At the heart of Black Mountain College, the experimental faculty at which Olson would become rector, he and Shahn plotted just such a 'domain of true lettering'. Writing to W. H. Ferry, the Director of Public Relations for the CIO-Political Action Committee in August 1951, Olson spells out the college's educational manifesto. Black Mountain College, he claims, is 'not at all local' but rather 'answering a need of the whole society':

What happens *between* things—what happens between *men*—what happens between guest faculty, students, regular faculty—and what happens *among* each as the result of each: for i do not think one can overstate—at this point of time, America, 1951—the importance of workers in different fields of the arts and of knowledge working so closely together some of the time of the year that they find out, from each other, the ideas, forms, energies, and the whole series of kinetics and emotions now opening up, out of the quantitative world.

And just because of the dispersions of the quantitative world, small place, whether, for a man and family it is Roosevelt, New Jersey, or for a group such as a college it is Black Mountain, a small place now offers this sort of chance, this sort of experimental locus.[38]

Olson's vision synthesizes physics, metaphysics, and politics. Faculty and students are a class of workers, a congregation of artisans undistinguished by rank but governed by chains of forces, 'the whole series of kinetics', as though they were subatomic particles. In this powerful defence of interdisciplinarity, the spaces between the arts, those 'between's and 'among's that Olson leans on, are imaged as transferrals of energy. It is from Alfred North Whitehead, a philosopher whose lexicon confers metaphysical abstraction

[37] William Carlos Williams, *Paterson: Book Five* (New York: New Directions, 1958), n.p.
[38] Charles Olson, 'Letter to W. H. Ferry, 7 August 1951', in *Selected Letters*, 138–45 (p. 141).

OLSON AMONG THE LETTERERS   155

on human terms like 'society' or 'community', a lexicon further stocked by particle physics, that Olson inherits this language.

Wedded to this vision, though, to ward off 'abstract definitions', are Democrat party politics. Roosevelt, New Jersey, was a model town, created during the Great Depression and later named after the president whose New Deal gave birth to it. Another New Deal body, the Farm Settlement Committee, commissioned Shahn to commemorate the town's founding in a mural. The town, then, offers to Olson the exemplar of a planned artistic and political community, and just as Shahn's mural lay at the heart of Roosevelt, his graphics, and the graphic arts, are to form the core of Black Mountain College:

> (1): Due to Ben's interest, and his perception that GRAPHICS is a shop core for work in the arts, there is a possibility that one of the fine printers will come here for, perhaps, two weeks and lecture, look over the equipment of the print shop, and give the lads some sense of what projects in printing the world, over there, needs. Already Ben and I have moved them away from too dandy a conception of projects to a little tough business like pamphleteering, how to design, write, print, and distribute such. The advantage of such a shop core would be immense, just because at this precise point—more, even, than any exhibit—the actualities of these kids' social and political world will be brought home to them—they will be reminded of the towns and cities and families from which they come—and which, at the peril of themselves, and the place, they forget, are altogether too apt to forget![39]

Graphics bears a great deal of structural weight in Olson's conceptual edifice. As 'shop core' it is a central atrium in a network of ateliers, as though Black Mountain College were a confederation of guilds, with poets, typographers, and painters all in adjoining workshops. Welded to this neo-medievalism, though, is a much more contemporary powerhouse, apt for the atomicity of Olson's imagination. 'Core' is first recorded by the OED two years earlier as meaning the active part of a nuclear reactor, in addition to its older meaning as the centre of an atom. This 'print shop' is to assume a compacted density only imaginable in a nuclear age. It is a 'precise point', which, despite its modest size, is to ingest 'the actualities of these kids' social and political world'. J. H. Prynne speaks of *The Maximus Poems* as a perverse form

---

[39] Charles Olson, 'Letter to W. H. Ferry, 7 August 1951', in *Selected Letters*, 142.

of homecoming, and what occurs in this hub is an inverted form of *nostos*.[40] Becoming hyperaware of every point and serif in Shahn's print shop, the students will awaken to the graphical constitution of American society. Lithuanian-born and Jewish, Shahn was reared on Hebrew lettering, and he speaks of his immigration to America as a 'cataclysmic change' and a typographical shock: 'Then there was the new world of letters and print; it seemed to me there were thousands of letters in the American alphabet, all shapes and styles and sizes.'[41] Through their formation in printing, the Black Mountain students are to lose their visual innocence, and to see what Shahn only saw as an immigrant: that American typography is not neutral but conditioned, and legible as sociopolitical script.

So much of Olson's programme as poet, critic, and educator is premised on this species of typographical awakening, of bringing lettering to sight that was once thought transparent. The early letters of *The Maximus Poems* articulate at once the poet's responsibility to reform print culture through typography and the marginality of avant-garde verse. These poems, I will claim, communicate a sense of material dispossession. 'Projective Verse' nurtures the conspiracy that scores of poets have written according to a typographical rule without ever realizing it; by ignoring print they came to be ruled by it. Olson rounds off his manifesto for the print shop with the addendum: 'There is also the hope that the faculty will be able to find the funds to restore an instructor in printing—or better, from my point of view anyhow, a full graphics-knowing man.'[42] This figure, a Maximus of projected faculties, sounds like a latter-day Renaissance Man, and Shahn, a mixed-media artist *avant la lettre*, sees graphics as fundamental to a holistic aesthetic: 'I believe that sensitivity is not departmentalized, and that art itself is not to be confined within hard boundaries.'[43] This conviction that Olson and Shahn share in the timeliness and reach of graphics resides in the word itself. Their usage of the term is in advance of common parlance. Prior to its first recorded use in 1960, 'graphics' denoted '[t]he technical use of diagrams and figures as an aid to mathematical calculation or to engineering or architectural design', though this definition has some felicity given Olson's sense that Black Mountain graphics are to miniaturize 'the quantitative world'. Denoting '[d]esign and decoration that involves typographic

---

[40] J. H. Prynne, 'Lecture on *Maximus IV, V, VI', Iron* (October 1971) <www.charlesolson.org/Files/Prynnelecture1.htm> [accessed 8 January 2017] (para. 12 of 12).

[41] Ben Shahn, *Ben Shahn*, 143, 144.

[42] Charles Olson, 'Letter to W. H. Ferry, 7 August 1951', in *Selected Letters*, 141.

[43] Ben Shahn, *Ben Shahn*, 161.

elements; the production of pictures, diagrams, etc., in association with text', its 1960 appearance in the journal *Design* already bleeds into other media: 'The type of credits designed by Saul Bass are an isolated example of good graphics for movies.' Six years later it will be affixed to the new visual horizon of the computer as 'computer-graphics'.[44] The adoption of the term, then, by Olson and Shahn several years before it would become current, pre-empts a new, more protean sense of the visual text. To be a student of 'graphics' is to be a student of typography, but also of the whole world of letters.

'Letter 5' is dispatched by an Olson who has taken on this mantle of graphical stewardship, keeping watch over Gloucester's print culture and that of the nation:

(as, in summer, a newspaper, now, in spring, a magazine)

though how Gloucester will know what damage . . . only Brown's window . . . This quarterly will not be read

The habit of newsprint
(plus possibly the National Geographic)
are the limits of
literacy[45]

The Maximus Poems are often a stylized, even mythic, form of letter writing, didactic missives like the dissertations of Maximus of Tyre, the second-century philosopher who gives his name to the poems' persona.[46] Sending imaginary letters to an imagined Gloucester, Olson often caustically notes how small his readership in the town in fact is. The world of letters conjured up seems that of a lost epistolary, like the correspondence of St. Paul or Erasmus. 'Letter 5', though, despite the pessimism that '[t]his quarterly will not be read', is woven into the real, contemporary print culture of Gloucester. Olson wrote the poem, a sustained philippic, a month after the publication in March 1953 of the second issue of *Four Winds*, a literary magazine edited by his fellow Gloucester poet Vincent Ferrini, a publication in which early

[44] *OED Online* <http://www.oed.com/view/Entry/80829?redirectedFrom=graphics#eid> [accessed 8 January 2017].
[45] Charles Olson, *The Maximus Poems*, n.p. [cf Charles Olson, *The Maximus Poems* (Berkeley, CA, 1983), 21] [I have reduced the point size of this quote for the sake of accurate lineation].
[46] George M. Butterick, *A Guide to the Maximus Poems*, 6.

versions of *The Maximus Poems* had appeared.[47] Ferrini earned his liveli-
hood as a frame-maker, as the letter goes on to relate, and Olson figures
Four Winds at the centre of a graphical malaise by overlaying multiple visual
frames. The magazine's 'damage' is magnified by being exhibited in the
window display of Brown's department store, and the eyes of Gloucester's
readership are already blinkered by the text blocks of newspapers and commercial layout of *National Geographic*, intellectual limits coalescing with
the uniform margins of mass typography. Sentinels of the town's graphic
decline, 'the eyes which watch you', Olson, along with the Gloucester painter
Helen Stein, are immune to the glossy mesmerism of 'the plate glass of
Brown's (that display)'. Their reading eyes have different vectors: 'Helen
Stein's eyes, and those others, Gloucester, who look, who still can look, /
look right straight down into yr pages.'[48] Ferrini's pages are now Gloucester's
pages, the town readable as print.

Vigilant though he may be, Olson is not a 'full graphics-knowing man'.
To claim an ocular superiority whereby he can discern cultural stagnation
through the lens of typography is not to be able to remedy the situation.
Olson boasts to Ferrini in 'Letter 5' that he was once a 'letter-carrier', implying that he knows better than his rival the town's networks of paper and
print—but, then again, only as a post-boy.[49] The pugilism of 'Letter 5' is still
shadow boxing; Gloucester is said to be both harmed by publications like
Four Winds and also blithely ignorant of them. 'Letter 5' stages a *logomachia*,
wherein the poem itself is a combatant, while also conceding defeat. 'This
quarterly will not be read'; but no more will *The Maximus Poems*, which
appear in that very publication. This sense of a material protest that is only
partially engaged is present in the typography. Chiding Ferrini and *Four
Winds*, Olson proclaims:

[47] George M. Butterick, *A Guide to the Maximus Poems*, 30–31.
[48] Charles Olson, *The Maximus Poems*, n.p.
[49] Charles Olson, *The Maximus Poems*, n.p.

Nor assuage yrself I use the local as a stick to beat you. Such pages
as you now have published twice, do not need one small Gloucester thing
to be a Gloucester magazine. The point of the fix of your cover
is otherwise (I prefer it, in fact, to the rhetoric of your title) :
North 42° 37′, West 70° 40′ It is enough Gloucester,
to say where it is,
had you also the will to be as fine as

> as fine as fins are

>> as firm as

> as firm as a mackerel is
> (fresh out of water)

>>> as sure

> as sure as no owner is
> (or he'd be to sea)

>>> as vulnerable

> (as vulnerable as I am
> brought home to Main St
> in such negligible company)[50]

This is a climax in the drama of print, as Olson modulates from long, prosy
lines to a shapely poise where parentheses, correlative clauses, and phrasing
assume a sudden graphical precision, an exactitude in line spacing, alignment, and couplet. These lines would seem to vaunt the acuity of Olson's
eyes, a typographical rigour that stands apart from Ferrini's concessions in
print. Gloucester's text seems to be seized and shaped into something better.
Yet, at the same time, there is a tone of resignation here. Surety appears as
its own negation, as the ship owner's lack of faith in his own vessel, divorced
from his own craft, and is paralleled with a 'vulnerable' Olson, distant from
his fellow townsfolk. Olson was compelled by the felicities of shape in nature,
such as the pendactylism of birds, and, the hand of man appearing only in
apophasis, the sudden shapeliness of these lines finds positive expression
in the mackerel's fins. An exemplar of better graphics is imagined here, but
Olson presents himself as dispossessed of it.

[50] Charles Olson, *The Maximus Poems*, n.p. [cf Charles Olson, *The Maximus Poems* (Berkeley, CA, 1983), 22, 26, 24].

3. The Poet and the Typographer: Frances Motz Boldereff, David Jones, and the Labour of Verse

This dispossession is written into much of Olson's unpublished and occasional verse, a series of poems that are plainly not what they proclaim to be. Olson dedicates the following putative ideogram to Ben Shahn:

TO A MAN WHO IS THE BEST GODDAMN PAINTER IN AMERICA
AND THE FACT THAT HE WAS A LITHOGRAPHER HAS TO DO
WITH HIS ELEGANCE, THIS

CHINESE WRITTEN CHARACTER

I cut stone
but it is another kind of stone
and with another line[51]

Poets, forestalling charges of *otium* and facility, have commonly enough laid claim to the intractability of language and the sheer effort of *poesis* by likening themselves to stonemasons, artisans, and engravers. Olson's declamation, though, rings hollower than Horace's 'exegi monumentum aere perennius' or Gautier's 'Sculpte, lime, cisèle / Que ton rêve flottant / Se scelle / Dans le bloc résistant'.[52] The imbalance between the lapidary capitals and circumlocutory weight of the dedicatory title and the leanness of Olson's own job description makes the poet sound like the poor relation. But more than that, the velleity of the capitalization and elegantly incised lineation, its wishful mimicry of inscription, makes type seem a flimsy after-image of carved and sculpted letters. Typography itself began as an ancillary art form, a technique of replication not origination. Print, for Renaissance typographers like Gutenberg and Aldus, mechanized the scribal artistry of the handwritten codex. Presses aped quills, and Shahn himself, though he turned his hand to typography, always regarded lithography, the handwritten letter, as the superior art. Modern practitioners still argue over whether calligraphy or carving is the true archetype, and that Olson's poem wants to be both, to be Chinese written character and stonecutting, points up the fact that his typescript is neither.

The lettering of the poet and designer David Jones is similarly caught between stone and print in his verse epics. Much more than Olson, Jones's

---

[51] Charles Olson, 'I cut stone', MS 22:947. Charles Olson Research Collection, Thomas J. Dodd Research Center, University of Connecticut Libraries.
[52] Horace, *Opera*, ed. Edward C. Wickham (Oxford: Oxford University Press, 1901), 86; Théophile Gautier, *Émaux et Camées* (Paris: Gallimard, 1981), 150.

career was divided between the worlds of poetry and typography. For not only is Jones published by Faber through the ministrations of Eliot, as well as lauded by Auden, he is also at the heart of British typographical reform through his apprenticeship and friendship with Eric Gill. Gill's imprint is stamped on the face of Jones's poems by the adoption of his font Perpetua for the body of the text. Yet Jones's verse does not emblematize Gill's aesthetics. Stonecutting, engraving, and inscription, arts practised by the Guild of St Joseph and St Dominic, the Roman Catholic art colony founded by Gill in which Jones was immured, bear upon the typography of *In Parenthesis* and *The Anathemata*, but in a mediated fashion. Like Olson's 'CHINESE WRITTEN CHARACTER', the dedication page of *In Parenthesis* adheres to the spatial logic of stonecutting, slabs of uppercase, unpunctuated lettering which admit of quite indecorous breaks of syntax, as in the isolated preposition and article in the following:

AND TO THE MEMORY OF THOSE
WITH ME IN THE COVERT AND IN
THE OPEN FROM THE BLACKWALL
THE BROADWAY THE CAUSEWAY
THE CUTS THE FLATS THE LEVEL THE

Inscriptional logic governs much of the body of the text as well:

Until dim flickerings light across; to fade where the revetment changes direction, and overhead wire catches oblique

Prose is justified in such a way that there are conspicuous splittings of words across the line break, as if in obedience to the economizing of space that guides the hand of the mason. Yet to say that the text *adheres* to such principles is to confuse the nature of the materials. Print can be obdurate, but it is not as unrelenting as stone. This is typography that aspires to the condition of masonry, printed as though under lapidary constraints.[53]

Letterer and poet, traditionalist and modernist, a disciple of Gill yet a writer whose pages resemble those of Olson, Jones is a figure who incarnates the harmonies and disharmonies between the sphere of lettering and the sphere of verse, and how the two collide in the twentieth century on both sides of the Atlantic. Despite his adoration of Roman inscriptions and their afterlife as the archetype of the printed letter, Jones never turned his hand to chiselling stone or cutting typefaces in the manner of Gill. In an article published in *The Tablet* in 1940, Jones pays homage to his mentor's lettering:

---

[53] David Jones, *In Parenthesis* (London: Faber and Faber, 1937), n.p., 49.

One thing is certain: as a carver of inscriptions he stands supreme. There the workman scaled the heights of pure form, and some of his inscribed stones possess the anonymous and inevitable quality we associate with the works of the great civilizations, where an almost frightening technical skill, for a rare moment, is the free instrument of the highest sensitivity—and the Word is made Stone.[54]

The chiselled letter is figured as the very type of sacramental art, incarnating something timeless and ineffable. Jones recalls that Gill's favoured example of this divine *signum* was the triangle, which, when accurately inscribed, the artist could transmit with absolute certainty, representing an unchanging form of rite and fore-time. Lettered stone, to Jones, seems especially susceptible to anamnesis because of Roman script's obduracy to sudden change. He notes: 'There is more affinity, aesthetically, between the inscribed stones of Roman Antiquity and [Gill's] inscribed stones, than between any two separated-by-centuries art-forms I can think of.'

But just as Olson claimed he was cutting stone while perched at his typewriter, Jones neither chiselled inscriptions nor cut typefaces. One of his first jobs when he joined Gill's Roman Catholic art colony, the Guild of SS. Joseph and Dominic at Ditchling, was to colour in the war memorial his mentor had inscribed in the chapel at New College, Oxford. And it was with a watercolour brush, not a chisel, that Jones formed his inscriptions. Painted inscriptions, the type of graphic art that Jones chiefly mastered, are alive with this hybridity. These living letters are calligraphic in their freedom, far looser and more limber than print, capricious in their spacing and realized in the liquidity of watercolour, yet nevertheless fashioned after stonework.[55] This is lettering that wants to be free and unfree at once. When Jones tries to define his war poem in the year of its publication, 1937, he says: 'This writing is called "In Parenthesis" because I have written it in a kind of space between—I don't know between quite what—but as you turn aside to do something.' He goes on to gloss this liminal space as that of the First World War, an interruption in the syntax of life, a trauma which the psyche keeps in brackets, and a punctuation proper to our 'curious type' of temporal existence. It is not only unclear when the poem was written— for it was not written *in* the war at all but after—nor in what psychological

[54] David Jones, *Epoch and Artist* (London: Faber, 2017), 300.
[55] Ariane Bankes and Paul Hills, *The Art of David Jones: Vision and Memory* (Farnham: Lund Humphries, 2015), 151–2.

Figure 8. David Jones, *IN PRINCIPIO ERAT VERBUM*, c.1951.
National Galleries of Scotland. Purchased 1976.

or spiritual state it was written, but also in what graphical space it is written. Between stonework and calligraphy, between typescript and printing, space changes what is written. Earlier in the preface to *In Parenthesis*, Jones attempts to delineate his method:

A new line, which the typography would not otherwise demand, is used to indicate some change, inflexion, or emphasis. I have tried to indicate the sound of certain sentences by giving a bare hint of who is speaking, of the influences operating to make the particular sound I want in a particular instance, by perhaps altering a single vowel in one word. I have only used the notes of exclamation, interrogation, etc., when the omission of such signs would completely obscure the sense. I hope the stress and changes intended will convey them.

Jones the letterer cedes to Jones the poet in this passage, and space warps between the two disciplines. For what typography *demands*, that a line of print be filled or a word broken—the calculations of typesetting and the rubrics of the profession, codes homologous to those of the engraver or the stonecutter—does not constrain the poet. In the same year that Olson publishes his poetic credo 'Projective Verse' (1950), Jones, in a much quieter fashion, discloses his own aesthetic tenets in a review entitled 'A Note on Mr Berenson's Views' in the *Dublin Review*. Admonishing Berenson for his classicism and fixed hierarchies, Jones appeals to an ancient legal distinction:

> In law there is the division between courts of Justice and courts of Equity—well, in the arts *all* cases have to be taken to Chancery; that is to say Chancery as once understood: a court where the equitable, as defined in the *Nicomachean Ethics*, was supposed to operate [...] But in the arts every case is particular and special to itself; the arts know only the unique.[56]

For all his praising of the mason's impersonality, Jones's typography shares the exceptionalism of his painted inscriptions, which have little of the utile reproducibility of Gill's lettering but, rather, flex and bend in their individual circumstances. They are equitable rather than being equal. Reflexes observed at the Guild of St Joseph and St Dominic are recalled and forgotten in Jones's verse. Letters look chiselled at one moment and at the next are formed according to 'some change, inflexion, or emphasis'. These are rules that are made to be broken; they cancel themselves out. To 'give a bare hint' of something is to sketch intentionally blurry outlines. Phonetic spelling may gesture to a particular speaker in Jones's poetry, but typography is more phantasmal. We see skeletons of choruses through indented layout; voices are singled out but anonymized by hanging in white space. This unspoken communication seems to take place in the very production of the book: at the end of the preface Jones appends this acknowledgement:

> PS I find I have neglected one thing that I very much wanted to say. There is a debt I owe to the printer who will print this for me. He is more than an aid, he is a collaborator, and I know no one else so aware of both the nature of a writing and of how to print it.[57]

Spectral in these lines is both the telepathic way in which Jones communes with his printer and the amorphous autonomy he ascribes to his

[56] David Jones, *Epoch and Artist*, 277.
[57] David Jones, *In Parenthesis*, xv, xi.

text. Verse shifts into prose and back again in Jones's oeuvre, chiefly through rearrangements of space, until those categories no longer seem valid. A 'writing'—text that remembers and forgets the lettering of the stonemason and the typographer—is what takes shape.

Such hybridic 'writings' are repeatedly sketched by Olson as he negotiates the terms between poetry and lettering. The typography of *The Maximus Poems*, in the manner of *In Parenthesis* or *IN PRINCIPIO ERAT VERBUM*, is measured as though under extreme material constraint while being free of the obstacles that face the mason or compositor. Olson's verse is preeminently 'equitable', to use Jones's term, in being fastidious with precise mensuration yet obdurately singular, pecular, and local. Like Jones, Olson had lifelong, often tempestuous, relationships with letterers. Recalling his British contemporary, Olson invokes the material rigour of the sister arts of stonecutting and type design, but he refuses to play by their rulebooks. His would-be ideogram typifies a series of poems entitled 'taos' and 'glyphs', which assume a graphical identity they cannot appropriate, as though they could transcend the visual poverty of typescript through sheer illocutionary force:

THE TAO

Inherent, three treasures, indwelling

the first is compassion,

the second is economy, that is to say, to manage a house
to keep things in order, husbandry

the third, it is that from which riseth courtesy, the word
it hath been emptied of meaning, humility, the root
to get back to it, to use it, humilitas

Because of his compassion
                    a man can become
                                        courageous
Because of his economy
                    a man can become
                                        generous
Because of his humility
                    a man can become leader
                                        wise[58]

---

[58] Charles Olson, 'The Tao', MS 21:891. Charles Olson Research Collection, Thomas J. Dodd Research Center, University of Connecticut Libraries.

The faux-Oriental didacticism of Pound's Chinese Cantos lies behind these poems, as does the older poet's veneration of the Chinese written character as a guiding light for modernist poetics. However, while *The Cantos* synthesize calligraphy and typography, confecting a symbology so catholic as to admit hieroglyphs, plainchant, and playing cards, *The Maximus Poems* remain within the confines of print. Desirous as these taos and glyphs are of appropriating a calligraphic aesthetic, Olson lacks Pound's confidence that the written form of such symbols can be annexed by the poet. Yet if typescripts fall short of calligraphy, they are also not quite typography. In copying the printed page, which itself copied the scribal hand, typescript might well be figured as a tertiary art form, a copy of a copy, a medium thereby imbued with a sense of material dispossession. Casting his eye over the work of these letterers, Olson knew he was dependent on their skills, and he started to doubt where his art ended and theirs began. This sense of verse's dependence on print, I will argue, impels Olson to reimagine the boundaries between the poet and the typographer, both in his personal relationships and his aesthetics. By thinking of verse as an art of measurement, Olson marries poetry and typography, and measuring, I will demonstrate, governs his compositional practice.

What hand the poet has in typography worried and occupied Olson throughout his life, both in theory and practice. Modernist poets must use typography, Olson tells us. Graphics men like Shahn are indispensable to a progressive education. Olson constantly berates and advises his typesetters. But, fraternizing with these letterers, does the poet become one? Or is the plangent materialism of 'Letter 5' the dominant note, a poet who sees a world comprised of print but is unable to make his mark in it: twice divorced from it, as an overlooked avant-garde poet, cut off from mainstream presses, and an evangelist for 'GRAPHICS' who cannot print his own pages?

This aporia in Olson's poetics came to life in his personal affairs. As he is formulating 'Projective Verse', Olson is corresponding with the typographer and scholar Frances Motz Boldereff. Enthused by a copy of *Call Me Ishmael*, Boldereff first writes to Olson in November 1949 on paper bearing the letterhead 'Frances Boldereff BOOK DESIGN Woodward, Penna.' In his reply the following month, Olson skirts over the praise of his own work to signal his interest in hers: 'My dear Frances Boldereff—It is generous of you. I am very curious to know what yr own work is—BOOK DESIGN.' The question of whose work should take precedence, and how a poet relates to a typographer, animates their letters throughout, intersecting with sexual longing and the dynamics of gender. Sex and typography are often hard to extricate. Excusing himself for his delayed visits, Olson writes:

> what seems now to be the thing to be faced is, how can you tolerate this olson system, with its crazy slow time, its intolerably long faiths, this space-system which is capable, i guess, of 40 days in a desert but which carries out such disciplines precisely not in deserts but in the gardens of its own delights

Three days later Olson will send Boldereff a first draft of 'Projective Verse', and he speaks of his courtship as though it were his new method of versification, a 'space-system' of finely calculated suspensions and absences, as if prosody and desire were scored on the same page.[59]

Boldereff responds rapturously to the draft, claiming that she can better apprehend his typing because of it, as though the essay were written to bring his distant voice closer to her and sound out her lover's intonations. How breath responds to type figures both intimacy and possession here. For Boldereff claims the essay as her own, asserting that it is born out of her own cerebrations: 'the main points [of "Projective Verse"] have points lying behind them which are all Motz points (I mean never stated by me but my critique of my time for myself) [...]'. Olson is indeed contriving and drafting the essay during the first flush of his correspondence with Boldereff, and he concedes a month prior to showing her the draft that 'one of my secret delights is to find myself suddenly not just using the motz vocabulary, but the twisting of the mouth, the exact heat and pressure of breath, the gestures, the works!' More than just mouthing her phraseology, Olson absorbs the pneumatics of her body and the physiology of her speech. This is no small admission for a poet founding a theory of verse on his own lungs.[60]

Despite this homage and act of erotic ventriloquism, Boldereff's art does not lie in her respiration; it lies in her mastery of print. Subversive though Olson's sexual mimicry may be, it still casts Boldereff as breathy and

---

[59] Charles Olson, 'Letter to Frances Boldereff, 22 November 1947'; 'Letter to Frances Boldereff, 29 December 1947'; 'Letter to Frances Boldereff, 8 February 1950'; 'Letter to Frances Boldereff, 11 February 1950', in Charles Olson and Frances Boldereff, *Charles Olson and Frances Boldereff: A Modern Correspondence*, ed. Ralph Maud and Sharon Thesen (Hanover, NH: Wesleyan University Press, 1999), 1, 2; 150–52 (p. 150), 162–63 (p. 162).

[60] Frances Boldereff, 'Letter to Charles Olson, 13 February 1950'; Charles Olson, 'Letter to Frances Boldereff, 31 January 1950', in Charles Olson and Frances Boldereff, *Charles Olson and Frances Boldereff*, 172–73 (p. 172); 139–43 (p. 142).

oracular, more bard than typographer, as though he impersonates her on the condition she exhibit this vatic maleness. Gender is a fraught issue between them. The letters oscillate from fierce independence to casual misogyny; vows to 'dynamite the PATRIARCHY' give way to passive adulation. While his esteem for Boldereff's designs never wavers, Olson will gender their respective vocations to ballast his own sense of *poesis*. A few months after a rupture in their relationship, Olson writes of the same essay Boldereff once laid claim to:

> To hell with it ['Projective Verse']. Why bother yr dear self with it. Only, it is, the work of a day, all there is, these days, that i am hammering, hammering, hammering, like some man condemned to die [...] So here I am. And there you are. And I sweat, sweat, sweat. And grow stronger each bloody day!

Those hammering lungs reassert the organs of verse, outmuscle Boldereff from his poetics by sheer force of breath. This is the bard resurgent, a self-sufficient masculinity with no reliance on type. Complaining to Boldereff about an inferior reprint of his volume *y & x* in May 1950, he writes: '(for a printer to let a dizzy woman mess up *print*—words on a page!)'. This phrase resurfaces several years later in his essay 'The Advantage of Literacy is that Words Can Be on the Page', an essay on the materiality of language, the wording already redolent of disputed ownership and sacrosanct male property. As he condescendingly offers the recently unemployed Boldereff his contacts in publishing, Olson says in coddling tones: 'look: olson is some pumpkin if he can't help his baby in that ancillary art to language, print [...]'.[61] Ancillary comes from *ancilla*, the Latin for maid-servant, so that graphic art is gendered and gently put in its place; the typographer as handmaiden to the poet. Sensing a dependence on typography and Boldereff, this is Olson stabilizing his poetic identity, protecting his fragile male ego, by warding off the supposed femininity of print.

[61] Charles Olson, 'Letter to Frances Boldereff, 10 July 1950'; 'Letter to Frances Boldereff, 4 April 1950'; 'Letter to Frances Boldereff, 11 February 1950', in Charles Olson and Frances Boldereff, *Charles Olson and Frances Boldereff*, 405–7 (p. 406); 295–97 (p. 296); 162–63 (p. 162).

Gendered as feminine, print flowers in Olson's verse, and typography is horticultural. Stymied by material delays, the printing of *y & x* is said to wilt, while 'Letter 9' of *The Maximus Poems* celebrates the printing of *In Cold Hell, In Thicket* as a vernal blossoming:

> the flowering plum
> out the front door window
> sends whiteness
> inside my house
>
> > as the news that the almond
> > was in bloom Mallorca
> > accompanied the news
> > that that book was in print
> > which I wish might stop
> > the workings of my city
> > where so much of it
> > was bred[62]

Neither artistic vocation, though, nor the gender of print is stable in 'Letter 9'. The printer of *In Cold Hell, In Thicket* is male rather than female; it is published by Robert Creeley's Divers Press in Mallorca. Printer upstages poet in Olson's letter of thanks to Creeley: 'I cldnt even look at the poems, was all eyes for the THING [...] to look & look at what you had done with the pages [...]'.[63] Olson expunges this provenance from the rhetoric of the poem. So insistent is Olson on the arborescence of its printing, its botanical grace, one might assume the edition sprang from the soil. 'Letter 9' begins in a combative mood, with Olson quoting a letter he had sent to Cid Corman about Ferrini. 'I had to clobber him', Olson writes, reigniting the print war of 'Letter 5'. Rather than bullish machismo, though, what carries over from 'Letter 5' to 'Letter 9' is an admission of material dispossession. The graphical accomplishment Olson hymns in the poem is one he had no hand in. Those aspects of book design which so thrill him—quality of paper, colour of type—were fashioned hundreds of miles away in Mallorca:

---

[62] Charles Olson, *The Maximus Poems*, n.p. [cf Charles Olson, *The Maximus Poems* (Berkeley, CA, 1983), 45].

[63] George M. Butterick, *A Guide to the Maximus Poems*, 69.

it was the reds of buds
sent me this spring,
lighting up the valleys

        as now the fruits do,
        and these pages have come in,
        of a white so right
        the print is brown
            I, dazzled[64]

Before he embarked upon *The Maximus Poems*, it was sound that was
to sprout from the soil of the page: 'It is my impression that *all* parts of
speech suddenly, in composition by field, are fresh for both sound and
percussive use, spring up like unknown, unnamed vegetables in the patch,
when you work it, come spring.'[65] Tilling, dispassionately, the ground of his
own speech, it was syllables that were to spring up in a sudden rhizomatic
flourishing. The egolessness of 'Projective Verse' was to be its disinterested
cultivation of sound. The objectivity of the poetics here, though, lies in the
poet awaiting the germination of print, an activity he has outsourced. The
fruits he harvests are typographical.

    The dialectic between poet and typographer dramatizes, then, in idea and
practice, how Olson figures the craft of verse, and how subjective an under-
taking it is. Typography cannot be eschewed, without regression, but the
poet's reliance on it disempowers him. Olson seems reduced to a specta-
tor of his own verse, blinded by Creeley's printing; but Olson inflects this
argument. After dazzlement comes a subtler recognition:

                  I, dazzled

as one is, until one discovers
there is no other issue than
the moment of
        the pleasure of
           this plum,[66]

[64] Charles Olson, *The Maximus Poems*, n.p. [cf Charles Olson, *The Maximus Poems* (Berkeley: University of California Press, 1983), 45, 46].
   [65] Charles Olson, *Collected Prose*, 244.
   [66] Charles Olson, *The Maximus Poems*, n.p. [cf Charles Olson, *The Maximus Poems* (Berkeley: University of California Press, 1983), 46].

The intertext behind these lines is Williams's lyric 'To a Poor Old Woman', which distils the momentary delight of its speaker finding 'a solace of ripe plums'.[67] Denise Levertov presents Williams's poem as a masterwork of modernist typography, detailing the gamut of nuances pressed upon by the lineation:

> They taste good to her.
> They taste good
> to her. They taste
> good to her.[68]

Williams's experiments with the machine were one of the other fruits to be picked in 'Projective Verse', and Olson's lines, as well as the typographical allusion to the triadic line the later Williams adopts, sound an act of homage that quietly rehabilitates the modernist poet-typist.

The ending of 'Letter 9' reinforces the earlier allusion to Williams, exhibiting Olson at his typewriter, so that a poem which began by figuring the poet as a recipient of his own work, disconnected from a material production which defined its idiosyncrasy and potency, re-establishes his role in its physical crafting:

> I measure my song,
> measure the sources of my song,
> measure me, measure
> my forces
>
>   (And I buzz,
>   as the bee does,
>   who's missed
>   the plum tree,
>   and gone and got himself caught
>   in my window
>
>   And the whirring of whose wings
>   blots out the rattle of
>   my machine)[69]

---

[67] William Carlos Williams, *An Early Martyr and Other Poems*, 22.

[68] Denise Levertov, *New & Selected Essays* (New York: New Directions, 1992), 82.

[69] Charles Olson, *The Maximus Poems*, n.p. [cf Charles Olson, *The Maximus Poems*, (Berkeley: University of California Press, 1983), 48].

Essential to the discipline of graphic art is measurement, as Shahn observes, relating his formation as a 'true letterer'. Skilled though he is at shaping letter-forms, Shahn is reproached for his defective spacing, and his foreman offers the analogy of a glass of water that needs to be poured equably across the line. Enlightened, Shahn realizes: 'That was it; letters were quantities, and only the eye and the hand can measure them. As in the ear and the sensibilities of the poet, sounds and syllables and pauses are quantities, so in both cases are the balancing and forward movement of these quantities only a matter of skill and feeling and art.'[70] Letterer and poet alike measure; their feel for mensuration is their art. Testifying to Bolderoff's skill, Olson likewise marries the two faculties: '[Bolderoff has] a profound understanding of the space which a page is, and what breath—to speak like a writer!—leading can give [...] For she knows her business (like a good writer knows syllables!).'[71] It is as a measurer that Olson vindicates himself at the close of 'Letter 9'. Sound is displaced from the poet's voice box to their notational instrument, the type-writer's buzz and rattle. To say 'I measure' is not to say 'I write in measure'. What was a medium in traditional prosody has become a verb. Mensuration supplants singing as the prime act of versifying here: the measurement of sound, not its production.

Before reciting 'Letter 9' at a 1965 conference at Berkeley, Olson affirms that book design is 'the most powerful political event', recalling the 'idiosyncrasy' of the Mallorca edition of his poems.[72] Convinced of the potency of graphics, Olson renounces any claims to autarky. This versifying is acutely self-aware, apprised of its reliance on the typographer and the printer, willing to formulate an aesthetic consonant with graphic art so as not to exile itself from the world of print through which it must pass. The formula 'I measure me' articulates a self-objectification, a voice that looks back on itself by gauging its extension on the page. The antagonist of 'Letter 9' is King Alfred, conqueror of an older Gloucester, 'Glow-ceastre', whose virile self-certainty provides a counter-image of the *poesis* Olson is gestating. Aprine Alfred is an unreformed Olson, the hammerer of breath in love with his own bulk, not the chastened poet that emerges here:

---

[70] Ben Shahn, *Ben Shahn*, 145.

[71] Charles Olson, 'Letter to Robert Giroux, 16 June 1950' in *Selected Letters*, 117.

[72] Charles Olson, *Mythologos: The Collected Lectures & Interviews*, ed. George F. Butterick, 2 vols (Bolinas, CA: Four Seasons Foundation, 1978), I, 119.

As of myself
I'd pose it,
today,
as Alfred at Ashdown, a wild boar
               (*aprino more*, Asser says)
versus
my own wrists and all my joints, versus speech's connectives, versus the tasks
I obey to,[73]

The letterer measures by hand and eye, according to Shahn, but the poet does so by ear. This vocational distinction, though, dissolves in 'Letter 9'. As Olson redrafted this poem, he *rearticulated* its typography, marking junctures in pen, adding joints to what was originally one long line from 'As of myself' to 'a wild boar'. This versifying is manual work. Labouring at the typewriter takes its toll on the wrists. Olson shifts the burden of verse from lungs to ligaments, from speech to its 'connectives', so that utterance becomes haptic and the strain felt *between* words rather than in them.

From the Objectivists to the Black Mountain poets, criticism of typography admitted the possibility of a more material form of scoring than that of the stave and bar; a scoring of wood rather than sheet music. Experimental mise-en-page was conceived of as a handicraft that engaged the eye and the wrists. Dissertating on Olson's *Maximus*, Robert Duncan figures prosody as kinaesthetic, a tensity at once visual and tactile: 'The discipline of the eye, clarity, is acknowledged measure [...] The hand is intimate to the measurings of the eye [...] the hand & eye estimate, and we feel what we see.' To measure speech is to bring it to order, according to Duncan; it is where the hard graft of form is felt, where material resistance is met. The proto-Maximus, he recollects, is a carpenter, and, inflecting the old Scots word for poet to connote artisanal handiwork, he asserts: 'Maximus is a *makar*; is then Olson, or his measure.'[74]

Theorizing his 'objectism', Olson espouses this analogy of woodwork: '[T]he necessity of a line or a work to be as wood is, to be as clean as wood is as it issues from the hand of nature, to be shaped as wood is when a man has had his hand to it.'[75] To think like a carpenter is to return to the rudiments of poetic measure, to grip the line afresh. In a hands-on 'craft lecture' of 1979

---

[73] Charles Olson, *The Maximus Poems*, n.p. [cf Charles Olson, *The Maximus Poems* (Berkeley: University of California Press, 1983), p. 47.

[74] Robert Duncan, *Collected Essays and Prose*, ed. James Maynard (Berkeley: University of California Press, 2014), 49, 53.

[75] Charles Olson, *Collected Prose*, 247.

entitled 'Technique and Tune-Up', Levertov likewise moves from notation to carpentry to rationalize modernist typography:

> Because there's no consensus about some of the tools of scoring—just as up till the eighteenth century there was virtually no consensus about musical scoring techniques—one can detect uncertainty and a hit-or-miss approach to these matters even in some of the major poets of our time. When I speak of consensus I'm not suggesting that people should write alike—only that it would be helpful if more poets would consider what typographical and other tools we do have at our disposal and what their *use* is. To point out that a carpenter's plane is not designed to be used as a knife sharpener or a can opener does not restrict how someone planes their piece of wood.

With uncommon perspicacity, Levertov discerns that the ferment of typographical experiment amongst 'major poets' has been accompanied by a dearth of theoretical reflection and an ad hoc heuristics. Were poets to assume the pragmatism of the woodworker and consider the instruments of their trade, they would realize that even the most elemental questions remain open: 'What makes a line be a line? How do you know where to end it if you do not have a predetermined metrical structure to tell you?' Refusing to believe that modernist lineation can be explained according to breath stops, and bemoaning the literalist reception of Olson's breath theory, Levertov intuits that, since the advent of free verse and the liberation of typography, the basics of poetic grammar remain indeterminate. She asks the same question Williams asked in 1951—'Why do some poems seem to be all over the page?'—but, rather than prescribing a typographical cure as Williams did with the regimen of his triadic line, she exhorts each poet to be their own measurer. Each poet must return to the drawing-board; to shatter and remould the stuff of print to apprehend the page space anew:

> Take a poem and type it up as a prose paragraph. Type it up again in lines, but not in its own lines—break it up differently. Read it aloud (observing the linebreak as roughly one-half a comma, of course—it is there to *use*, and if you simply run on, ignoring it, you may as well acknowledge that you want to write prose, and do so). As you perform this exercise or experiment you will inevitably begin to *experience* the things that linebreaks do—and this will be much more useful than being *told about* them.[76]

---

[76] Denise Levertov, *New & Selected Essays*, 94.

Breaking up print and putting it back together, the poet is to construct their poetics through a do-it-yourself empiricism. Culling granular apprehensions of type from this bottom-up reconstruction, they are to husband them till they form a graphical language.

It is through slow patient measurement that Olson's verse is formed. These cogitations of how graphics relates to poetics and how the eye might measure verse are not the preserve of speculation; they were applied, hands-on. Early lyrics by Olson frequently dramatize style's formation, and in composing 'A B C s', Olson returns to alphabetic fundamentals (see Figure 9). Text is viewed embryonically in this poem.[77] 'The word forms on the left', as though typography is still gestating; margins, the vectors of reading, yet to be set. Words have their graphemes prised apart, so that their semantic elasticity— that cabbage can denote both the vegetable and Olson's childhood friend—is apprehended by defamiliarizing their graphical shape. Levertov claims that by fine-tuning indentation and line breaking the poet can inflect the reader's 'eye-ear-mouth coordination', like rewiring a nervous system, and this poem returns to 'synapse' and 'registration', as if re-engineering our linguistic reflexes.[78] Hannah Sullivan has convincingly argued that 'writers in the modernist period revised more than their predecessors in several senses: more frequently, at more points in the lifespan of the text, more structurally and experimentally (rather than through lexical substitution alone), and more self-consciously'.[79] Attempting to realize his typographical designs impels Olson to a similarly meticulous and innovative form of correction. Fastidiously, Olson tinkers with the typography, splicing lines with the typewriter then suturing them together with pencil arrows. Whole sections are re-lineated in autograph marginalia. Line spacing is twice recalculated, with abbreviated numerals hovering between exact increments, oscillations from '2sp' to '3sp' carefully marked. The poet of 'Letter 9' who proclaims 'I measure my song', a humble worker bee rattling at the keys of his typewriter, is no fictional construct. The virtues of the typographer, the attritive calculation of a Boldereff or a Shahn, are being put to service in Olson's atelier.

[77] This is the sole extant draft of the first lyric of 'The ABCs' written in 1948. The Olson Papers in the Dodd Center also contain typescripts of two 'sequels', parts two and three, dated 10 April and June 1950 respectively. The layout shown in Figure 9, with the autograph modifications realised, is accurately reproduced in published versions.
[78] Denise Levertov, *New & Selected Essays*, 97.
[79] Hannah Sullivan, *The Work of Revision* (Cambridge, MA: Harvard University Press, 2013), 22.

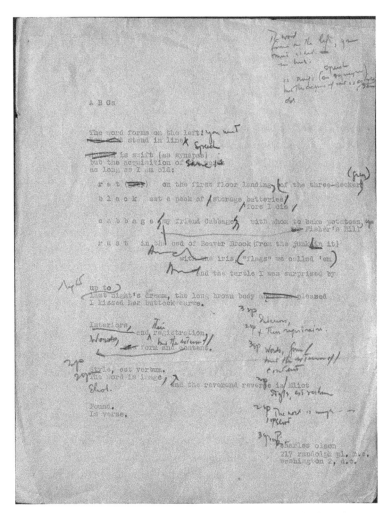

Figure 9. Charles Olson, 'The ABCs', box 14, folder 378, Charles Olson Research Collection. Thomas J. Dodd Research Center, University of Connecticut Libraries. Works by Charles Olson published during his lifetime are copyright the Estate of Charles Olson; previously unpublished works are copyright the University of Connecticut. Used with permission.

Weeks after drawing up the foundational treatise of his poetics in 'Projective Verse', Olson, in consultation with Boldereff, planned to elaborate and enlarge the already ambitious typographical system that essay proposed. Not only was an architectonic of type to be more fully schematized, but any consideration of notating the voice or graphing the breath was to be omitted. Breath poetics seemed wholly forgotten. By labouring to realize his complicated typographical designs and his abortive schemes to create a poetics of typeface, Olson refigured poetic labour from the effort of breath to the work of print. Volume 1 of *The Maximus Poems* broods over the vitality of print culture and the poet's disconnection from it. Emulous of the printer's art, Olson aspires not only to imitate the mensurational rigour of the typographer in his drafting but to master the whole repertoire of graphic design. Showing off his microscopic appreciation of Boldereff's printing of Whitman, and punning on the blades of *Leaves of Grass*, he boasts '(you see, baby, how the olson can acquire a skill the motz eyes have, to look so sharp a blade is clear!)'.[80] Maximus appears to us first as a 'lance', 'a metal hot from boiling water', and Olson whets his gaze as though it were a knife, as if his vision were incising not merely absorbing Boldereff's lettering.[81] Olson claims to have contracted Boldereff's graphical acuity, and, not content with the 'space-precisions' of the typewriter, he now eyes typeface:

> If I am right in the argument abt what the typewriter has offered the poet in composition, then it seems to me to follow that, in the printing of language which is projective, there ought to be another convention accepted by the reader—that type-face may change page to page[82]

This passage confirms what is inherent in the poetic thinking of the *Maximus Poems*, in its tense ruminations of printing and typing, poetics and billboards: that Olson sees a continuum between versification and printing. Verse and typography cannot be considered as two discrete arts, with the poet blasé about the type their words become, believing sound to be the only materialization of language, and that this form, Platonic and inviolable, lives on, untouched by its incarnation on the page.

Typeface is the aspect of typography that most eludes the modernist poet. Though Pound and Cummings readily annex spacing and layout with little deference to the know-how of professional typographers, they rarely meddle with letterforms. (The Genoa edition of Cavalcanti discussed in the first

---

[80] Charles Olson, 'Letter to Frances Boldereff, 15 February 1950', in Charles Olson and Frances Boldereff, *Charles Olson and Frances Boldereff*, 173–81 (p. 174).
[81] Charles Olson, *The Maximus Poems*, n.p. [cf Charles Olson, *The Maximus Poems* (Berkeley: University of California Press, 1983), 5.
[82] Charles Olson, 'Letter to Frances Boldereff, 15 February 1950', in Charles Olson and Frances Boldereff, *Charles Olson and Frances Boldereff*, 175.

chapter is an important, but atypical, exception.) The reasons for this are both practical and aesthetic. Typewriters, of course, have only one font, so that typescript could not act as a blueprint for the design of typeface as it did for layout. Governing typeface would mean supervising almost every stage of the poem's printing, allowing the printer no creative input whatsoever. Even Cummings at his most uninhibited never shifts typeface in a poem, and Levertov, despite her enthusiasm for the usage of typographical tools, considers it stylistically vulgar, a 'clumsy overemphasis', to switch fonts.[83] This provides a yardstick for Olson's audacity here. Referring to his early volume *y & x*, Olson claims that, for all their training, he has a better eye for type than his printers: 'master printer Lescaret was right in setting *preface*—and wrong for all the rest, altogether wrong Why? astre italic gets a broadside quality in p., and for the rest is altogether too lush, too decorative [...]'.[84] Convinced that the composition of verse and its printing are indissolubly bound, that poetry is a part of visual culture, prey to the incursions of newsprint and ad-men, Olson assumes the vocation of the 'full graphics-knowing man'. Olson drafts the job description of a complete poet-typographer, a figure who has assimilated the talents of the designer and printer, and holds unrivalled sway over the space of the page.

What Olson articulates is a reconception of what the work of poetry is. Within Williams's and Levertov's formulation that poetry is all over the page resides an anxiety that visual poetry has no traction, a lubricated glibness that places no restraints on versification. To audit speech, to isolate and assay each syllable, is manifestly laborious; to press the space bar on a typewriter is not. So, too, the production of sound is intimately physiological, each breath conceivable as a discharge of energy; the hard graft of typography, though, seems distanced from the poet's body, outsourced to the labours of the printing house. In his letter to Boldereff, and in an unpublished, contemporaneous 'Note on Typeface' that details the same programme, Olson thinks through these objections. Ideally, Olson says, this poet-typographer would compose like a contemporary Greek poet the sculptor Michael Lekakis told him of, a figure writing verse in his own print shop, his words immediately set in the typeface he designates. Rather than dispatching his typescripts to a publisher, the poet would centralize all

[83] Denise Levertov, *New & Selected Essays*, 100.
[84] Charles Olson, 'Letter to Frances Boldereff, 15 February 1950', in Charles Olson and Frances Boldereff, *Charles Olson and Frances Boldereff*, 175.

production around their own writing body, materially present at the coal-face of the press.[85] Olson was a trained orator, a champion debater proud of his vocal projection, but he had also studied physical theatre and posture exercises under the tutelage of Constance Taylor at the Gloucester School of the Little Theatre.[86] Countering the charge that typography is frictionless, requiring only the pressure of the fingers on the keys, Olson figures it as a somatic art, proffering the analogy of dance. Drawing on Projesh Banerji's *The Dance of India*, and possibly conversations with the Black Mountain dance instructor Nataraj Vashi, Olson proposes that typography assume the totalizing concinnity of Hindu dance, where deity, time signature, time of day, and mood are brought into synchronicity. Unlike the prestidigitation of 'Hindu finger-hand mime', typography should embrace the whole body. One of Olson's earliest experiments in typography was the script for a hybrid of ballet and drama drawing on Melville's *Moby Dick*, a piece titled *The Fiery Hunt*, which he described as a 'dance-play'. In a rare case of direct typograph-ical allusion between modernist poets, the epilogue to the dance-play, with its stepped lines, archaic syntax, and internal rhyme, strongly suggests that Olson drew on Pound's version of Cavalcanti's 'Donna mi prega' as a model, a translation he knew well and whose vision of an augmented physiology is recalled in *The Maximus Poems* (see Figure 10).

The typography of *The Fiery Hunt* choreographs a *Gesamtkunstwerk* that enlarges even Pound's figuration of sensory holism, its stepped lines sug-gesting cues for dance steps in a poetics that is (like the canzone's fusing of medieval codex and modernist printing) radically old and radically new, summoning up the *feet* of Greek prosody while also engineering a distinctly Black Mountain synthesis of disparate arts centred on graphics.[87] Graphics, as in Olson's conception of Ben Shahn's print shop at Black Mountain, is again a 'shop core', a point of synaesthetic convergence, choreographing its sister arts. Not only does Hindu dance with its exhaustive correspondences model the widening ambit of Olson's poetics, where no aspect of the printed page is to remain indeterminate, but it imagines a communal kinetics of har-monized movement. Correlative to facile typography is the slipperiness, the indiscipline, of the contemporary reader: 'the eye runs away with all reading now, no? and the eye is altogether too fast [...]'. The full ambition of Olson's scheme is not only that the poet ought to work harder, fully present in the

---

[85] Charles Olson, 'Letter to Frances Boldereff, 15 February 1950', in Charles Olson and Frances Boldereff, *Charles Olson and Frances Boldereff*, 175.

[86] George M. Butterick, *A Guide to the Maximus Poems*, 92.

[87] This is the sole extant version of this unpublished work.

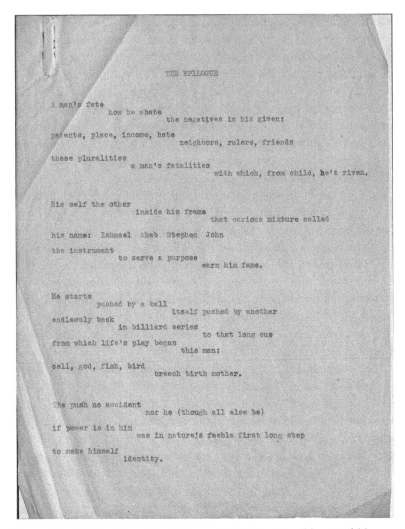

THE EPILOGUE

A man's fate
            how he abate
                        the negatives in his given:
parents, place, income, hate
                        neighbors, rulers, friends
these pluralities
            a man's fatalities
                        with which, from child, he's riven.

His self the other
            inside his frame
                        that curious mixture called
his name: Ishmael Ahab Stephen John
the instrument
            to serve a purpose
                        earn him fame.

He starts
            pushed by a ball
                        itself pushed by another
endlessly back
            in billiard series
                        to that long cue
from which life's play began
                        this man:
cell, god, fish, bird
            breach birth mother.

The push no accident
            nor he (though all else be)
if power is in him
            was in nature's feeble first long step
to make himself
            identity.

Figure 10. Charles Olson, 'The Epilogue to *The Fiery Hunt*', box 21, folder 884, Charles Olson Research Collection. Thomas J. Dodd Research Center, University of Connecticut Libraries. Works by Charles Olson published during his lifetime are copyright the Estate of Charles Olson; previously unpublished works are copyright the University of Connecticut. Used with permission.

crafting of his books, scrutinizing every letter, but that this dynamism will be transferred to his readership. Subtly modulating 'a "family of type-face"', inculcating the tensity of metre in print, the rigours of this new graphics are to change the pace of the reading eye and oblige it to see with greater weight of purpose.[88]

Olson, though, never realizes this programme for a modulation of font because of how entrammeled he is otherwise by the exactions of his typographical design. Fourteen years later, Jonathan Williams, Olson's former student, signals that Olson still had this programme in mind for a prospective complete edition of *The Maximus Poems*. Williams speaks of the printer being 'minimized' by Olson's typographical hegemony, and, already despairing that Olson's work 'demands more than 99% of all the printers to achieve them in type', refuses to countenance any modulation of font to compound existing difficulties.[89] Typeface, Olson comes to learn, is already implicated in an architectonic of horological complexity. The choice of type realigns the fine details of spacing he sweats over in typescript. As he collaborates with Barry Hall of Cape Goliard Press on printing volume II of *Maximus*, Olson agonizes over the choice between Bembo face and Garamond, opting for the former as he discerns in it an innate energy the latter face lacks. As he sees proofs of the poems in Bembo, though, Olson is pained by the recalibration of his spacing it entails: 'The *real* agony [...] is the bloody Bembo double-space (actually also *the leading of single-space* is too open for my harder taste) either in this font—or, in some necessity of modern type-setting I don't understand.'[90] Olson, in fact, recognizes the labour expended in graphic design even without his proposed innovations, and seems apprised of the common weft between font and spacing. He concludes his letter to Boldereff:

> The trick, (excuse the old man, he's thinking out aloud to you, mistress printer, and not making statements but asking his baby questions for his own furtherance) is the subtlest kind of changes, the sort of narrow range of change you surely made a triumph of in the P.S. Catalogue & LEADING (pun: leading on, the dance!
>
> my motto for the lovely lady, today:
> LEAD ON, THE DANCE![91]

---

[88] Charles Olson, 'Letter to Frances Boldereff, 15 February 1950', in Charles Olson and Frances Boldereff, *Charles Olson and Frances Boldereff*, 175.

[89] MS 222, Charles Olson Research Collection. Thomas J. Dodd Research Center, University of Connecticut Libraries.

[90] Charles Olson, 'Letter to Barry Hall, 12 July 1968', in *Selected Letters*, 405–6 (p. 405).

[91] Charles Olson, 'Letter to Frances Boldereff, 15 February 1950', in Charles Olson and Frances Boldereff, *Charles Olson and Frances Boldereff*, 175.

The P.S. catalogue is a library catalogue of the holdings of Pennsylvania State University designed by Boldereff. Olson elsewhere commends Boldereff to the publisher Robert Giroux for having 'learned her trade in the hardest kind of discipline, the Jersey City house that does the N.Y. telephone books.'[92] So encompassing is Olson's eye for graphics that modernist verse can find inspiration in the mundanity of library catalogues and telephone books. The ocular diligence of a designer of directories is an exemplar for a poet wishing to instil rigour in visual poetry. Boldereff is moved at times to ardent declarations of the dynamism of her art, as though she needs to prove the physicality of her work. Recently made redundant, she declares: 'I have this terrible vitality and I must create with those spaces and lines or I go mad [...]'. Over the course of their relationship, and while hard at work on *The Maximus Poems*, Olson needs no convincing of the typographer's assiduity. He may have gleaned the term leading from Boldereff, who defines it as 'the spacing between lines [...] that is what makes type readable, beautiful, etc.'[93] It becomes talismanic in his aesthetic lexicon and, as he notates and renotates the line spacing of his drafts and reviews the proofs of his poem, a cumbersome task. Leading is derived from the practice of placing lead strips between rows of type to create interlinear spaces. It gives mineral weight to the language of typography, a metallic edge to the layout of the page. Olson acknowledges this etymology. Writing to Barry Hall about the proofing and copy-editing of the *Maximus II*, he bewails:

I have adjusted, as best I could – crying, in some cases, on page after page (in notes to yourself) out to you if there isn't some 1 1/2 space or some way to shrink or sweat the leading. (In most cases I have just had to abandon double-space.) So you will see—& I shall have the whole thing mailed to you just the very moment I finish. (It's devilish work—I average at best 33 pages a day—& as you know I was somewhat held up by that hospital spell [...] The problem then is mainly this leading—& *anything* you can possibly do to improve it—to "dry out" the over-distance between lines, will give us both a better press and, for me, a longer life of my poems.[94]

[92] Charles Olson, 'Letter to Robert Giroux, 16 June 1950', in *Selected Letters*, 117.
[93] Frances Boldereff, 'Letter to Charles Olson, 2 February 1950'; 'Letter to Charles Olson, 4 February 1950', in Charles Olson and Frances Boldereff, *Charles Olson and Frances Boldereff*, 143–45 (p. 145); 147–48 (p. 147).
[94] Charles Olson, 'Letter to Barry Hall, 12 July 1968', in *Selected Letters*, 406.

Olson set out to be a hammerer of breath in 1950, but as he labours over the *Maximus Poems*, it is the lead of the printing press that offers resistance. The pages of his poems are said to 'shrink', 'sweat', and 'dry out' as though forged in a foundry. Material hardness and aesthetic worth meld as typographical effort offers 'a longer life of my poems'. Having posited breath as the energy of verse, Olson comes to acknowledge the material labour of typography, a poetics of diligent measurement and painstaking eye effort.

4. 'Metric then is mapping': Olson, Prynne, and the Language of Space

As he gauges the leading of his lines in fractions of a pica, what is Olson seeking to measure *through* the page? What is a language of space, so minutely calculated, supposed to articulate? Typographers weren't the only measurers Olson esteemed. In 1952, having abandoned his earlier ambition to become an academic, his doctoral labours published as *Call Me Ishmael*, Olson advised the Melville scholar Henry Murray how to communicate his research:

> please merely *tell* what you have found out—there is no necessity at all to wrap it up in the ordinary packages of discourse—no need to make any ANY generalizations: the MAP of Melville's PSYCHE is in your hands to make, and it needs to be made as quietly and as carefully and as modestly (the modesty got nothing to do with anything but the scrupulousness with which the continents are drawn, the soundings are indicated—exactly as disciplined as an Admiralty chart [...][95]

Forgoing discursive formats and academic generalizations, Murray ought to replace the familiar packaging of scholarly rigour with another model of discipline: the spatial exactitude of cartography. Mensurational rigour in 'Projective Verse' was notational, the 'stave and bar' of the musician. Here, though, 'soundings' aren't the measurements of sound, but those of bathymetry, of the ascertainment of the sea's depths. Melville's 'PSYCHE', which Olson venerated for its unique sense of space, cannot be apprehended in the propositional shape of conventional scholarship; it can only be laid

---

[95] Charles Olson, 'Letter to Henry Murray, 16 February 1952', in *Selected Letters*, 148–58 (p. 152).

out and traced in the form of a map. In a taut passage in 'Some Notes on Olson's *Maximus*', published in 1962, Robert Creeley interprets Olson's poetry as a cartographic enterprise:

> In *Maximus* the "portrait" is a place, Gloucester, with all that may thereto be related—first of all, men, since "polis is / eyes…", and then the "measure" of those men and that place, as:
>
> > I measure my song
> > measure the sources of my song,
> > measure me, measure
> > my forces …
>
> or the literal "mapping" of "Letter, May 2, 1959", and as well, the sense that "metric then is mapping, and so, to speak modern cant, congruent means of making a statement …"[96]

That iterative and stubborn measuring, in Creeley's estimation, is a project of map-making in verse. This laconic summa of Olson's poetics may seem too hastily compiled, involving, as it does, choice excisions from four different poems, stitched up in a single sentence. Its concision, though, is hard-won. Creeley is binding together a mass of cogitations on poetics, linguistics, and philosophy accumulating for over a decade. This presentation of the poet as a cartographer is founded on a sustained consideration of the interrelation of language and space and the inadequacy of inherited linguistic forms. Through his correspondence with J. H. Prynne, this chapter will now propose, Olson formulated a critique of the linearity of poetry and a programme to spatialize language. It is through typography, though, rather than syntax, I will argue, that Olson pursues this project in his verse.

Realigning words on a page affects the apprehension of syntax as well as rhythm, especially when, as in Olson's verse, normative punctuation is periodically suspended or dispensed with altogether. Moreover, the conviction that language should be spatialized, disposed on the page like a map, is not the sole preserve of prosody and 'COMPOSITION BY FIELD'. The idea germinates likewise in the Black Mountain poets' essays and musings on linguistics. Metrics morphs into a philosophy of language set down geometrically in Creeley's quote from *Maximus*—'"metric then is mapping, and

[96] Robert Creeley, *Collected Essays*, 114.

so, to speak modern cant, congruent means of making a statement'"—and Olson proposes Murray write cartographically because of the failings of ordinary discourse and generic propositions. The *locus classicus* of Olson's critique of discursive formulae is his 1950 essay 'Human Universe'. Propositions are a debilitating inheritance, Olson claims, bequeathed by the Greeks:

> We have lived long in a generalizing time, at least since 450 B.C. And it has had its effects on the best of men, on the best of things. Logos, or discourse, for example, in that time, so worked its abstractions into our concept and use of that language that language's other function, speech, seems so in need of restoration that several of us go back to hieroglyphics or to ideograms to right the balance.[97]

Olson owes this sweeping claim to his patron philosopher Whitehead, who breaks with the dispassionate technicality of his lexis when discussing the malignity of Aristotelian logic: 'The *evil* [my emphasis] produced by the Aristotelian "primary substance" is exactly this habit of metaphysical emphasis upon the "subject-predicate" form of proposition.'[98] This diagnosis, and the vituperative force behind 'evil', is shared by Olson, and Aristotle will appear as an antagonist, tagged with expletives, throughout his future writings. The syntax of logic is totalizing; it has enclosed the cosmos in a 'UNIVERSE of discourse':

> It [discourse] is [the Greeks'] word, and the refuge of all metaphysicians since—as though language, too, was an absolute, instead of (as even man is) instrument, and not to be extended, however much the urge, to cover what each, man and language, is in the hands of: what we share, and which is enough, of power and beauty, not to need an exaggeration of words, especially that spreading one, "universe".

Two spatial dynamics are opposed here: one is pathological, the 'spreading' universalizing of discourse; the other is geometrical, the innate extensiveness of language. The former has displaced the latter; stretched out to an 'absolute', language is 'not to be extended'. Olson reshapes this dichotomy later in the essay. Discourse is not only miasmic in its dispersion, but

---

[97] Charles Olson, *Collected Prose*, 155.
[98] Alfred North Whitehead, *Process and Reality: An Essay in Cosmology* (New York: The Free Press, 1978), 30.

simultaneously reductive, like a simplified geometry. It has inculcated a way of living and writing where man abstracts from 'the full content some face of it, or plane, some part'. Olson continues: 'It comes out a demonstration, a separating out, an act of classification, and so, a stopping, and all that I know is, it is not there, it has turned false'. This false geometry, collapsed to the one-dimensionality of propositional content, has whittled down experience to a single plane. The cosmos is multidimensional; what is needed is a language that can operate on 'several more planes than the arbitrary and discursive which we inherit can declare'.[99]

Radical solutions, admits Olson, present themselves in graphical languages, in pictography or ideography: '[...] several of us go back to hieroglyphics or to ideograms to right the balance'.[100] It should be noted that Olson does not suggest a recourse to some primal orality, to some ur-phonics untouched by the Fall into Logic. As speech is tainted by print in 'Projective Verse', so it is tainted by logic in 'Human Universe'; in both essays it is a revolution in written characters, experimental typography in one, ancestral glyphs in the other, that is deemed salvific. One of those who go back to written characters as a linguistic panacea is, of course, Ezra Pound. J. H. Prynne inherits from Olson the credo that language, above all poetic language, must be spatialized, and in his correspondence with the elder poet formulates why this is the case. Prynne begins with Pound and his turn to the Chinese ideogram. Prynne first writes to Olson on 4 November 1961, betraying in that letter his considerable erudition in philology and foreign languages. In his second letter to Olson later that month, he deploys this learning to expose the simplifications and misapprehensions in Pound and Fenollosa's understanding of Chinese grammar, but, beyond this act of whistle-blowing, Prynne is compelled by the metalinguistics of their theory. Fenollosa's treatise, Prynne recalls, was not a work of empirical linguistics, but a metaphysics of language, which, bolstered by Pound's annotations, could alchemize poetic style with the occult energies in words. Fenollosa discerned in Chinese a propositional simplicity, a subject-predicate distillation, homologous to the 'transferences of force from agent to object in natural phenomena'. Prynne concludes: 'Hence the simple declarative sentence with its one transitive & active verb, furnishes the kinetic type'. Noting that his grammatical critique has a kinship with Olson's, Prynne voices his dissatisfaction with the linearity of the 'simple

[99] Charles Olson, *Collected Prose*, 156, 157.
[100] Charles Olson, *Collected Prose*, 156.

declarative sentence'. Fenollosa's sentence, like the Aristotelian proposition, has a hegemonic narrowness: 'Things are nouns, and particular substantives of this order are storehouses of potential energy, hoard up the world's available motions.' Far from revivifying Western linguistics with the energies of oriental languages, the formula produced by Fenollosa's treatise establishes its own 'UNIVERSE of discourse' founded on linguistic one-sidedness. 'But there are other energies', Prynne protests. This one-track model falsifies the dendrite maps of energy found in nature: the circulation of glucose or the irradiation of oxygen.[101]

Prynne rehabilitates the declarative sentence later in this letter with the proviso that it plot an exact sense of place, a deictic groundedness which he ascribes to Heidegger. In his later correspondence, though, he reverts to his initial misgivings. Prynne relates a debate about the 'kinetic thrust of the verse line' he had recently had with his Cambridge colleague, the poet and critic Donald Davie. Davie had eagerly welcomed Olson's early critical writings and told Prynne, from whom he had received the essay, that he had scrutinized 'Projective Verse' more closely than any dissertation on poetics since Fenollosa's treatise. Prynne writes:

My aim was to convince Donald of how wrong Fenollosa was about the transitive dynamics of Chinese sentence-structure, and also even to suggest that Pound himself came (in practice) to realise this: that the monolinear sequence offers too little breadth of narrative, too little space in which to deploy the larger patterns of awareness. The locus, that is, as well as the vector (or, as I revert to it, the noun as well as the verb).

The 'monolinear sequence', whether logical, as a proposition, or grammatical, as a declarative sentence, is too constrictive for the dimensions of modern epic. Consciousness, figured as those 'larger patterns of awareness', is not motored by a syllogistic ratio, able to be tabulated as statements, but knows spatially, through its orientation in the world. Prynne, like Olson, was a devotee of Maurice Merleau-Ponty, a philosopher whose theory of knowledge is premised on a replacement of the Cartesian cogito with *je peux*, signifying the capacity to act in a sensory world. To map this epistemological shift, as well as the projected faculties of modernist epic, language needs to operate geometrically; nouns and verbs are to interrelate like loci and vectors. This may sound like the daydream of a philosophical language,

---

[101] J. H. Prynne, 'Letter to Charles Olson, 4 November 1961' and 'Letter to Charles Olson, 26 November 1961', MS 206. Charles Olson Research Collection, Thomas J. Dodd Research Center, University of Connecticut Libraries.

as though Prynne believes contemporary metaphysics, Whitehead's cosmology or Merleau-Ponty's *être au monde*, can dissolve the chemical bonds of language and restructure it topologically. It is consonant with the utopian strains of this idea that Prynne says Pound's verse transcends the 'monolinear sequence' in its 'paradisiac nodes'. What would such verse actually look or sound like? Prynne, in fact, contrives that Pound's verse is spatialized within the confines of normative syntax: through structures of nominalizations and gerunds, which Prynne terms either 'nominal-gerundial' or 'a form of parallelistic gerundial patternment'.[102] In *'John Burke'* in the first volume of *The Maximus Poems*, Olson analyses the syntax of his own verse, and as Prynne says of Pound's, he asserts that it has sloughed off the confines of 'the monolinear sequence' through a latticework of nominalization:

A FOOTNOTE TO THE ABOVE,

> To speak in Yana-Hopi about these matters
> with which I, as Maximus, am concerned
> (which is Gloucester, and myself as here-
> a-bouts, in other words in *Maximus* local
> relations are nominalized) one would talk,
> Yana being a North California tongue, &
> Hopi is a language peculiarly adjusted to
> the topological as a prime and libidinal
> character of a man, and therefore of all of his
> proximities: metric then is mapping, and so,
> to speak modern cant, congruent means of
> making a statement), I, as Mr. Foster, went
> to Gloucester, thus:
>
> > "And past-I-go
> > Gloucester-insides
> > being Fosterwise of
> > Charley-once-boy
> > insides"[103]

Yana and Hopi are Native American languages whose grammatical idiosyncrasies Olson gleaned from reading the American linguist and

---

[102] J. H. Prynne, 'Letter to Charles Olson, 9 May 1963', MS 222. Charles Olson Research Collection. Thomas J. Dodd Research Center, University of Connecticut Libraries.

[103] Charles Olson, *The Maximus Poems*, n.p. [cf Charles Olson, *The Maximus Poems* (Berkeley: University of California Press, 1983), 149].

anthropologist Edward Sapir, specifically his monograph *Language*, first published in 1921.[104] Prynne's space language mentions only two grammatical classes, noun and verb, which he parallels with locus and vector; the topological speech of Yana, according to Sapir, likewise has only two parts of speech, noun and verb. What look like adjectives are, in fact, verbs.[105] The hyphenated adjective 'past-I-go' is the Yana version of 'I went', and this 'verbal adjective' premodifies the substantive 'Gloucester-insides'. When 'local relations are nominalized', as Olson claims happens in *The Maximus Poems*, prepositions that mark place and direction, as in 'Doctor Foster went to Gloucester', are welded to object nouns to form hyphenated nominalizations like 'Gloucester-insides'. These nominalizations fuse proper nouns, real people, and real places with their orientation and relatedness; they form a topological grammar, a language disposed like a map.

When the space grammar of Yana is transplanted into English, though, abominations of phrasing are sired. Olson knows this, of course, and none of the syntax of *The Maximus Poems* resembles this fantastical interlude. This discombobulated nursery rhyme, the Gloucester of children's verse set beside the Gloucester of modernist epic, is a self-deflating ecphrasis, allowing Maximus to play the licensed fool, commenting on the drama's tragic action in an aside of trenchant levity. The moral, though, is serious. Olson cares very deeply about fashioning a topological language in English, and the episode shows quite clearly what happens if you try to do so by rewriting the rules of syntax. Prynne's blueprint for radical nominalization seems unworkable for Olson. Around three weeks after discarding 'monolinear sequence' in favour of locus and vector, Prynne writes again to Olson with a slightly inflected linguistic scheme. He dives straight into those scholastic pyrotechnics of which Pound was so enamoured:

Dear Charles Olson,

          Energy was a will idea all right, even if they thought of it as <u>amor</u> or <u>lux</u>, setting the universe in an order of luminous tendential movement.

After quoting from the thirteenth-century theologian and philosopher Robert Grosseteste, famed for his metaphysics of light *De Luce*, and from the

[104] George M. Butterick, *A Guide to the Maximus Poems*, 202.

[105] J. H. Prynne, 'Letter to Charles Olson, 9 May 1963', MS 222. Charles Olson Research Collection. Thomas J. Dodd Research Center, University of Connecticut Libraries.

commentary of a contemporary scholar, Edgar de Bruyne, Prynne proposes
that such *splendor formae* might not yet have faded from the world:

> I suspect that we may not even have lost this, having simply rendered it
> into a language of more paramount abstraction; what, after all, lies just
> further than the enclosed notes just snatched out of the unknown? Vector
> as gerund, perhaps, and the universal field an interplay of intentions with
> the placement of proper nouns.

Gerundial vectors had little interest for Olson, but he did agonize over 'the
placement of proper nouns.'[106] After the death of his wife Bet in a car accident
in 1964, Olson resolved to inscribe a dedication to her at the front of the second edition of the second volume of *The Maximus Poems*. By 1968, Olson
has disowned the 1960 edition of volume II on account of the typographical inadequacy of its printing, and he was working on a reissue with Barry
Hall of Cape Goliard Press. He wrote to Hall spurning the stock solemnity
of a 'cold (& dry)' inscription he had previously sent him, saying, 'I want
something so moving & expressive'; he encloses the following:

Single space—narrower
(& *not* that s.s. of the book's type
except a (*equally narrow double space*) before the last line

[enclosed]

Bet

for Bet

for

Bet

For Bet[107]

What is so moving about this dedication is that it looks like a draft from
Maximus. That tireless care Olson takes over the placement of the words of
his verse suffuses the cosseting of this proper noun, as if affect and alignment
were one and the same. In a 1971 lecture on volume II of *The Maximus
Poems*, a year after Olson's death, Prynne speaks of a love that dilates both

---

[106] J. H. Prynne, 'Letter to Charles Olson, 29 May 1963', MS 222. Charles Olson Research
Collection, Thomas J. Dodd Research Center, University of Connecticut Libraries.
[107] Charles Olson, 'Letter to Barry Hall, 21 September 1968', in *Selected Letters*, 406–7
(p. 406).

language and the senses: 'Pound realized when he came to Cavalcanti: he realized that that Cavalcanti poem really had some understanding of the condition of love which could be extended through the language into the absolute curvature of the way a person's mind was open to what he heard and to what he saw and to what he felt.'[108] Pound, rendering Cavalcanti's poem, was also seeking a language of space, but to map the projections of *amor* he turned to typography, not gerundial vectors. Seeking a 'prime and libidinal' language, Olson feels for the smallest gradations of space—give it 'your *carefullest* care' he pleads with Hall as he palps each single space and double space—but this language does not unfold in linguistic convolutions; it moves in the intimacies of typography.[109]

5. 'Literal, real realty': Typography, Topology, and Property

Prynne's lecture on *Maximus* concludes with a vision of *l'amor che move il sole e l'altre stelle*: 'It is the singular, then, that makes it possible to consider the question of love as a complete part of the cosmos, and as love for the planet, as love for the whole.'[110] In local attention to spacing, in this affective bond with the minutiae of layout, inheres a passion for cosmogony. The typographical vision of *The Maximus Poems* is dizzyingly ambitious; it is meant to map out a whole world. Systems of typography, this book has suggested, tend to grandiose aspirations: perfect notations of sound, graphical renderings of thought. The expansiveness of cartography married with a passion for cosmology lends a grandiloquence to Olson's typographic designs. This is symptomatic of the poetics of the time. The Prynne of the 1971 *Maximus* lecture often sounds like a highly erudite mystic. Yet we need to keep pace with the grandeur of the vision to discern it at all, especially, as this chapter will go on to discuss, as Olson makes recurrent recourse to terms like 'real' and 'literal'. Cribbing from Olsonian nomenclature, the tonality of this poetics might be said to be projective. Olson intimates there is an aspirant quality in his poetics at the conclusion of his unpublished sequel to

---

[108] J. H. Prynne, 'Lecture on *Maximus IV, V, VI*' <http://charlesolson.org/Files/Prynnelecture2.htm> [accessed 8 January 2017] (para. 4 of 7).

[109] Charles Olson, 'Letter to Barry Hall, 21 September 1968', in *Selected Letters*, 406.

[110] J. H. Prynne, 'Lecture on *Maximus IV, V, VI*' <http://charlesolson.org/Files/Prynnelecture2.htm> [accessed 8 January 2017] (para. 6 of 7); Dante, *Paradiso*, ed. and trans. Robin Kirkpatrick (London: Penguin, 2007), 326.

'Human Universe', 'Human Universe II', where he returns to Edward Sapir, Whitehead, and 'Yana-Hopi' to flesh out his project for a language of space: 'And the projective – knowledge of our future act or change (or change of our condition as we stand here) is only to be proven – is not yet nor can it be a statement [...]'.[111] A non-propositional language, a spatial one, Olson implies, does not make the same truth claims as one that makes 'statements'. Projective has the sense of prospective, as if it is geared towards a utopian congruence of world and word without claiming to have achieved it, but needing that prospect lest verse stand still. Olson's mature poetics conceive of space as mapping rather than notation. The experimental typography of Olson's later poems, especially those comprising *Maximus IV, V, VI*, critiques conventional cartography, which is deemed to be warped by ownership and property.

The broadest prospects for poetry are descried in 'Projective Verse – II', a long essay which Olson drafts and redrafts but which, despite its being more fully worked out than many of his published essays, never finds its way into print. Speculative and ambitious, substituting the oracular brio of its prequel of 1950 for a metaphysical steeliness inherited from Whitehead, the essay marks out the scale of Olson's vision, an amplitude most discernible in passages like the following:

> The character of this art is ultimate. For it happens to coincide with the way things are. I don't propose here to make the case. I wish only to pull anyone's attention to the fact, that if a poem is taken in its aspect as thing, and the qualitative is left where it is always is, & has to be—implicated in the thing and only expressing itself by it—the power comes into the poet's hands.[112]

Olson derives this Orphic power, this belief that the poet's art coincides with 'the way things are', from an amplification of what prosody means. Prosody must keep step with advances in complex geometry and philosophy of science because its numbers are to cohere with all the myriad quantifications of the human universe. Following Whitehead, human and cosmos, mind and motion, are conceived as a sprawling tentacular network whose dimensions the poem must delineate: 'A poem must do equal justice to atomism, to

---

[111] Charles Olson, 'Human Universe II', MS 31:1586. Charles Olson Research Collection, Thomas J. Dodd Research Center, University of Connecticut Libraries.

[112] Charles Olson, 'Projective Verse II', MS 34. Charles Olson Research Collection. Thomas J. Dodd Research Center, University of Connecticut Libraries.

continuity, to causation, to memory, to perception, to quantitative as well as well as qualitative forms, and to extension (measureable existence in field). The most <u>active</u> or <u>creative</u> import of quantity, extension itself [...]'. In the morphing of the word 'quantity', the expansion of what prosody is to cover is readily apparent. While for Pound, who urged young apprentices to cut their teeth in composing sapphics, the term still denoted the *macra* and *brevia* of classical metres, according to Olson this usage has obsolesced for the modern versifier:

> We have replaced the old metronome of measure [...] [a]nd what has come in is quantity not as some antiqueness of classical languages (weighing syllables as durations of time in inflectional speech) but space itself, with its character and structure, lying in time alone intersecting it, so that art in verse today is light signals and mass points, both of which needs rigidity and restores flux to this creation so that it too is experiential (instead of highfallutin, and aesthetic (!) noble and all that.

Space comes in, and typography, its function and possibilities, is transfigured in 'Projective Verse – II'. The theoretician of 1950 still clung to the topos that the page was like sheet music, and, properly disposed, the printed text could notate the total acoustics of the poem. Prosody was the entire sound-world of verse, phonocentric metrics honed to pinpoint accuracy; *macra* and *brevia* were still quanta of sound to be recorded. The 'stave and the bar' along with 'the old metronome of verse' is dispensed with in 'Projective Verse – II'. Olson abandons the analogy of musical notation to which so many poets and critics turn to define experimental typography. Quantity and duration have nothing to do with minims and crotchets or dactyls and trochees in this essay; they always signify space and time, imagined geometrically via Whitehead's theory of extension. The sole vestige of this musical lexicon is 'rest', but even that term denotes something closer to a node in a network than a pause on a bar line. Sound isn't erased from verse in this treatise, but its presence or absence is more felt than heard, and a 'rest' is described as 'what amounts in our art to both traction and silence'.[113]

A contempt for 'highfallutin' artifice, for any stylistic pieties, spurred the author of the original 'Projective Verse, led him to liken verse to a play of forces, a 'high energy construct'. This disdain for traditional aesthetics—glossed as 'noble and all that'—and, indeed, the experience of actually

---

[113] Charles Olson, 'Projective Verse II', MS 34. Charles Olson Research Collection, Thomas J. Dodd Research Center, University of Connecticut Libraries.

composing *The Maximus Poems*, unwritten at the time of the first treatise, impels Olson to delete voice, music, and song from this account of versifying. Poetry is spoken of as the stuff of physics, as though verse were the conglomeration and dispersal of matter in a miniature cosmos:

> Because [conservative poets] don't start wide enough to go for the target, to give themselves launching platform, there are no eliminations, none of the pleasure (to the reader) of what's left out, the 'silences' (spaces) which embody the light, which draw it up. The poem does not travel through anything it merely accretes to itself substance.

A critique of typography is interwoven into this passage. Conventional typography merely lumps together preformed, inert blocks of text, 'rigid bodies of verse', while experimental typography embraces a dialectic of white space and black text, of light and substance. The birth of a world of space, set free from traditional numbers, is storied in the short essay 'THE LIE OF 10, OR THE CONCEPT OF ZERO'. Poetic form capitulates to mere expediency in adhering to simple quantities:

> 10 is nothing anywhere else but handy and boring – dollars and tallies, and statistics etc: and overlays and creates bad psyches and bad verse (Dante was clear 11 syllables etc – and the Alexandrine stinks as does 10 in English – the dead pentameter, da dum da dum da dum da dum da dum

In this numerical fable the advent of zero, which Olson likens to the adoption of the number in Western mathematics from its Arabic source, destabilizes fixed formal quantities. Loosed from the tens and twelves of metrics, Olson sees himself drawing a new world with his fingertips:

> The Cosmos rushes in. All flows, right by my fingertip, which doesn't raise itself. Therefore nothing enters. If I lift it, wow: I'm changed. Nothing will be the same again. At least it won't be as it was. It is.[114]

The punning on nothing here, divested of any Shakespearean solemnity, registers a light-headedness and a levity, as though Olson is apprised of the

---

[114] Charles Olson, 'Projective Verse II', MS 34; Charles Olson, 'THE LIE OF 10, OR THE CONCEPT OF ZERO', MS 16: 576. Charles Olson Research Collection, Thomas J. Dodd Research Center, University of Connecticut Libraries.

ease with which he can sprawl into the page under this rubric and a slight sense of vertigo at the possibilities. He goes on to schematize this airy space at the bottom of the typescript (see Figure 11).

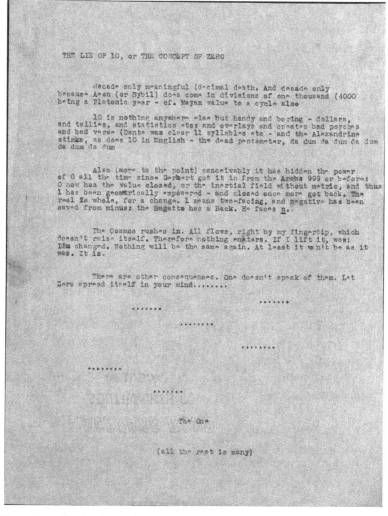

Figure 11. Charles Olson, 'THE LIE OF 10, OR THE CONCEPT OF ZERO', box 16, folder 576, Charles Olson Research Collection, Thomas J. Dodd Research Center, University of Connecticut Libraries. Works by Charles Olson published during his lifetime are copyright the Estate of Charles Olson; previously unpublished works are copyright the University of Connecticut. Used with permission.

When quantity goes out, space comes in. In 1969, while Olson is pushing his verse to the outer limits of typographical possibility in the drafts for the third volume of *The Maximus Poems*, the Belgian poet and artist Marcel Broodthaers produces an artist's book of Mallarmé's *Un coup de dés*, in which the text is replaced with black lines, reducing the poem to the pure shape of its mise-en-page. These stepped ellipses likewise furnish the bare typographical blueprint for an unwritten poem. Implicit in the erasure of text is a radical shifting of structural weight to typography, the supposition that layout can form the primary building block of a new order of verse.

The poem most conscious of Olson's cosmogonic ambition, his project to build a world of space, is 'A Maximus' (see Figure 12). This is one of Olson's most careful constellations of nouns.[115] Olson is intractable about the correctness of its disposition. Having drawn up the poem in pencil manuscript, he retains the layout in several subsequent typescripts, refraining from his habitual tinkering. '[Spacings here exactly in same proportions as here]' and 'Print [as is]', he writes in the margins of the setting typescript. Preparing the poem for publication with Jonathan Williams in the mid-1960s, he scribbles 'all these spaces too fucking awful' on a page proof with slight inaccuracies in line-spacing, and then fulminates in block capitals which cover the whole sheet: 'I REQUIRE HERE UTTERLY AND ABSOLUTELY IDENTICAL spacing to attached XEROX of MS'.[116] Olson is so enraged by these discrepancies because the poem is a microcosm of the spatial cartography of *The Maximus Poems* as a whole; its dimensions are synecdochic of the calculated measurements of the poem at large. That topological language of substantives disposed in a spatial field which Olson and Prynne envisioned is here realized on the page. The nodes are the *dramatis personae* of the principal actors of his verse: his rival poet Vincent Ferrini, whom he 'clobbered' in 'Letter 5'; the explorer John Smith, whose 'ADVERTISEMENTS' he praised in 'Letter 15'; and even the plum tree of 'Letter 9' whose arborescence symbolized the printing of 'IN COLD HELL, IN THICKET'. This constellation is an ecphrastic map of the whole poem, miniaturizing Olson's scheme to hold his cosmos in graphical equipoise. This ecphrasis, like the hybrid of Yana-Hopi and 'Doctor Foster went to Gloucester', is premised on

---

[115] This typescript is preceded by an autograph manuscript where Olson plots this layout in pencil. There is a subsequent typescript without any autograph additions, followed by a fair-copy setting typescript and an early page proof. The earlier annotated typescript shown in Figure 11 has its typography accurately reproduced in the published versions.

[116] Charles Olson, 'A Maximus', MS 2:63. Charles Olson Research Collection, Thomas J. Dodd Research Center, University of Connecticut Libraries.

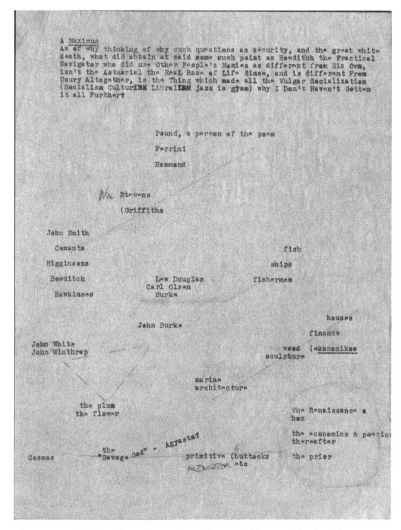

Figure 12. Charles Olson, 'A Maximus', box 2, folder 63, Charles Olson Research Collection, Thomas J. Dodd Research Center, University of Connecticut Libraries. Works by Charles Olson published during his lifetime are copyright the Estate of Charles Olson; previously unpublished works are copyright the University of Connecticut. Used with permission.

a self-awareness of Olson's poetic enterprise. There is a grain of self-parody in the inclusion of 'Cosmos' as a node in his chart, and the underlining in the title 'A Maximus' expresses this ambivalence. Underlining is often shorthand in typescript for italicization, so the title can be read 'A *Maximus*', as though the poem were a bibliographic miniature; the indefinite article and the maintenance of the underlining in the printed version tempers this claim while allowing it to stand.

'A Maximus' typifies an ingrained dynamic in *The Maximus Poems* which its experiments in typography manifest. This cartography of the page is animated by Olson's thinking on territory and economics: how to chart and reclaim ownership. After transmogrifying English syntax in the baroque parody of a Yana-Hopi nursery rhyme, the subsequent poem lays out a language of space to which Olson is seriously committed. '*Letter, May 2, 1959*' is another typographical map, and it is also a property map, transcribing the buildings and boundaries of seventeenth-century Gloucester, their locations and proprietors. Olson keenly enumerates how these settlers measured their property. Metrical feet are the surveyor's footsteps in that poem, the '230 paces' or '300 paces' in which land is registered and assigned. Olson was compelled by the shape ownership assumes and how it is graphed on the page.[117] Admiralty charts and topographies are interspersed with account books and inventories. The map of 'A Maximus' is prefaced by a revision of Pound's anti-Semitic economic demonology ('isn't the Actuarial the ReaL Base of Life and is different from Usury altogether') and of the predatory accountancy of Nathaniel Bowditch, a navigator and mathematician who made himself trustee of 'other people's monies.' Accountancy has its own typography, which is, in its way, expressive. Later in *Maximus IV, V, VI*, after another map, comes this inventory of the Gloucester merchant Benjamin Ellery, from whose account book Olson culls this list of subcategories:

The Account Book of B Ellery
    vessels
    goods
    voyages
    persons
    salaries
    conveyances[118]

This is the mise-en-page of commodification, a tabulation that equates assets liquid and solid, thing conveyed and mode of conveyance. Millimetres

---

[117] Charles Olson, *Maximus Poems IV, V, VI* (London: Cape Goliard Press, 1968) n.p. [cf Charles Olson, *The Maximus Poems* (Berkeley: University of California Press, 1983), 150.
[118] Charles Olson, *Maximus Poems IV, V, VI*, n.p. [cf Charles Olson, *The Maximus Poems* (Berkeley: University of California Press, 1983), 204.

separate categories: fractional indentations where 'persons' are aligned with 'goods' but kept apart from 'salaries' by hair-line spaces. This account book is another type of property map: a graphic where the discrete qualities of men and cargo are consigned to the narrowest minima of typographical variance.

The preamble to 'Human Universe – II' synthesizes the topology of its famous prequel with a theory of economics. It begins:

> Human Universe – II
>> topology: that all things are actually placed, in place of one
>>> sort or another, literally; and that this in itself,
>>> that they are and they do suffer deformation
>>> are moved do moved (motility or abused or exploited or
>>> simply moved; or that things moved then join or did
>>> join identical object condition, no matter what
>>> for sale, to be seen gone to etc.[119]

Styled as a metaphysical treatise *à la mode*, this essay follows Whitehead in its grafting of mathematical lexis onto speculative philosophy. From *Process and Reality* is taken the notion of a primal extension, a metaphysical lattice-work that is prior to time and space. As Whitehead puts it, 'The extensiveness of space is really the spatialization of extension; and the extensiveness of time is really the temporalization of extension.'[120] Of course, it should be noted, however immaterial 'extension' to supposed to be here, that the very term, the lexicon of Whitehead's prose, is inalienably spatial. (Try imagining, expressing, or drawing a non-spatial extension). Olson moulds Whitehead's concept into a theory of topological resilience, a spatial identity in things that cannot be erased. The abuse and exploitation of mercantilism, the deracination of people and the uprooting of goods, are figured as deformations, but deformations like those of mathematical topology: shapes twisted and reconfigured, but whose transformations can accounted for, however complex the equations. The eye that can discern these deformations, says Olson, has 'a point-by-point mapping power of such flexibility that whatever stays the same, no matter where it goes and into whatever varying conditions, it can follow'. The typography of 'A <u>Maximus</u>' possesses this cartographic percipience. Even in the atomization of its spacing, it traces ley lines of

[119] Charles Olson, 'Human Universe II', MS 31:1586. Charles Olson Research Collection, Thomas J. Dodd Research Center, University of Connecticut Libraries.
[120] Alfred North Whitehead, *Process and Reality*, 340.

economic causality and constellations of value. The diagonal alignment of 'fish / ships / fishermen' maps the fixed stars of Gloucester's economy, its south-westerly course corresponding with 'houses / finance / wood sculpture / marine architecture', alignments underscored in the typescript with pencil lines. Such charting is true metrics for Olson, not trochees and iambs: a dispassionate map of the world's quantities. Such a map of objects, claims Olson, 'supplies its own metrical, quantity isn't dead old reason, it is moved about in exchange, public-place is a genuine action, ekonomics is a reason, the transfer from quantity to goods is legit, something has happened and congruence is its name'. Metrics and economics are 'legit' when expressed as 'congruence', when their full geometry is allowed to unfurl. This map-making in type is its own manner of audit, but unlike the graphical constriction of Ellery's account book with its constrictive mercantile equivalences, the topos of exchange is allowed to sprawl in all its extended complexity.

What Olson's exploded typography charts, then, is a hidden mappemonde, a geometry in the 'human universe' that is ordinarily occluded. There is a defiance in the sense of topology in 'Human Universe – II': that things have a spatial identity which, however modified and misappropriated, persists. In the hands of another poet this might lead to a blood-and-soil, chthonic nationalism, but Olson, a poet of migrations, ever linking Gloucester with its distant roots, wards off such politics with the pliancy of his scheme, its deformations and transformations, its tolerance of change. Conservative plottings of space have their own agenda. The closed typography of account books and inventories is not transparent or neutral, but wedded to economic simplifications. Disburdening himself from the strictures of Fenollosa's grammar, Prynne considers how the natal extensiveness of language may be earned, and what 'so articulates the sentence that it may move with purpose & effect along its own line'. Prynne shapes this projective sentence after a primal act of freedom, a casting-off from land into sea: 'And if it needs no question how the rocks on the shore may allow us to push on them to start out to sea, how is the human agent so endowed, with the right to function as the noun (the pro-noun) subject of the sentence (of his own life)? [...]'. But this nautical map of human and linguistic agency, of untrammelled navigation in a sea of possibility, is not the one 'humanity' has to steer by. Prynne continues:

Commonly of course humanity is not so endowed, lives on the most fragile of credit, on a purely virtual instrument devised and maintained

by the tacit agreement of others never to ask to see the map for themselves. Access to the fundament is earned by the mind's geologers, the
passions which will forge out availably valid starting points, and lend
them to those few others prepared to profit. Writers have always done
this, and poets have always gone deeper & more tenaciously than any
into these soundless risks.[121]

Like the inherited forms of grammar, most people's spatial ambit is predetermined; in Prynne's account, their field of activity is plotted in lines of
credit. Space is coextensive with the flow of capital, and the chart of this
fact is withheld by those in power. Cartography here is occult, conspir-
atorial, 'maintained by the tacit agreement of others', the proxy mapping
of financiers. Literature, though—poetry pre-eminently—retains a superior
discernment of space. As in Olson's 'Human Universe – II', topology is also
economics. Poets, heuristically, map out rival charts of value, communicate
their insights like creditors who 'lend them to those few others prepared
to profit'. Prosodic experiment is bathymetrical here; a sounding out of
uncharted spaces; a plumbing of 'soundless risks'.

Writing to Olson a year later, in February 1963, Prynne nurtures this conviction about the cartographical privilege of poets. Wishing to 'celebrate the
geographic in between: expanse' and pull together a 'first gathering of the
lines', Prynne lays out his first numbered meditation in a verbless drift of
noun phrases, an apt exordium for his credal faith in substantives: '1. The
sense of history as field: the convergence of necessities & the imagination,
the shaping of a language to climate, coast-line: process held down firmly
enough to yield the substantive kernels of it, the megaliths, the primary
nodes. The spaces are intimate, the reality formal (even for us cartographic)
[…]'. Prynne whispers to Olson that reality for them is formal as a quantum
physicist might say that to their peers, intimating a hermetic perception of
structure opaque to the common eye. That pronoun 'us' and the hushed
parentheses are telling, sequestering this map-making amongst a cenacle
of poets. It was Pound, Prynne goes on to say, who 'set up a great cartographic' and who adumbrates this clandestine art. What sets them apart is
their sense of time, of the deep time of geology and archaeology, as space:
ancestral 'megaliths' are contemporary for them, the 'primary nodes' of
their maps. Modernists, Prynne claims, have dissented from a sequential
sense of time, which he terms a 'chronologic conspiracy'. This discrepant

---

[121] J. H. Prynne, 'Letter to Charles Olson, 26 November 1961', MS 206. Charles Olson
Research Collection. Thomas J. Dodd Research Center, University of Connecticut Libraries.

metaphysics he dates from Wyndham Lewis's critique of Henri Bergson's *durée* in *Time and Western Man*. Bergson had proffered melody as a schema for *durée* in his *Essai sur les données immédiates de la conscience*, a liquid concatenation of past moments, but Lewis sees in this musicalized self an enervating repetitiousness and a stultifying determinism, to which he opposes an ontology of things 'standing apart – the wind blowing between them'. Quoting 'Projective Verse', Prynne sees Olson's field poetics as the heir to Lewis's draughty expanse and concludes: 'So that time is a governing absolute within the process, the immersal in the poem and its coming to be; but the achieved kinetics of the thing on the page are tensions, which is the idiom of poem as construct or diagram rather than passage or transit [...]'.[122] Lecturing on Olson's *Maximus*, Prynne keeps insisting that the poet's sense of land and territory bucks quotidian definitions: '[B]y land I do not mean that superficial notion of terrain, but the whole compact history of the planet [...]'.[123] Apprised of hidden historical densities, Olson's verse converts time into space. The energy of composition and research, 'the immersal in the poem', is transmuted into typographical constructs, 'the achieved kinetics of the thing on the page'. Eyeing the terrain of Gloucester with a sense of its impacted histories, geological, economic, nautical, Olson spurns conventional property maps for the deep cartography of poetry.

Volume II of *The Maximus Poems* is devoted to this subterranean cartography as it maps out the defunct settlement of Dogtown, abandoned since 1830, its land subsumed by present-day Gloucester and Rockport. Olson charts the ossific presence of Dogtown in the soil of Gloucester by thickening the texture of the page:

Dogtown the <u>under</u>
vault heaven
is Carbon Ocean   Dogtown the <u>under</u>
is Annisquam   vault – the 'mother'
               rock : the Diamond (Coal) the Pennsylvanian

                              Age   the soft
                              (Coal) LOVE[124]

---

[122] J. H. Prynne, 'Letter to Charles Olson, 3 February 1963', MS 206. Charles Olson Research Collection. Thomas J. Dodd Research Center, University of Connecticut Libraries.

[123] J. H. Prynne, 'Lecture on *Maximus IV, V, VI*', <www.charlesolson.org/Files/Prynnelecture1.htm> [accessed 8 January 2017] (para. 12 of 12).

[124] Charles Olson, *Maximus Poems IV, V, VI*, n.p. [cf Charles Olson, *The Maximus Poems* (Berkeley: University of California Press, 1983), 180.

As throughout *The Maximus Poems*, this expanded unit of text, three discrete sections of print, spans what is elsewhere the allotment of a verse line:
the time it takes the reading eye to pass from one margin to another. Two
directions of reading are overlaid, downward and rightward, and Olson does
not cleanly segment them so they flow sequentially, like the stepped text
blocks of '*I, Maximus of Gloucester, to You*', but has them overlap, the second
block beginning halfway down the first one, parallel with 'is Carbon Ocean'
rather than beneath 'is Annisquam'. Phrasing and lexis is repeated, the visual
echoing of words inducing a kind of stereoscopy, as though a singular block
of text has been stratified into three. Noun phrases are recurrently staggered,
broken over line endings, and 'the Pennsylvanian Age' divided by a blank
line of print. This is the slow, iterative compaction of geological time, typography decelerating and imbricating the kinetics of reading, so that the heavy,
carbonic formation of Dogtown can be discerned. The upper and lower road
of Dogtown, Olson posits in '<u>Letter 72</u>', accreted with glacial speed, con-
crescing beneath the ground from moraine, and like the buried forms of
geology, Olson plots the property boundaries of the settlement's long dead
townsfolk (see Figure 13).

By comparing topographic surveys he acquired from the City Engineer's Office with the map of Dogtown drawn up by Joshua Batchelder,
an eighteenth-century surveyor, Olson locates the homes of Bennett, Davis,
Hilton, and Elwell beneath the surface of modern-day Gloucester, reckoning
their latitudes, 'above 75" and 'inside 125", and the feet between their properties.[125] The 'garden of Ann' is that of Ann Robinson, the wife of Samuel Davis,
and 'Elizabeth' may allude to Olson's own wife.[126] The poem is an epithala-
mion, a hymn to marital and territorial harmony, each property founded
on the 'love & hand-holding' of matrimony. Olson figures his reclamation
of the Edenic contours of the land as a redirecting of the lines of typography. Arrows, present from the first pencil manuscript right up to the printed
version, signal the orientations of reading. The right-facing arrow overlays
the placement of Bennett's on a line of topography with the placement of
the print line on the page. Topographical and typographical reading merge,
as though both acts of looking demarcate place and assign boundaries. The

---

[125] This typescript is preceded by an autograph pencil manuscript with many of the same
graphical features as later typescripts and the printed versions. There are four later extant typescripts, some of which omit the arrows but maintain the lineation. There is also a xeroxed
copy of an early typescript that contains the pencilled arrows, suggesting Olson wished to
incorporate them into the published version.

[126] George M. Butterick, *A Guide to the Maximus Poems*, 328.

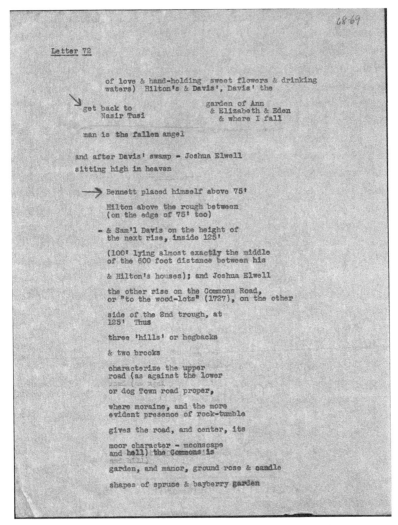

Figure 13. Charles Olson, 'Letter 72', box 2, folder 84, Charles Olson Research Collection, Thomas J. Dodd Research Center, University of Connecticut Libraries. Works by Charles Olson published during his lifetime are copyright the Estate of Charles Olson; previously unpublished works are copyright the University of Connecticut. Used with permission.

unfamiliar bearing of the diagonal vector marks the phantasmal mapping invoked here. Olson not only descries the skeletons of defunct homesteads, but the exhortation "get back to / Nasir Tusi" refers to the Islamic theologian whose angelology haunts *Maximus IV, V, VI*, a doctrine where all earthly souls have an eternal counterpart.[127] Behind the layout of contemporary Gloucester, then, is the abiding spectre of Dogtown: beneath the clean lines of modern topography is the Edenic after-image of the settlers' properties, an uncanny double vision written into the diagonal typography, the two blocks of text unloosed from sequential reading, hanging in mirrored equipoise.

Reorienting the bearings of reading, Olson's typography maps out space warped by its impacted past, its economic and geological histories—a topography alien to the settled amnesia of the property map. The map of Gloucester morphs as Dogtown resurfaces; it skews and denatures our sense of space and print. Olson has his own adjective for this disjointed sense of space: kooky. Filmed at his home in Gloucester for a documentary in 1966, Olson reads out another poem on the deep time of Dogtown's geology. 'That's a lovely poem,' he comments, 'kooky, like; just made of nothing but Shaler's geology.' After the kookiness of geology, Olson immediately relates the kookiness of getting lost:

> And one day I was up … I got lost, by the way. Everybody laughs about … and in fact, people get lost and die. And like I'm supposed to know, like, everything. But here I am, the first time up on top of a goddamn field, I couldn't find my way out … like any other goddamn fool, blueberry picker or anybody else! They have to send fire departments up there and boy scouts. I mean, it's a kooky thing.[128]

Explaining how Dogtown should be laid out on the page in *Maximus IV, V, VI*, Olson retains the term with a slight inflection of its suffix to describe his typography:

> The problem here is the *disparateness* of the whole work: the book *depends* upon these *kooked balances* throughout. Each poem needs to be set individually for itself on each page, irregularly though that may seem, and going against normal justifying. I have in as many instances as possible included or had xerox'd my original mss. so that *all spaces both between words as well as between lines* – as well as *location on the page* may be followed.

---

[127] George M. Butterick, *A Guide to the Maximus Poems*, 354.
[128] Charles Olson, *Muthologos*, I, 181.

Olson hails Melville for his disruption of chronometry, for his fracturing of clock time through his newfound sense of space, and in another version of this letter, Olson likens these 'kooked balances' to the jewels and cogs of watchmaking.[129] Time is flattened in this frozen horology, its springs and escapements laid out on the page. Temporal flux is spaced out in typographical design. Unearthing the morainal genesis of Dogtown or its buried polity, making these deep times contemporary, unbalances settled chronometry. This kooky time generates a kooked typography. 'Normative justifying' would be a false form of measurement. Demotic and carefree as kookiness sounds as an aesthetic watchword, this metaphor of an offset chronometer does not license a formal laxity or a carefree inexactitude in layout. Rather, Olson insists on the concinnity of his design, its mensurational accuracy. Later in the 1966 documentary where he attests to the kookiness of his verse, a member of the camera crew gestures to a composite map of Dogtown in Olson's bedroom. 'That's not a map, that's a topgraphical [sic] creation!' Olson responds. Asked by the interviewer Richard Moore whether it is a 'working chart for the new *Maximus*', Olson demurs, but he goes on to relate the cartography of Dogtown's eighteenth-century surveyor, Joshua Batchelder, to his own mapmaking in verse:

> Well, each one of them [entries on the poet's map] is the extent of the property of each of the houses that I was able to start with, the exact location in rods and poles of this marvellous fellow named Batchelder, who did this with chains—they called them chains—for measurement. (They do still.) And poles for rods, right; a pole is a rod, I think. And the chain bearers carry the lengths. So that you could be ... I just found that I could be extremely precise about something, by the way, that's become a piece of absolute ... I mean the thing—like we spoke earlier of the covered wagon that's covered America. I mean that cuteness which has ruined all. Literal, real realty—realty and personality, too! [Laughs.] That's what I'm talking ... that's what this thing is, is an attempt to just introduce some accuracy into shit. Cute shit. Cute, nominative crap.

Dogtown is not a 'cute name', Olson earlier affirms, and he execrates the shallowness of conventional mapmaking, its prettifying onomastics, and the '[c]ute, nominative crap' of its reliance on naming. This is a wishful map of

---

[129] Charles Olson, 'Note on typesetting', MS 159. Charles Olson Research Collection, Thomas J. Dodd Research Center, University of Connecticut Libraries.

America, the 'covered wagon' of romanticized pioneers. True cartography is patient measurement, the precision of Batchelder's surveying with chains and rods. '[T]he literal is an invention of language and power the same as numbers', Olson asserts in a 1965 lecture, and he uses the same adjective when stipulating the measurements of his typography.[130] His spacings must be preserved as accurately as possible, he tells his printer in 1968, to maintain *'the "flat" literal effect those poems require'*.[131] A flat literality is what an accurate map promises: a precise translation of place onto the dimensions of a page. Plotting 'literal, real realty' beneath maps of real estate and 'normative justifying', Olson's typography lays claim to a kookier space, a layout apprised of the alien precisions, the impacted forces of geology and migration, that shape the land.

---

[130] Charles Olson, *Muthologos*, I, 186, 188, 94.
[131] Charles Olson, 'Letter to Barry Hall, 12 July 1968', in *Selected Letters*, 405.

Conclusion

Experimental Typography, Typographical Revivals, and *Die neue Typographie*

Many of the most esteemed typographers and graphic designers of the last century were wholly contemptuous of the idea that experimental typography existed at all. They may well have disapproved of this book. They deemed that modernism in printing was, at best, a passing aberration and that the art of mise-en-page was not susceptible to sudden change. Contemporaneous with the graphical experimentation of Anglo-American poets, though, typography at large was reimagined. When the contemporary historian of design and practising typographer Robert Bringhurst refers to the nineteenth century as a 'dark and inflationary age in typography and type design', he is espousing a view that dominates the twentieth century.[1] In Britain, the vanguard of reform featured the Catholic engraver and book designer Eric Gill who sought to remedy the perceived malaise of the preceding century through a synthesis of artisanal know-how and utilitarian pragmatism; the principles of typographical reform were promulgated by Beatrice Warde through essays, lectures, and journals like *The Fleuron*; and as typographical consultant for the Monotype Corporation, Stanley Morison oversaw the cutting of a new family of typefaces apt for mass dissemination and shaped by his reformist principles. Likewise, in Europe and Russia, artists, designers, and teachers, especially those affiliated with the Bauhaus school, chiefly Jan Tschichold, Moholy-Nagy, and El Lissitzky, proclaimed the birth of *Die neue Typographie* and articulated visions of a technologized typography refitted after the analogues of photography, recording, and telecommunications. Poet and typographer are traditionally separate vocations, but much of this book has been concerned with

---

[1] Robert Bringhurst, *The Elements of Typographic Style* (Point Roberts, WA: Hartley & Marks, 2005), 28.

The Graphics of Verse. Daniel Matore, Oxford University Press. © Daniel Matore (2023).
DOI: 10.1093/oso/9780192857217.003.0005

how the former encroached upon the domain of the latter. But it is salutary to think about how the typographer, sceptical or intrigued, might have glanced at what the poets were up to. Typography and graphic design have their own standards, traditions, and knowledge independent of literature. While neither being drawn to one profession or the other, nor favouring innovation or conservatism, it is instructive to examine these two traditions side by side. What this conclusion will consider is how the visual experiments of modernist poets concord with or dissent from the canons and tastes of professional typography in order to cast the graphics of verse into sharper relief as well as to lay claim to the transatlanticism of this visual flourishing.

Implicated though they are in various reforms and revivals, twentieth-century typographers often baulk at the notion that what they are doing is, properly speaking, innovatory. In his concise treatise *First Principles of Typography*, written in 1936, Morison, who oversaw the production of Times New Roman, opines:

> It is of the essence of typography and of the nature of the printed book *qua* book, that it perform a public service. For single or individual purpose there remains the manuscript, the codex; so there is something ridiculous in the unique copy of a printed book, though the number of copies printed may justifiably be limited when a book is the medium of typographical experiment [. . .] Typography today does not so much need Inspiration or Revival as Investigation.

Print is inhospitable to experiment, and the medieval scribe, following Morison's reasoning, has more artistic licence than the modern typographer. The *raison d'être* of typography, since Gutenberg mechanized the codex, is mass replication. *Ipso facto*, its aesthetics are subject to public ratification. Printing for one's own eyes is to ape the culture proper to manuscripts. Morison continues:

> No printer should say, 'I am an artist, therefore I am not to be dictated to. I will create my own letter forms,' for, in this humble job, such individualism is not helpful to an audience of any size. It is no longer possible, as it was in the infancy of the craft, to persuade society into the acceptance of strongly marked and highly individualistic types—because literate society is so much greater in mass and correspondingly slower in movement. Type design moves at the pace of the most conservative reader. The good

type-designer therefore realises that, for a new font to be successful, it has to be so good that only very few recognise its novelty.[2]

Securus judicat orbis terrarum, St Augustine's famous pronouncement on church doctrine, might well be adopted as the motto of typographical aesthetics.[3] Only through ecclesial and catholic consensus is change to occur. Typography, as many of its practitioners and students imply, is the property of the whole body of the literate public. Connoisseurship in poetry, fine art, or music may be licensed by the selectiveness of their audiences. Print, though, cannot be limited to a *soirée*, an occasional séance, or a solitary communion; it is quotidian and ubiquitous. The eyes which scan the daily newspaper are the same as those which are alerted by the traffic sign and those which read a book of verse. Typography is constrained by all these proliferating viewings. According to this conservative standpoint, experiment must be below the threshold of common perception.

It could therefore be claimed that typography must at once be a high art and a low art, since unwittingly the common reader assents to newness in typography and at the same time the connoisseur descries the tasteful slightness of what has been inflected. Five years earlier, Gill adumbrated Morison's principles in his *Essay on Typography*, though the bibliographical difference between the two monographs—that Gill's is a limited edition hand-press book set in a custom-made typeface, while Morison's is a mass-produced volume published by Cambridge University Press—manifests a discrepancy in their ideologies. Gill argues that it is right that typography is founded on corporate assent, but it ought not to depend on the masses:

> The more serious the class of book [the typographer] prints, the wider the public to whom he appeals, so much the more solemn and impersonal and normal will & should be his typography. But he will not call that book serious which is merely widely bought, & he will not call that a wide appeal which is made simply to a mob of forcibly educated proletarians. A serious book is one which is good in itself according to standards of goodness set by infallible authority, and a wide appeal is one made to intelligent people of all times and nations.

[2] Stanley Morison, *First Principles of Typography* (Cambridge: Cambridge University Press, 1936), 2, 5.

[3] John Henry Newman, *Apologia Pro Vita Sua*, ed. Ian Ker (London: Penguin, 2004), 116.

Typographer was, for Gill, an uncomfortable mantle to bear. The *Essay* attempts to justify how an artisanal worker, a craftsman at home with stone and wood, can, in good conscience, work with print, with the demotic compromises of typography. A segregation between the two worlds, between handiwork and industrialism, between the codex and the printed book, is often the only settlement to which Gill can acquiesce: 'The conflict between Industrialism & the ancient methods of handicraftsmen which resulted in the muddle of the 19th century is now coming to its term [. . .] The two worlds can see one another distinctly and without recrimination, both recognizing what is good in the other—the power of Industrialism, the humanity of craftsmanship.'[4] There are moments, though, when the artisan transcends the mob of the temporal world and, loosed from commercialism, communes with the 'infallible authority' of the ages, a sainthood of 'all times and nations'.[5] The conservatism of Morison's typography was predicated on its publicity and serviceability, in step with the slow gyrations of the contemporary readership and the drift of collective memory. Gill's typography, though, is slower still. Its audience is dead; its aesthetics are those of eternity, a mystical body of typographical connoisseurs.

Conservatism, then, would seem to be a virtue particular to typography, native to it. The treatises of Gill and Morison enunciate a thesis ingrained in the theory and criticism of typography. They are reformers who do not believe in reform. Where classicism in another art form—say, painting— might espouse transcendent ideals which admit of quite different material permutations, so that the same critic might descry *harmony* in Raphael and Picasso, despite their wildly incongruous techniques, the classicism of typography does not allow for such local variation. Typographical conservatism holds that the principles of good design are immutable and that its incarnations in print can but scarcely diverge. A fifteenth-century page by Aldus Manutius and an eighteenth-century page by John Baskerville ought not to look all that different. Letters are identities: they call for recognition far more urgently than melodies or figures, and so the dictates of legibility constrict innovation.

Accordingly, when Bringhurst introduces his history and taxonomy *The Elements of Typographic Style*, perhaps the most esteemed recent volume of

[4] Eric Gill, *An Essay on Typography* (London: Sheed & Ward, 1931), 67, 1.
[5] Gill, *An Essay on Typography*, 67.

its kind, the conservatism of mise-en-page is not classed as a historically conditioned theory, a peculiar strain of thought, but as the natural state of print:

> The principles of typography as I understand them are not a set of dead conventions but the tribal customs of the magic forest, where ancient voices speak from all directions and new ones move to unremembered forms [...] Letterforms change constantly yet differ very little, because they are alive. The principles of typographic clarity have also scarcely altered since the second half of the fifteenth century, when the first books were printed in roman type. Indeed, most of the principles of legibility and design explored in this book were known and used by Egyptian scribes writing hieratic script with reed pens on papyrus in 1000 BCE.

He continues: 'Typography is the craft of endowing human language with a durable visual form, and thus with an independent existence.'[6] Since the expected serviceability of typography moulds its aesthetics, typographers are called upon to work both inside and outside of history. Their handiwork gains traction by very close contact with preceding and contemporary printing, but they are to shape something that will not be anachronistic for readers decades hence. So wedded is Adorno's *Aesthetic Theory* to the idea that the 'concept of art is located in a historically changing constellation of elements' that it is haunted by the spectre of the death of art.[7] A phenomenon predicated on transience seems itself doomed to pass away. Typography, by contrast, seems undying. Not quite canonized by the honorific of great art, it thereby wards off such attendant evanescence.

   Does, then, experimental typography exist? Are twentieth-century poets likewise constrained by the innate conservatism of print? How can such a recalcitrant medium be made the organon of radical change? One answer to this is vocational. As editors, many modernist poets became acquainted with recent typographical fashions and lent their support to different schools. Eliot, at the helm of Faber, has been said to have had 'whatever typeface he liked' and to have followed American tastes in supporting the revival of the eighteenth-century typeface Bell as well as rejecting the original typeface

---

[6] Robert Bringhurst, *The Elements of Typographic Style*, 9, 10, 11.
[7] Theodor W. Adorno, *Aesthetic Theory*, trans. Robert Hullot-Kentor (London: Bloomsbury, 2014), 2.

of his poem *Coriolan* in favour of a modern sans serif.[8] Yeats, like Pound, rejected the gothic types of William Morris or the Irish half uncial for the Cuala Press in favour of the clarity of another eighteenth-century revival, the roman face Caslon.[9] Nevertheless, modernist poets were not trained, apprenticed, and schooled as typographers. They could not draw or cut new typefaces. They did not study primers on when text ought to be set ragged and when it ought to be justified, nor did they consult handbooks on when to letterspace and when not to, or on how many characters to fit onto the average line. Not only were they wholly ineligible for membership of that cenacle of great typographers, they were moreover exiled from the community of everyday graphic designers. The patrimony of typography did not therefore weigh on their minds and shoulders. Hermetic rules on paginal dimensions, for instance, are easily broken if one does not even know such rules exist. Unschooled in such traditions, these poets were liberated from the conservatism of print.

Cursory glances at the pages of modernist verse betray this freedom. Judged by the wisdom of typographical handbooks, they are not stylish, nor are they pretty. As such, the apparently reactionary retort of the critic Edmund Wilson that Cummings's poems are 'hideous on the page' is more insightful than it first seems.[10] Beauty and ugliness, categories that inhere even in some of the most radical typography of designers like Tschichold, had little if any hold over these poets. Beauty in typography is the fruit of a discipline to which these poets did not adhere. It is an architectonic founded on the harmony of manifold constituents whose synthesis requires years of training. It is rare to find a modernist poet commend the beauty of their own typography, or indeed to denounce the ugliness of it. These categories simply did not pertain. Were Gill to look at a page designed by Olson, he would have been appalled; conversely, were Olson to look at a page designed by Gill, though he might have admired the workmanship, he couldn't have used it for his own poetry. If we compare the textbooks and editions of graphic designers with the essays and verse of twentieth-century writers, it becomes clear that a good page for the typographer is not a good page for the poet. Yet

---

[8] John Tranter, 'Lost Things in the Garden of Type', <http://jacketmagazine.com/02/gardtype.html> [accessed 3 April 2017] (para. 16 of 45); T. S. Eliot, *The Poems of T. S. Eliot*, ed. Christopher Ricks and Jim McCrue (London: Faber and Faber, 2015), 816.

[9] Nicola Gordon Bowe, 'The Iconic Book in Ireland, 1891–1930', in *The Oxford History of the Irish Book, 1891–2000* (Oxford: Oxford University Press, 2011), 390–412 (p. 393).

[10] Edmund Wilson, 'Wallace Stevens and E. E. Cummings', in *Critical Essays on E. E. Cummings*, ed. Guy Rotella, (Boston: G. K. Hall, 1984), 43–46 (p. 45).

the discrepancy is not simply one of the scrupulousness of the former and the sloppiness of the latter. Incisive scrutiny, good eyes, the gift of discerning hairline spaces, and an indefatigable mania for exactitude were qualities which these poets richly possessed, as the fastidiousness of their drafting and proofing attests, but they did not employ these virtues according to any recognized rulebook. Local, idiosyncratic calculations, particular to their own poetics or the style of a given poem, as when Cummings plots the precise arc of 'the/sky/was' or Olson maps out his desired arrangement of substantives in 'A Maximus', guided them, rather than shared canons of good practice.

Legibility and illegibility likewise warp under the influence of poetics. These are categories that are as cardinal to experiments in the typography of verse as they are to the aesthetics of graphic designers. However, what Olson means by the legibility of the page is quite different to that which Morison extols. Rhyme and rhythm are prized at times for their unintelligibility in modernist verse, precious because they are on the cusp of inaudibility. Typography is less often measured by this particular axiology, not least because its pedigree is often questioned; it is not a readily accepted art of verse. The arbitration of mass viewing, though, which Morison and Gill felt bear upon them, does not have the same weight. The eyes of the public more often are to be educated, shown how and at what pace to read. His translation of Cavalcanti's *Rime* is an exemplar of legibility for Pound, not because they are easy on the eye, but because they bring the hidden layers of the poem to light through their shape. For modernist poets, the legibility of their typography is more often an index of how form, thought, and idea assume graphical form. Informational transfer is a facet of legibility for typographers; breaking words and phrasing, rupturing syntactic flow, is often considered a taboo in typographical primers. This principle, though, is radicalized when placed in the hands of twentieth-century poets. Typography *reads* poems rather than making them *readable*; it interprets them rather than presenting them. Illegibility, too, is transmuted. Though poets like typographers of the twentieth century turned away from the Arts and Crafts Movement—from dense text blocks, blackletter, and neo-medievalisms, from that 'Kelmscott mess of illegibility' as Pound phrases it—they nevertheless frustrated vision in a manner which most graphic designers would have found rebarbative.[11] Many of Cummings's unpublished poems read right to left, and verbal recognition is increasingly impeded in his verse of the late 1920s and 1930s,

---

[11] Ezra Pound, 'Letter to Kate Buss, 12 May 1923', in *The Letters of Ezra Pound 1907–1941*, ed. D. D. Paige (New York: Harcourt, Brace, 1950), 186-87 (p.187).

until it becomes almost cryptogrammatic, an effortful deciphering. Morison's judgement that autograph codices are more apt for experiment than the printed book is incidentally borne out by the posthumously published third volume of *The Maximus Poems*, which features poems whose lines spiral like the shell of a mollusc, so difficult to render in print that facsimiles of Olson's manuscripts are used instead. It is readers who are to conform to typography, in the eyes of these poets, not typography to readers. Bringhurst, in the manner of a Renaissance humanist, argues that the continuity of typographical aesthetics is founded on the anatomy of the body. '[T]he eye, the hand and the forearm', their ambits and reflexes, determine the span of the text.[12] Typographical experiment in verse, though, demands that bodies shift to the contours of the text, that straining and exercising the eyes is salutary.

The history of typography and the history of verse, despite these divergences, do seem to intersect at one point. 'Anglo-American' is a term this book has often employed to delineate the strain of typographical experiment with which it is occupied, and the term has been adopted in part because of the transatlanticism of poets like Pound and to suggest a filiation with the mise-en-page of postwar British poets such as Prynne and Hill. Scholars of typography like Robin Kincross have downplayed Britain's role in modernist typography and stressed the centrality of continental Europe to typographical experiment. Likewise, Jan Tschichold the typographer as much as William Carlos Williams the poet perceived the United States as a symbolic bastion of typographical newness, as a citadel of neon signs and visual energy. But while some of the most prominent British theorists and practitioners of typography, such as Stanley Morison and Beatrice Warde, extolled the primacy of book typography over display typography and espoused a graphical conservatism, British poets like Hope Mirrlees and David Jones penned some of the most visually experimental texts of the last century and were at the vanguard of graphical innovation. These British typographical landmarks are already present in the first half of the twentieth century and long predate postwar collaborations like that of Charles Olson and J. H. Prynne, as explored in the third chapter. A drive for semantic atomicity through typography is already present in Mirrlees's *Paris: A Poem* of 1920 over a decade before it manifests in Cummings's *No Thanks* of 1935. Likewise, the tension between measurement and freedom peculiar to typographic experiment is evident in Jones's *In Parenthesis* of 1937, several years before it resurfaces as Olson begins writing *The Maximus*

---

[12] Robert Bringhurst, *The Elements of Typographic Style*, 10.

Poems in the 1950s. Aesthetic preoccupations like advertising, holophrasis, and inscription, as I suggested in earlier chapters, are shared between British and American poets as they unsettled the canons of typography. Even as they pursued individual authorships fiercely without claiming to have influenced one another, British and American poets possessed a common experimental verve in their typography, and the former often anticipated the preoccupations of the latter.

Finding causation in nationality, or setting up British poets in contest with American poets, is therefore deceptive and limited, not least because so many modernist poets abjured their countries of birth and formed international collectives. Metre rather than nationality offers a more robust index for tracing poets who were drawn to typographical experiment. Poets who remain most loyal to metre, whether British or American—such as W. B. Yeats, W. H. Auden, Wallace Stevens, or Robert Frost—tend to steer clear of typographical experiment. Poets such as Pound, Williams, Jones, or the early Mirrlees, who disassociate themselves from accentual-syllabic metres, are often compelled to innovate their mise-en-page. Freeing verse, whether that means approximating quantitative metres or incorporating the rhythms of speech and prose, attracts typographical experiment. This is, though, far from absolute. Exceptions abound, many of which this book has already discussed. Cummings's *Tulips & Chimneys* is a synthesis of accentual-syllabic prosody and typographical experiment. The kinetics of many of his sonnets, indeed, depend on this very interplay between the torsions of print and the strains of metricality. Likewise, a work like Hart Crane's *The Bridge* figures the interpolation of ambient voices into the taut metrical weft of its neo-Elizabethan verse through warping its typography.[13] Such correlations give a sense of the lie of the land, but broad generalizations offer little insight into individual authorships. Eliot, in turning away decisively from the incipient typographical experiment of *The Waste Land* (such as the markedly isolated 'Do' and 'But' and the hectoring capitalization of the bartender in 'A Game of Chess', and the fragmented interpolation 'la la' and iterations of 'burning' at the end of 'The Fire Sermon'), might be seen as offering an alternative patronage to that of Pound.[14] Lawrence Rainey has noted that Eliot approached the Cambridge publisher Maurice Firuski to publish a limited edition version of *The Waste Land*, encouraged, in part, by the typographical

[13] Hart Crane, *Complete Poems*, ed. Brom Weber (Newcastle Upon Tyne: Bloodaxe, 1984).
[14] T. S. Eliot, *The Poems of T. S. Eliot* (London: 2015), 59–61, 66; cf T. S. Eliot, *Poems 1909–1925* (London: Faber and Faber, 1925), 70–73, 79.

standard of the imprint and that the poet communicates the importance of the layout in a letter to Firuski dated 26 February 1922, speaking of 'certain spacings essential to the sense'.[15]

British and American typographies were unified by certain institutional connections, relationships which had a bearing on the mise-en-page of twentieth-century poets. The Monotype Corporation, responsible for producing many of the last century's most famous typefaces, originated in Pennsylvania in 1887, before setting up a branch in London in 1897. Its British branch employed Morison as a typographical consultant and Warde as publicity manager, and commissioned Gill to design faces like the eponymous Gill Sans and Perpetua. The two branches of the Monotype Corporation, as Robin Kinross has chronicled, enjoyed distinct identities: the American one was notable for the designs of its consultant Frederic Goudy, the majority of which were display faces used for advertising; the British one, under Morison's direction, was renowned for its recreations of historical faces suitable for book typography. Morison, indeed, thought of his American counterpart as an antagonist and felt that the virtue of Times New Roman lay in its dignified impersonality in comparison with the individualist peculiarity of Goudy's faces.[16]

Cross-pollination, though, was widespread, and poets were some of its vectors. However much American poets like Pound and Olson were at odds with Morison's asceticism and decorousness, they nevertheless imbibed some of the typographical culture of British Monotype. Renaissance typography, the faces of Aldus Manutius and Francesco Griffo, was a guiding light for Pound as much as for Morison. A year before the publication of Canto XXX and its commemoration of the Aldine Press as a motor of intellectual rebirth, British Monotype had redesigned Bembo, the face cut by Griffo and commissioned by Aldus in 1495, for the twentieth century.[17] *The Cantos* in this instance adumbrate and are impressed by the living history of graphic design. Pound continues to laud Aldine typography throughout the 1930s, bewailing the execrable state of contemporary book culture without acknowledging that the foremost British type foundry is continuing to resurrect his and other humanists' fonts and designs. Olson, similarly, when he comes to elect the typeface which will be used throughout *The Maximus*

---

[15] Lawrence Rainey, *Institutions of Modernism: Literary Elites and Public Culture* (New Haven, CT: Yale University Press, 1998), 102–3.

[16] Robin Kinross, *Modern Typography: An Essay in Critical History* (London: Hyphen Press, 1992), 47-8.

[17] Robin Kinross, *Modern Typography*, 64.

Poems, chooses between two of Monotype's historical recreations, Garamond and Bembo, ultimately opting for the latter.[18] Typeface—the aspect of typography over which poets had the least control, the graphic art which they could not co-opt and hijack—is aptly where they are most in keeping with the times. It is where the posture of the heroic poet-typographer battling against the malaise of contemporary graphical culture, Pound's image of the poet manning a linotype on the ruins of the Stock Exchange, looks most precarious.[19]

Conservative typography is propelled by the same reasoning as experimental typography. Though the editions of the Golden Cockerel Press and Cape Goliard Press look irreconcilably dissimilar, common axioms can be discerned.[20] While many typographers baulked at the term 'experimental', the word 'modernist' could be fitted to variant purposes. Utility might impel as much as inhibit innovation. Robin Kinross inverts the topos that typography is inherently conservative; instead of an oxymoron, modern typography might be read as a pleonasm. 'If the printing process was one of the main facilitators in the development of the modern world', he writes, 'then the phrase "modern typography" may be an unnecessary duplication of sense. Is not *all* typography modern?'[21] Gutenberg's invention is invoked as the creation myth of wildly divergent philosophies of design. Functionality as a principle can justify adhering to a narrow family of serifed typefaces for the sake of readerly comprehension as much reconfiguring the dimensions of the page to turbo-charge communication. Passages from Beatrice Warde's famous 1930 lecture 'The Crystal Goblet, Or Why Printing Should Be Invisible', though written in defence of Morison's aesthetics, could well have been plagiarized by Bauhaus typographers for their own manifestos. Warde proposes the analogy of a wine connoisseur who chooses a clear crystal glass for his vintage rather than an opaque but more decorative drinking vessel. She continues:

> Now the man who first chose glass instead of clay or metal to hold his wine was a "modernist" in the sense in which I am going to use that term. That

---

[18] Charles Olson, 'Letter to Barry Hall, 12 July 1968', in Charles Olson, *Selected Letters*, ed. Ralph Maud (Berkeley: University of California Press, 2000), 405-6 (p. 405).

[19] 'Letter to Ford Madox Ford, 22 March 1938', in *Pound/Ford: The Story of a Literary Friendship* ed. Brita Lindberg-Seyersted (London: Faber and Faber, 1982), 159–160 (p.160).

[20] The Golden Cockerel Press was particularly associated with Eric Gill and fine-press printing, while Cape Goliard Press was involved with postwar modernist poetry and Olson's *Maximus Poems*.

[21] Robin Kinross, *Modern Typography*, 7.

is, the first thing he asked of this particular object was not "How should it look?" but "What must it do?" and to that extent all good typography is modernist. Wine is so strange and potent a thing that it has been used in the central ritual of religion in one place and time, and attacked by a virago with a hatchet in another. There is only one thing in the world that is capable of stirring and altering men's minds to the same extent, and that is the coherent expression of thought. That is man's chief miracle, unique to man. There is no "explanation" whatever of the fact that I can make arbitrary sounds that will lead a total stranger to think my own thought. It is sheer magic that I should be able to hold a one-sided conversation by means of black marks on paper with an unknown person halfway across the world. Talking, broadcasting, writing, and printing are all quite literally forms of *thought transference*, and it is this ability and eagerness to transfer and receive the contents of the mind that is almost alone responsible for human civilization.[22]

What is striking about this passage is how close Warde is to the more outlandish typographical theories of modernist poets. This metaphor of frictionless transparency can justify anodyne simplicity, typography so inconspicuous that we do not see it, an analogy guilty of a suspect dualism of form and content, as though words were windows through which we peer to discern the referents that stand behind. Frictionless transparency, though, summons up telecommunication: typography as limpid signals that beam from mind to mind. It is this faith in distant intuitive communication, that, belying its inky presence, print is like an aerial stream of data, which impels modernist poets to refigure it into all manner of eccentric permutations. The crystal goblet is a close cousin to the radio antenna.

Die neue Typographie, Jan Tschichold's name for the waves of experimental design emanating from the Bauhaus and the Russian Constructivists, comes into being by asking the very same question Warde poses: 'What must it do?' Typography becomes defamiliarized, its conventions come unstuck, when this question is asked of it. It would be naive and modish, though, to think that this question never occurred to typographers before the twentieth century. Indeed, the corollary of the tenet that typography has always been a service art is that printing has been functional for centuries. It is

[22] Beatrice Warde, 'The Crystal Goblet, or Why Printing should be Invisible', in Helen Armstrong, ed., *Graphic Design Theory: Readings from the Field* (New York: Princeton Architectural Press, 2009), 39-43 (p. 40).

a modernist art *avant la lettre*. The discrimination Warde draws between how it should look and what it must do is unsound. An eighteenth-century typographer like John Baskerville, in setting an edition of Virgil's *opera*, is instinctively mindful of both utility and elegance. Neither, conversely, can we say that the young Tschichold even at his most radical ceases to care about the harmoniousness of his designs. A better formulation would be that typographical modernism prioritises function over form. Strictures on layout, received improprieties, give way; letters slope or enlarge incrementally because in so doing they might say more or speak more quickly.

The engineer was a tutelary presence not only for poets but also for typographers. Resident though he is in a neo-medieval guild, Gill urges his peers to look to the factories for inspiration. 'Fancy lettering', he prophesies, 'will be as distasteful to the artist as it will be to the engineer—in fact it is more than probable that it will be the artists who will give the lead.' He continues:

> Artists no less than engineers are forced to question the very roots of workmanship, to discover the first word, the word that was at the beginning. And we can only pray that those who employ industrial methods of manufacture will pursue those methods to a logical and stern conclusion—thus only can our age leave a monument worthy of its profane genius and mechanical triumph—and that those who refuse the blandishments of power or the ease of irresponsibility will discover that in its ultimate analysis the only justification for human work is an intrinsic sanctity.[23]

This 'logical and stern conclusion', though, will not be prosecuted by Gill himself. His world of letters is Manichean: typographers in thrall to industry ought to produce ever more utilitarian specimens of printing while enclaves of artisans labour away at beautiful lettering undisturbed. Gill only moonlights in the world of Industry; he sees himself as a part-time engineer. Separate though he would like these professions to be, he cannot switch off his artisanal reflexes on the floor of the printing press. He may cut Gill Sans, heir to Johnson's sans serif for the London Tube and cousin to the universal alphabets of Bauhaus, but he would never set this face in the errant patterns attempted by his European contemporaries. Tschichold, however, proposes that typographers be full-time engineers. His history of aesthetics does not allow artisans and engineers to cohabit:

---

[23] Eric Gill, *An Essay on Typography*, 22, 24.

Instead of recognizing and designing for the laws of machine production, the previous generation contented itself with trying anxiously to follow a tradition that was in any case only imaginary. Before them stand the works of today, untainted by the past, primary shapes which identify the aspect of our time: Car Aeroplane Telephone Wireless Factory Neon-advertising New York! These objects, designed without reference to the aesthetics of the past, have been created by a new kind of man: **the engineer!** The engineer shapes our age. Distinguishing marks of his work: economy, precision, use of pure constructional forms that correspond to the functions of the object.[24]

Tschichold dissertates with the syntax of advertising, a breathless flurry of asyndetic phrases: 'Car Aeroplane Telephone Wireless Factory Neon-advertising New York!' Referring to 'these objects', he does not just equalize their variant referents, so that a city is equated to a radio, but he makes their graphic signs into disposable tokens. Words are cast as factory-fresh inventions, newly minted counters with no prehistory.

It is consequently in the manner of a modernist poet that Tschichold the professional typographer holds forth about his métier. His 1930 manifesto is not at all ignorant about the history of design: he furnishes a potted history of typography from Aldus to Jugendstil. The New Typography as he envisages it, however, is not an accretive excogitation of previous forms; it isn't freighted with historical memory. It rather sets the clock back to zero to intuit timeless universals:

Modern engineering and standardized machine manufacture have of necessity led to the use of precise geometric forms. The final and purest shape of a product is always built up from geometric forms. The new age has created an entirely new visual world, and has guided us to the primary elements of human expression: geometric shape and pure exact form[25]

It is from outside of typography that typography discovers its true nature. Sedimented wisdom, accumulated *savoir faire*, counts for very little in this manifesto. Calqued from Bauhaus ideology is the belief that under a rational gaze an art form will configure itself to its optimal shape according to its purposefulness. Dormant in typography, buried in its inner logic, is an

---

[24] Jan Tschichold, *The New Typography: A Handbook for Modern Designers*, trans. Ruari McLean (Berkeley: University of California Press, 2006), 11.

[25] Jan Tschichold, *The New Typography*, 12.

originary simplicity more readily discerned by an unskilled outsider than a skilled designer. Typography is the native tongue of this aesthetics far more than fine art, music, architecture, or literature because it approaches geometry.

Poets revolutionize typography because in Tschichold's account an ignorance about the history of typography, its received rules and canons, is needed to revivify it. Uninitiated and untrained, theirs are the fresh eyes that see through the dutiful transparency of print and ask what its shape is for:

> It is to a 'non-technician', the Italian poet F. T. Marinetti, the founder of Futurism, that the credit must be given for providing the curtain-raiser for the change-over from ornamental to functional typography. [Tschichold quotes, in French, Marinetti's 'Lettre d'une jolie femme à un monsieur passéiste'] The types have not been chosen for formal-aesthetic, decorative reasons; their carefully thought-out optical impact expresses the content of the poem. The types generate a hitherto unknown visual strength. For the first time typography here becomes a functional expression of its content. For the first time also an attempt was made in this book to create 'visible-poetry', instead of the old 'audible-poetry', to which in any case nobody had listened for a long time.[26]

Marinetti's pre-eminence is contestable here. Tschichold may have elected him because Futurist *paroliberismo* manipulates typeface far more than visual poetry in English or French, and thus Marinetti is more comprehensive an exemplar than poets who restrict themselves to spacing or layout. Olson, Mirrlees, Pound, Jones, Williams, or Cummings, though, might justifiably have been laurelled as well. For it is poetic thinking rather than the work of any one pioneer that Tschichold is identifying. It is poetry's acute awareness of metacommunication to which Tschichold is paying homage. An allergy to complacent diction and a style that to the letter is hyperconscious of itself, these are the traits which engender 'visible poetry'.

Typography becomes poetry in the twentieth century, and, it is feared, poetry becomes typography. Tschichold is rightly cognizant of a change in the nature of print. Yet his proposed binary between ornamental and functional typography still falls short. Printed public notices throughout the nineteenth century, in their patterning of bold face and relatively sized fonts,

---

[26] Jan Tschichold, *The New Typography*, 53.

sought to communicate information in a hierarchical and efficient manner. Accordingly, Tschichold's celebrated film posters for the Palast Palace in Berlin, for example, do not break from typographical history; their diagonal lines and sloping text rather extend the grammar of the functionality of poster art. Functionality in typography well predates the Bauhaus. Poetry, par excellence, seems to undergo the 'change-over' Tschichold describes. It is the epicentre of the ructions in print culture at large. Though their chronologies align, there is far greater a schism between the typography of Algernon Charles Swinburne and that of E. E. Cummings than between Art Nouveau posters and those of the Bauhaus. But what emerges between Swinburne and Cummings, between the nineteenth and the twentieth century, is not simply functionality. Neither poetry nor, indeed, graphic design can be said to have ready-made contents—contents that were once decorated by art typography and became rationally expressed in functional typography. Form, aesthetics, sound—all of these categories which Tschichold wishes to supersede—are not cancelled out by modernist typography. This is a utopian dream which modernist poets themselves grasp at.

Typography is not thought transference; it is not a pellucid communication of ideas through the optics of print. This is an ideal to which poets are drawn. Such a possibility impels the experimentation of these versifiers. To strew the page with precisely reckoned intervals of nouns requires a faith in a pristine language of print. Yet the inadequacy of calling such typography functional is self-evident. Poetry does not have a function. However much modernist poets might liken themselves to engineers, there is no science of the efficacy of print. To calculate the dimensions of the text, the mathematics of stepped lines and spacing, is not to be engaged in a functional enterprise. Typography that functioned reliably, whose spacing exactly notated sound or whose typefaces were clearly mimetic, would be just as moribund as decorative typography or as predictable as Marianne Moore found pictorial poetry.[27] If there were a code or legend ready to hand, if sizes of font equalled incrementally louder volumes, or Perpetua equalled sanctity, typography wouldn't be an art at all. It may be tempting to say that because Pound speaks of his typography as a rhythmical system when it plainly fails to function as such that he has failed as a poet. The opposite, though, would be the case. If his mise-en-page were a guide to reading his verse that humbly did a good

[27] Marianne Moore, 'People Stare Carefully', in *Critical Essays on E.E. Cummings*, ed. Guy Rotella, pp. 46–49 (p. 46).

and predictable job, it would be in no way poetic. To ask what experimental typography does is just as self-defeating as to ask what heroic couplets do. This is not to sanctify ambiguity and vagueness. It is to read through mise-en-page, line by line, poem by poem, as this book has striven to do. Typography might trace an erotic interplay with imagined bodies in one volume and a quest for the atomicity of experience in another; a scripting of paradisiac sound-worlds in one poem and elsewhere a palimpsestuous act of translation; an economic critique at one moment and later a mapping of buried geographies. Though cast alternately as systematic perfection or incoherent failure, typography finds expression between these two poles. While poets believed they were solidifying sound and thought in print, it is the amorphousness and mobility of typography that make it poetic.

Bibliography

Archival Collections [cited]

Ezra Pound Papers, Beinecke Rare Book and Manuscript Library, Yale University

Pound, Ezra, 'Canto XVII', box 70, folder 3175, and box 70, folder 3177.
Pound, Ezra, 'Canto XXXVI', box 73, folder 3284.
Pound, Ezra, 'Cavalcanti's Rime', box 81, folder 3583 and box 236, folder 37.
Pound, Ezra, 'Homage to Sextus Propertius', box 126, folder 5201.
Pound, Ezra, 'The Pisan Cantos', box 76, folders 3394 and 3400.
Pound, Ezra, 'Unpublished note', box 130, folder 5436.

E. E. Cummings Papers, Houghton Library, Harvard University

Cummings, E. E., 'Babylon slim', MS Am 1823.5 (38) and MS Am 1823.7 (23).
Cummings, E. E., 'logeorge', MS Am 1823.7 (21).
Cummings, E. E., 'Notes on reading', MS Am 1823.7 (25).
Cummings, E. E., 'Poems 1923–1954', bMS Am 1823.4 (114).
Cummings, E. E., 'The Poetry of Silence', MS Am 1892.6 (94).
Cummings, E. E., 'the sky was', bMS Am 1823.5 (359).
Cummings, E. E., 'two brass buttons', MS Am 1823.7 (23).

Charles Olson Research Collection, Thomas J. Dodd Research Center, University of Connecticut Libraries

Olson, Charles, 'The ABCs', MS 14:378.
Olson, Charles, 'Conqueror', MS 14:449.
Olson, Charles, 'The Epilogue to The Fiery Hunt', MS 21:884.
Olson, Charles, 'Human Universe II', MS 31:1586.
Olson, Charles, 'I cut stone', MS 22:947.
Olson, Charles, 'Letter 72', MS 2:84.
Olson, Charles, 'THE LIE OF 10, OR THE CONCEPT OF ZERO', MS 15:576.
Olson, Charles, 'A Maximus', MS 2:63.
Olson, Charles, 'Note on typesetting, MS 159.
Olson, Charles, 'Projective Verse II', MS 34.
Olson, Charles, 'The Tao', MS 21:891.

Prynne, J. H., 'Letter to Charles Olson, 4 November 1961' and 'Letter to Charles Olson, 26 November 1961', MS 206.
Prynne, J. H., 'Letter to Charles Olson, 3 February 1963', MS 206.
Prynne, J. H., 'Letter to Charles Olson, 9 May 1963', MS 222.
Prynne, J. H., 'Letter to Charles Olson, 29 May 1963', MS 222.

Published Works

Adorno, Theodor W., *Negative Dialectics*, trans. E. B. Ashton (London: Routledge and Kegan Paul, 1973).

Adorno, Theodor W., 'Punctuation Marks', *The Antioch Review*, 3 (1990), 300–5.

Adorno, Theodor W., *Minima Moralia: Reflections on Damaged Life*, trans. E. F. N. Jephcott (New York: Verso, 2005).

Adorno, Theodor W., *Aesthetic Theory*, trans. Robert Hullot-Kentor (London: Bloomsbury, 2014).

Albright, Daniel, *Quantum Poetics: Yeats, Pound, Eliot, and the Science of Modernism* (Cambridge: Cambridge University Press, 1997).

Albright, Daniel, *Untwisting the Serpent: Modernism in Music, Literature, and Other Arts* (Chicago: University of Chicago Press, 2000).

Anderson, David, *Pound's Cavalcanti: An Edition of the Translations, Notes, and Essays* (Princeton, NJ: Princeton University Press, 1983).

Apollinaire, Guillaume, 'Nos Amis Les Futuristes', *Les Soirées de Paris* (1914), 78–79.

Apollinaire, Guillaume, 'Simultanéisme-Librettisme', *Les Soirées de Paris* (1914), 322–25.

Apollinaire, Guillaume, *Calligrammes: poèmes de la paix et de la guerre (1913–1916)* (Paris: Mercure de France, 1918).

Apollinaire, Guillaume, 'L'Esprit nouveau et les poètes', *Mercure de France* (1918), 385–96.

Apollinaire, Guillaume, *Calligrammes* (Paris: Gallimard, 1966).

Apollinaire, Guillaume, *Œuvres en prose complètes*, ed. Michel Decaudin (Paris: Gallimard, 1991).

Armstrong, Helen (ed.), *Graphic Design Theory: Readings from the Field* (New York: Princeton Architectural Press, 2009).

Atheling, William, 'Music', *New Age*, 21 February 1918, 334–35.

Atheling, William, 'Music', *New Age*, 28 March 1918, 434.

Atheling, William, 'Music', *New Age*, 7 March 1918, 377–78.

Atheling, William, 'Music', *New Age*, 25 March 1920, 338–39.

Atheling, William, 'Music', *New Age*, 18 April 1918, 486.

Atheling, William, 'Music', *New Age*, 25 November 1920, 44.

Atheling, William, 'Music', *New Age*, 9 December 1920, 68.

Attridge, Derek, *The Rhythms of English Poetry* (London: Longman, 1982)

Attridge, Derek, *Moving Words: Forms of English Poetry* (Oxford: Oxford University Press, 2013).

Bankes, Ariane, and Hills, Paul, *The Art of David Jones: Vision and Memory* (Farnham: Lund Humphries, 2015).

Barthes, Roland, *Le degré zéro de l'écriture* (Paris: Éditions du Seuil, 1972).

Barthes, Roland, *Oeuvres complètes: Tome IV 1972–1976*, ed. Éric Marty (Paris: Seuil, 2002).

Bass, Eden, 'Songs of Innocence and Experience: The Thrust of Design', in *Blake's Visionary Forms Dramatic* (Princeton, NJ: Princeton University Press, 2017).

Beasley, Rebecca, *Ezra Pound and the Visual Culture of Modernism* (Cambridge: Cambridge University Press, 2007).

Beeching, Wilfred A., *The Century of the Typewriter* (Bournemouth: British Typewriter Museum Publishing, 1990).

Bell, Ian F. A., *The Critic as Scientist: The Modernist Poetics of Ezra Pound* (London: Methuen & Co., 1981).

Benda, Julien, *Belphégor: essai sur l'esthétique de la présente société française* (Emile-Paul Freres Editeurs: Paris, 1918).

Benjamin, Walter, *Illuminations*, ed. Hannah Arendt, trans. Harry Zorn (London: Pimlico, 1999).

Berry, Eleanor, 'Visual Form in Free Verse', *Visible Language*, 1 (1989), 89–111.

Berry, Eleanor, 'The Emergence of Charles Olson's Prosody of the Page Space', *Journal of English Linguistics*, 1 (2002), 51–72.

Blanchot, Maurice, *L'espace littéraire* (Paris: Gallimard, 1955).

Bohn, Willard, *The Aesthetics of Visual Poetry 1914–1928* (Cambridge: Cambridge University Press, 1986).

Boldereff, Frances, and Olson, Charles, *Charles Olson and Frances Boldereff: A Modern Correspondence*, ed. Ralph Maud and Sharon Thesen (Hanover, NH: Wesleyan University Press, 1999).

Bornstein, George, *Poetic Remaking: The Art of Browning, Yeats, and Pound* (University Park: Pennsylvania State University Press, 1988).

Bornstein, George, *Material Modernism: The Politics of the Page* (Cambridge: Cambridge University Press, 2001).

Bradford, Richard, *The Look of It: A Theory of Visual Form in English Poetry* (Cork: Cork University Press, 1993).

Bradford, Richard, 'Cummings and the Brotherhood of Visual Poetics', in *Words into Pictures: E. E. Cummings' Art Across Borders*, ed. Jiří Flajšar and Zénó Vernyik (Newcastle: Cambridge Scholars Publishing, 2007), 2–26.

Bringhurst, Robert, *The Elements of Typographic Style* (Point Roberts, WA: Hartley & Marks, 2005).

Bucknell, Brad, *Literary Modernism and Musical Aesthetics: Pater, Pound, Joyce, and Stein* (Cambridge: Cambridge University Press, 2001).

Bunting, Basil, *Complete Poems* (Tarset: Bloodaxe, 2000).

Burke, Christopher, *Active Literature: Jan Tschichold and New Typography* (London: Hyphen Press, 2007).

Bush, Ronald, *The Genesis of Ezra Pound's Cantos* (Princeton, NJ.: Princeton University Press, 1976).

Bush, Ronald, 'La filosofica famiglia: Cavalcanti, Avicenna, and the "Form" of Ezra Pound's Pisan Cantos', *Textual Practice*, 4 (2010), 669–705.

Butterick, George F., *A Guide to the Maximus Poems of Charles Olson* (Berkeley: University of California Press, 1978).

Butterick, George F., *Editing the Maximus Poems* (Storrs: University of Connecticut Library, 1983).

Byers, Mark, 'Environmental Pedagogues: Charles Olson and R. Buckminster Fuller', *English* (2013), 248–68.

Byers, Mark, 'Egocentric Predicaments: Charles Olson and the New York School of Music', *Journal of Modern Literature*, 4 (2014) 54–69.

Byron, Mark, 'A Defining Moment in Ezra Pound's *Cantos*: Musical Scores and Literary Texts', in *Literature and Music*, ed. Michael J. Meyer (Amsterdam: Rodopi, 2002), 157–82.

Carpenter, Humphrey, *A Serious Character: The Life of Ezra Pound* (London: Faber and Faber, 1988).

Carruth, Hayden, 'Hung Over, Like a Dali Watch', *Nation*, 8 April 1950, in Charles Doyle (ed.), *William Carlos Williams: The Critical Heritage* (London: Routledge & Kegan Paul, 1980), 218–21.

Cavalcanti, Guido, *Sonnets and Ballate of Guido Cavalcanti*, trans. Ezra Pound (London: Stephen Swift, 1912).

Cavalcanti, Guido, *Rime*, ed. and trans. Ezra Pound (Genova: Edizoni Marsano, [1931/2]).

Childs, John Steven, *Modernist Form: Pound's Style in the Early Cantos* (London: Associated University Press, 1986).

Claudel, Paul, *Cent phrases pour éventails* (Paris: Gallimard, 1942).

Cocteau, Jean, *Le Cap de Bonne-Espérance* (Paris: Gallimard, 1967).

Cohen, Milton A., *Poet and Painter: The Aesthetics of E. E. Cummings's Early Work* (Detroit: Wayne State University Press, 1987).

Cookson, William, *A Guide to the Cantos of Ezra Pound* (London: Crook and Helm, 1985).

Crane, Hart, *Complete Poems*, ed. Brom Weber (Newcastle Upon Tyne: Bloodaxe, 1984).

Creeley, Robert, *The Collected Essays of Robert Creeley* (Berkeley: University of California Press, 1989)

Creeley, Robert, *Selected Poems* (Berkeley: University of California Press, 1991)

Creeley, Robert, and Olson, Charles, *Charles Olson and Robert Creeley: The Complete Correspondence*, ed. George F. Butterick, 10 vols (Santa Barbara, CA: Black Sparrow Press, 1980).

Cummings, E. E., *Tulips and Chimneys* (New York: Thomas Seltzer, 1923).

Cummings, E. E., *XLI Poems* (New York: Dial Press, 1925).

Cummings, E. E., *Is 5* (New York: Boni and Liveright, 1926).

Cummings, E. E., *No Thanks* (New York: Golden Eagle Press, 1935).

Cummings, E. E., *Tulips & Chimneys* (Mount Vernon, NY: Golden Eagle Press, 1937).

Cummings, E. E., *Collected Poems* (New York: Harcourt, Brace, 1938).

Cummings, E. E., *I: Six Nonlectures* (Cambridge: Harvard University Press, 1953).

Cummings, E. E., 'Freedom, Joy & Indignation: Letters from E. E. Cummings', *Massachusetts Review*, 4 (1963), 497–528.

Cummings, E. E., *Selected Letters of E. E. Cummings*, ed. F.W. Dupee and George Stade(London: Andre Deutsch, 1972).

Cummings, E. E., *Tulips & Chimneys: The Original 1922 Manuscript with the 34 Additional Poems from &*, ed. George James Firmage (New York: Liveright, 1976).

Cummings, E. E. *Etcetera: The Unpublished Poems of E. E. Cummings*, ed. George James Firmage and Richard S. Kennedy (New York: Liveright, 1983).

Cummings, E. E., *Complete Poems 1904–1962*, ed. George J. Firmage, (New York: Liveright, 1994).

Cummings, E. E., and Pound, Ezra, *Pound/Cummings: The Correspondence of Ezra Pound and E. E. Cummings*, ed. Barry Ahearn (Ann Arbor: University of Michigan Press, 1996).

Cureton, Richard, 'E. E. Cummings: A Study of the Poetic Use of Deviant Morphology', *Poetics Today*, 1 (1979), 213–44.

Cureton, Richard, 'Visual Form in E. E. Cummings' *No Thanks*', *Word & Image*, 3 (1986), 245–77.

Davie, Donald, *Ezra Pound* (Harmondsworth, UK: Penguin, 1976).

De Gourmont, Remy, *Le problème de style* (Paris: Societé du Mercure de France, 1907).

Derrida, Jacques, *De la grammatologie* (Paris: Éditions de Minuit, 1967).

Derrida, Jacques, *L'écriture et la différence* (Paris: Éditions de Seuil, 1979).

Derrida, Jacques, *A Derrida Reader: Between the Blinds*, ed. Peggy Kamuf (New York: Columbia University Press, 1991).

Divoire, Fernand, 'Case: Mallarmé', trans. Ezra Pound, *The Dial* (September 1920), 514.

Dolmetsch, Arnold, *The Interpretation of the Music of the XVII & XVIII Centuries* (London: Novello, 1915).

Doolittle, Hilda, *Collected Poems: 1912–1944*, ed. Louis L. Martz (Manchester: Carcanet Press, 1984).

Doyle, Charles (ed.), *William Carlos Williams: The Critical Heritage* (London: Routledge & Kegan Paul, 1980).

Drucker, Johanna, *The Visible Word: Experimental Typography and Modern Art 1909–1923* (Chicago: University of Chicago Press, 1994).

Duncan, Robert, *Collected Essays and Prose*, ed. James Maynard (Berkeley: University of California Press, 2014).

Eliot, T. S., 'Reflections on Vers Libre', *New Statesman* (3 March 1917), 518–19.

Eliot, T. S., *The Poems of T .S. Eliot*, ed. Christopher Ricks and Kim McCrue, 2 vols (London: Faber and Faber, 2015).

Epstein, Josh, *Sublime Noise: Musical Culture and the Modernist Writer* (Baltimore, MD: John Hopkins University Press, 2014).

Fenollosa, Ernest, *The Chinese Written Character as a Medium for Poetry*, ed. Ezra Pound (San Francisco: City Lights Books, 1964).

Fisher, Margaret, *Ezra Pound's Radio Operas* (Cambridge, MA: MIT Press, 2002).

Ford, Ford Madox, and Pound, Ezra, *Pound/Ford: The Story of a Literary Friendship* ed. Brita Lindberg-Seyersted (London: Faber and Faber, 1982).

Foucault, Michel, *L'archéologie du savoir* (Paris: Gallimard, 1969).

Foucault, Michel, *Surveiller et punir* (Paris: Gallimard, 1975).

Fredman, Stephen, *The Grounding of American Poetry: Charles Olson and the Emersonian Tradition* (Cambridge: Cambridge University Press, 1993).

Friedman, Norman, *E. E. Cummings: The Art of His Poetry* (London: Oxford University Press, 1960).

Friedman, Norman, *(Re)valuing Cummings: Further Essays on the Poet, 1962–1993* (Gainesville: University of Florida Press, 1996).

Gautier, Théophile, *Émaux et camées* (Paris: Gallimard, 1981).

Gill, Eric, *An Essay on Typography* (London: Sheed & Ward, 1931).

Ginsberg, Allan, *Deliberate Prose: Selected Essays 1952–1995*, ed. Bill Morgan (London: Penguin, 2000).

Golston, Michael, *Rhythm and Race in Modernist Poetry and Science* (New York: Columbia University Press, 2008).

Gould, George M., *Concerning Lafcadio Hearn* (Philadelphia: George W. Jacobs & Co., 1908).

Heidegger, Martin, *Basic Writings*, ed. David Farrell Krell (London: Routledge and Kegan Paul, 1978).

Heidegger, Martin, *Parmenides*, trans. Andre Schuwer and Richard Rojcewicz (Bloomington: Indiana University Press, 1992).

Henry, Barbara, 'The Design and Typography of Leaves of Grass (1860)' *Huntington Library Quarterly*, 4 (2010), 601–12.

Hui, Alexandra, *The Psychophysical Ear: Musical Experiments, Experimental Sounds, 1840–1910* (Cambridge, MA: MIT Press, 2013).

Hulme, T. E., *The Collected Writings of T. E. Hulme*, ed. Karen Csengeri (Oxford: Clarendon Press, 1994).

Izenberg, Gerald N., *Modernism and Masculinity: Mann, Wedekind, Kandinsky through World War I* (Chicago: University of Chicago Press, 2000).

James, William, *The Principles of Psychology*, 3 vols (Cambridge, MA: Harvard University Press, 1981).

Jarrell, Randall, '... "Paterson" has been getting rather steadily worse', *Partisan Review*, 6 (1951), in Charles Doyle (ed.), *William Carlos Williams: The Critical Heritage* (London: Routledge & Kegan Paul, 1980), 238–41.

Jones, David, *In Parenthesis* (London: Faber and Faber, 1937).

Jones, David, *The Anathemata: Fragments of an Attempted Writing* (London: Faber and Faber, 1952).

Jones, David, *Use and Sign: An Essay* (Ipswich: Golgonooza Press, 1975).

Jones, David, *The Sleeping Lord and Other Fragments* (London: Faber and Faber, 1995).

Jones, David, *Epoch and Artist* (London: Faber and Faber, 2017).

Kahn, Douglas, and Whitehead, Gregory (eds.), *Wireless Imagination: Sound, Radio and the Avant-Garde* (Cambridge, MA: MIT Press, 1992).

Katz, Daniel, 'From Olson's Breath to Spicer's Gait: Spacing, Pacing, Phonemes', in *Contemporary Olson*, ed. David Herd (Manchester: Manchester University Press, 2015), 77–88.

Kennedy, Richard S., *Dreams in the Mirror: A Biography of E. E. Cummings* (New York: Liveright, 1994).

Kennedy, Richard S., *E. E. Cummings Revisited* (New York: Twayne, 1994).

Kenner, Hugh, *The Pound Era* (London: Faber and Faber, 1972).

Kenner, Hugh, *The Mechanic Muse* (New York; Oxford: Oxford University Press, 1987).

Kindellan, Michael, 'Poetic Instruction', in *Contemporary Olson*, ed. David Herd (Manchester: Manchester University Press, 2015), 89–102.

King, Henry, 'Ezra Pound and the Music on the Page', *PN Review*, 3 (2011), 54–57.

Kinross, Robin, *Modern Typography: An Essay in Critical History* (London: Hyphen Press, 1992).

Kittler, Friedrich A., *Gramophone, Film, Typewriter*, trans. Geoffrey Winthrop-Young and Michael Wutz (Stanford, CA: Stanford University Press, 1999).

Lennard, John, *But I Digress: The Exploitation of Parentheses in English Printed Verse* (Oxford: Clarendon Press, 1991).

Lessing, Gotthold Ephraim, *Laocoön, Nathan the Wise and Minna von Barnhelm* (London: Dent, 1930).

Levertov, Denise, *O Taste and See: New Poems* (New York: New Directions, 1964).

Levertov, Denise, *New & Selected Essays* (New York: New Directions, 1992).

Lewis, Wyndham, *BLAST: Review of the Great English Vortex*, 1 (1914).

Lewis, Wyndham, *BLAST: Review of the Great English Vortex*, 1 (1915).

Lewis, Wyndham, and Pound, Ezra, *Pound/Lewis: The Letters of Ezra Pound and Wyndham Lewis*, ed. Timothy Materer (London: Faber and Faber, 1985).

Love, Heather A., 'Cybernetic Modernism: Ezra Pound's Poetics of Transmission', *Modernism/modernity*, 1 (2016), 89–111.

Mallarmé, Stéphane, 'Un coup de dés jamais n'abolira le hasard', *Cosmopolis*, 6 (1897), 417–27.

Mallarmé, Stéphane, *Les poésies* (Bruxelles: Edmond Deman, 1899).

Mallarmé, Stéphane, *Un coup de dés jamais n'abolira le hasard* (Paris: Gallimard, 1914).

Mallarmé, Stéphane, *Igitur, Divagations, Un coup de dés* (Paris: Gallimard, 1976).

Mallarmé, Stéphane, *Correspondance complète 1862–1871 suivi de Lettres sur la poésie 1872–1898 avec des lettres inédites*, ed. Bertrand Marchal (Paris: Gallimard, 1995).

Mallarmé, Stéphane, *Oeuvres complètes*, ed. Bertrand Marchal, 2 vols (Paris: Gallimard, 1998).

Mallarmé, Stéphane, *Collected Poems and Other Verse*, trans. E. H. and A. M. Blackmore (New York: Oxford University Press, 2006).

Marinetti, F. T., 'L'Immaginazione senza fili e le parole in libertà', *Lacerba* 12 (1913), 121–24.

Marinetti, F. T., 'Distruzione della sintassi – Immaginazione senza fili – Parole in libertà', in *I manifesti del futurismo* (Firenze: Edizioni di Lacerba, 1914), 133–146.

Marinetti, F. T., 'Manifesto tecnico della letteratura futurista', in *I manifesti del futurismo* (Firenze: Edizioni di Lacerba, 1914), 88–96.

Marinetti, F. T., 'Lo splendore geometrico e meccanico nelle parole in libertà', *Lacerba*, 6 (1914), 81–83.

Marinetti, F. T., *Zang Tumb Tuuum* (Venezia: Edizioni Futuriste di Poesia, 1914).

Marinetti, F. T., *Teoria e invenzione futurista*, ed. Luciano De Maria (Arnoldo Mondadori Editore, 1968).

Marinetti, F. T., *Marinetti: Selected Writings*, ed. R. W. Flint, trans. R. W. Flint and Arthur A. Coppotelli (London: Secker & Warburg, 1971).

Maxim, Hudson, *The Science of Poetry and the Philosophy of Language* (New York: Funk & Wagnalls, 1910).

McGann, Jerome, *The Textual Condition* (Princeton, NJ: Princeton University Press, 1991).

McGann, Jerome, *Black Riders: The Visible Language of Modernism* (Princeton: Princeton University Press, 1993).

McGann, Jerome, 'Pound's *Cantos*: A Poem Including Bibliography', in *A Poem Containing History: Textual Studies in The Cantos*, ed. Lawrence S. Rainey (Ann Arbor: University of Michigan Press, 1997).

Merleau-Ponty, Maurice, *The Phenomenology of Perception*, trans. Colin Smith (London: Routledge, 2002).

Merleau-Ponty, Maurice, *Œuvres*, ed. Claude Lefort (Paris: Éditions Gallimard, 2010).

Merritt, Robert, *Early Music and the Aesthetics of Ezra Pound: Hush of Older Song* (Lewiston, NY: Edwin Mellen Press, 1993).

Middleton, Peter, *Physics Envy: American Poetry and Science in the Cold War and After* (Chicago: University of Chicago Press, 2015).

Millard, A. J., *America on Record: A History of Recorded Sound* (Cambridge: Cambridge University Press, 1995).

Mirrlees, Hope, *Paris: A Poem* (London: Hogarth Press, 1919 [1920]).

Mirrlees, Hope, *Collected Poems* (Manchester: Carcanet, 2011).

Mitchell, W. J. T., *Iconology: Image, Text Ideology* (Chicago; London: University of Chicago Press, 1986).

Moore, Marianne, 'Two Poems', *The Dial* (1921), 33–34.

Moore, Marianne, *The Complete Poems of Marianne Moore* (London: Faber and Faber, 1956).

Moore, Marianne, *The Poems of Marianne Moore*, ed. Grace Schulman (London: Faber and Faber, 2003).

Moore, Marianne, 'People Stare Carefully', in *Critical Essays on E. E. Cummings*, ed. Guy L. Rotella (Boston, MA: G. K. Hall, 1984), 46–49.

Moraru, Christian, '"Topos/typos/tropos": Visual Strategies and the Mapping of Space in Charles Olson's Poetry', *Word & Image*, 3 (1998), 253–66.

Morison, Stanley, *First Principles of Typography* (Cambridge: Cambridge University Press, 1936).

Newman, John Henry, *Apologia Pro Vita Sua*, ed. Ian Ker (London: Penguin, 2004).

Nikolova, Olga, 'Ezra Pound's Cantos De Luxe', *Modernism/modernity*, 1 (2008), 155–77.

Nørgaard, Nina, 'The Semiotics of Typography: A Multimodal Approach', *Orbis Litterarum*, 2 (2009), 141–60.

Olson, Charles, *The Maximus Poems 1–10* (Stuttgart: Jonathan Williams, 1953).

Olson, Charles, *The Maximus Poems* (London: Cape Goliard Press, 1960).

Olson, Charles, *Human Universe and Other Essays*, ed. Donald Allen (San Francisco: The Auerhahn Society, 1965).

Olson, Charles, *Maximus Poems IV, V, VI* (London: Cape Goliard Press, 1968).

Olson, Charles, *The Maximus Poems: Volume Three* (New York: Grossman, 1975).

Olson, Charles, *Mutholagos: The Collected Lectures & Interviews*, ed. George F. Butterick, 2 vols (Bolinas, CA: Four Seasons Foundation, 1978).

Olson, Charles, *The Maximus Poems*, ed. George F. Butterick (Berkeley: University of California Press, 1983).

Olson, Charles, *The Collected Poems of Charles Olson: Excluding the Maximus Poems* (Berkeley: University of California Press, 1987).

Olson, Charles, *Collected Prose*, ed. Donald Allen and Benjamin Friedlander (Berkeley: University of California Press, 1997).

Olson, Charles, *Selected Letters*, ed. Ralph Maud (Berkeley: University of California Press, 2000).

Ortega y Gasset, José, *The Dehumanization of Art and Other Essays on Art, Culture, and Literature* (Princeton, NJ: Princeton University Press, 2019).

Parkes, M. B., *Pause and Effect: An Introduction to the History of Punctuation in the West* (Cambridge: Scolar Press, 1992).

Peppis, Paul, *Literature, Politics and the English Avant-garde: Nation and Empire, 1901–1918* (Cambridge: Cambridge University Press, 2000).

Perloff, Marjorie, *The Dance of the Intellect: Studies in the Poetry of the Pound Tradition* (Cambridge: Cambridge University Press, 1985).

Perloff, Marjorie, 'After Free Verse: The New Nonlinear Poetries', in *Close Listening: Poetry and the Performed Word*, ed. Charles Bernstein (New York: Oxford University Press, 1998), 86–111.

Peters, John Durham, *Speaking into the Air: A History of the Idea of Communication* (Chicago: University of Chicago Press), 1999.

Plotinus, *Select Works of Plotinus*, trans. Thomas Taylor, ed. G. R. S. Mead (London: G. Bells and Sons, 1914).

Pound, Ezra, *A Lume Spento* (Venice: A. Antonini, 1908).

Pound, Ezra, *Exultations* (London: Elkin Mathews, 1909).

Pound, Ezra, 'A review of *the Science of Poetry and the Philosophy of Language* by Hudson Maxim', *Book News Monthly* (1910), in *Ezra Pound's Poetry and Prose: Contributions to Periodicals*, ed. Lea Baechler, A. Walton Litz, and James Longenbach, 11 vols (London: Garland, 1991), I, 40–41.

Pound, Ezra, *The Spirit of Romance* (London: J. M. Dent & Sons, 1910).

Pound, Ezra, *Canzoni* (London: Elkin Mathews, 1911).

Pound, Ezra, 'Prolegomena', *Poetry Review*, 2 (1912), 72–76.

Pound, Ezra, 'A Review of *High Germany* by Ford Madox Hueffer', *Poetry Review*, 1 (1912).

Pound, Ezra, *Ripostes* (London: S. Swift and Co., Ltd., 1912).

Pound, Ezra, 'How I Began', *T.P.'s Weekly*, 6 June 1913, 707.

Pound, Ezra, 'In a Station of the Metro', *Poetry*, 1 (1913).

Pound, Ezra, *Des Imagistes: An Anthology* (London: Poetry Bookshop, 1914).

Pound, Ezra, 'Vorticism', *Fortnightly Review* (1 September 1914), 461–71.

Pound, Ezra, *Gaudier Brzeska: A Memoir* (London: John Lane, 1916).
Pound, Ezra, *Gaudier-Brzeska: A Memoir* (London: Laidlaw & Laidlaw, [1939]).
Pound, Ezra, 'Arnold Dolmetsch', *The Egoist*, 7 (1917), 104–5.
Pound, Ezra, *Lustra* (New York: Knopf, 1917).
Pound, Ezra, *Pavannes and Divisions* (New York: Alfred A. Knopf, 1918).
Pound, Ezra, 'The Island of Paris: A Letter', *The Dial* (September 1920), 406–11.
Pound, Ezra, 'The Island of Paris: A Letter', *The Dial* (December 1920), 635–39.
Pound, Ezra, 'The New Therapy', *New Age* (16 March 1922), in *Contributions to Periodicals*, IV, 222–23.
Pound, Ezra, *Antheil and the Treatise on Harmony* (Paris: Three Mountains Press, 1924).
Pound, Ezra, 'Mr. Dunning's Poetry', *Poetry*, 6 (1925), 339–45.
Pound, Ezra, *Personae: The Collected Poems of Ezra Pound* (New York: Boni and Liveright, 1926).
Pound, Ezra, 'Practical Suggestions', *Poetry*, 6 (1929), 327–33.
Pound, Ezra, *A Draft of XXX Cantos* (London: Faber & Faber, 1933).
Pound, Ezra, *Eleven New Cantos XXXI—XLI* (New York: Farrar and Rinehart, 1934).
Pound, Ezra, *Make It New* (London: Faber and Faber, 1934).
Pound, Ezra, 'The Printing Press Was Invented', *Poetry*, 1 (1936), 55.
Pound, Ezra, *The Fifth Decad of Cantos* (New York: Farrar and Rinehart, 1937).
Pound, Ezra, *Polite Essays* (London: Faber and Faber, 1937).
Pound, Ezra, *The Pisan Cantos* (New York: New Directions, [1948]).
Pound, Ezra, *The Letters of Ezra Pound 1907–1941*, ed. D. D. Paige (New York: Harcourt, Brace, 1950).
Pound, Ezra, *ABC of Reading* (London: Faber and Faber, 1951).
Pound, Ezra, *The Translations of Ezra Pound* (London: Faber and Faber, 1953).
Pound, Ezra, *Literary Essays of Ezra Pound*, ed. T. S. Eliot (London: Faber, 1954).
Pound, Ezra, *Pound/Joyce: The Letters of Ezra Pound to James Joyce, with Pound's Essays on Joyce*, ed. Forrest Read (London: Faber and Faber, 1968).
Pound, Ezra, *Literary Essays of Ezra Pound*, ed. T.S. Eliot (New York: New Directions, 1968).
Pound, Ezra, *Guide to Kulchur* (New York: New Directions, 1970).
Pound, Ezra, *Selected Prose 1909–1965*, ed. William Cookson (London: Faber and Faber, 1973).
Pound, Ezra, *Collected Early Poems of Ezra Pound*, ed. Michael John King (London: Faber and Faber, 1977).
Pound, Ezra, *Ezra Pound's Poetry and Prose: Contributions to Periodicals*, ed. Lea Baechler, A. Walton Litz, and James Longenbach, 11 vols (London: Garland, 1991).
Pound, Ezra, *The Cantos* (New York: New Directions, 1996).
Pound, Ezra, *Personae: The Shorter Poems of Ezra Pound* (London: Faber and Faber, 2001).
Pound, Ezra, and Zukofsky, Louis, *Pound/Zukofsky: Selected Letters of Ezra Pound and Louis Zukofsky*, ed. Barry Ahearn (London: Faber and Faber, 1987).

Propertius, *Elegies*, trans. H. E. Butler (London: William Heinemann, 1912).

Propertius, *Elegies*, ed. and trans. G. P. Goold (Cambridge, MA: Harvard University Press, 1990.)

Prynne, J. H., *Poems* (Hexham: Bloodaxe Books, 2015).

Prynne, J. H., 'Lecture on *Maximus IV, V, VI*' <http://charlesolson.org/Files/Prynnelecture1.htm>.

Rainey, Lawrence, *Institutions of Modernism: Literary Elites and Public Culture* (New Haven, CT: Yale University Press, 1998).

Rainey, Lawrence S., *Ezra Pound and the Monument of Culture: Text, History and the Malatesta Cantos* (Chicago: University of Chicago Press, 1991).

Rainey, Lawrence S., 'Eliot Among the Typists: Writing The Waste Land', *Modernism/modernity*, 1 (2005), 27–84.

Rilke, Rainer Maria, 'Primal Sound', in Friedrich A. Kittler, *Gramophone, Film, Typewriter*, trans. Geoffrey Winthrop-Young and Michael Wultz (Stanford, CA: Stanford University Press, 1999), 38–42.

Roberts, Andrew Michael, et al., 'Space and Pattern in Linear and Postlinear Poetry', *European Journal of English Studies*, 1 (2013), 23–40.

Rotella, Guy (ed.), *Critical Essays on E. E. Cummings* (Boston, MA: G. K. Hall, 1984).

Rousselot, Jean-Pierre, *Synthèse phonétique* (Paris: Publications de la Parole, 1901).

Saussure, Ferdinand de, *Premier cours de linguistique générale (1907): d'apres les cahiers d'Albert Riedlinger* (Oxford: Pergamon, 1996).

Sawyer-Lauçanno, Christopher, *E.E. Cummings: A Biography* (London: Methuen, 2005).

Sayre, Henry M., *The Visual Text of Williams Carlos Williams* (Urbana: University of Illinois Press, 1983).

Shahn, Ben, *Ben Shahn*, ed. John D. Morse (London: Secker & Warburg, 1972).

Sherman Paul, *Olson's Push: Origin, Black Mountain and Recent American Poetry* (Baton Rouge: Louisiana State University Press, 1978).

Sherry, Vincent, *Wyndham Lewis, Ezra Pound and Radical Modernism* (New York: Oxford University Press, 1993).

Sherry, Vincent, *The Great War and the Language of Modernism* (Oxford: Oxford University Press, 2003).

Spinoza, Benedict de, *Ethics*, ed. and trans. Edwin Curley (London: Penguin, 1996).

Sullivan, Hannah, *The Work of Revision* (Cambridge, MA: Harvard University Press, 2013).

Swanner, Seth, 'The Beauty of Ho(me)liness', *Studies in Philology*, 3 (2018), 544–79.

Swinburne, Algernon Charles, *Poems and Ballads* (London: John Camden Hotten, 1866).

Swinburne, Algernon Charles, *Poems and Ballads* (London: Chatto and Windus, 1912).

Tschichold, Jan, *The New Typography: A Handbook for Modern Designers*, trans. Ruari McLean (Berkeley: University of California Press, 2006).

Van Dijk, Yra, 'Reading the Form: The Function of Typographic Blanks in Modern Poetry', *Word & Image*, 4 (2011), 407–15.

Von Hallberg, Robert, *Charles Olson: The Scholar's Art* (Cambridge, MA: Harvard University Press, 1978).

Warde, Beatrice, 'The Crystal Goblet, or Why Printing should be Invisible', in Helen Armstrong, ed., *Graphic Design Theory: Readings from the Field* (New York: Princeton Architectural Press, 2009), 39-43.

Webster, Michael, 'Magic Iconism: Defamiliarization, Sympathetic Magic and Visual Poetry (Guillaume Apollinaire and E. E. Cummings)', *European Journal of English Studies*, 5 (2001), 97-113.

Wershler-Henry, Darren, *The Iron Whim: A Fragmented History of Typewriting* (Ithaca, NY: Cornell University Press, 2007).

Whitehead, Alfred North, *Process and Reality: An Essay in Cosmology* (New York: The Free Press, 1978).

Williams, William Carlos, 'Della Primavera Transportata al morale', in *Imagist Anthology 1930* (London: Chatto & Windus, 1930), 129–36.

Williams, William Carlos, 'Rain', in *Imagist Anthology 1930* (London: Chatto & Windus, 1930), 145–48.

Williams, William Carlos, *An Early Martyr and Other Poems* (New York: The Alcestis Press, 1935).

Williams, William Carlos, *Paterson: Book One* (New York: New Directions, 1946).

Williams, William Carlos, *Paterson: Book Two* (New York: New Directions, 1948).

Williams, William Carlos, *Paterson: Book Three* (New York: New Directions, 1949).

Williams, William Carlos, *Paterson: Book Four* (New York: New Directions, 1951).

Williams, William Carlos, *Paterson: Book Five* (New York: New Directions, 1958).

Williams, William Carlos, *The William Carlos Williams Reader*, ed. M. L. Rosenthal ([London]: Macgibbon & Kee, 1966).

Williams, William Carlos, *The Embodiment of Knowledge*, ed. Ron Loewinsohn (New York: New Directions, 1974).

Williams, William Carlos, *The Collected Poems of Williams Carlos Williams*, ed. A. Walton Litz and Christopher MacGowan (London: Paladin, 1991).

Williams, William Carlos, *Paterson* (Manchester: Carcanet, 1992).

Wilson, Edmund, 'Wallace Stevens and E. E. Cummings', in *Critical Essays on E. E. Cummings*, ed. Guy Rotella, (Boston: G. K. Hall & Co., 1984), 43–46.

Zukofsky, Louis, *"A" 1–12* (London: Cape, 1966).

Zukofsky, Louis, *A–14* (London: Turret Books, 1967).

Zukofsky, Louis, *Prepositions +: The Collected Critical Essays* (Hanover, NH: University Press of New England, 2000).

Index